D1300304

GRAND TRUNK CORPORATION

CANADIAN NATIONAL RAILWAYS IN THE UNITED STATES, 1971-1992

GRAND TRUNK CORPORATION

CANADIAN NATIONAL RAILWAYS IN THE UNITED STATES, 1971-1992

DON L. HOFSOMMER

Michigan State University Press

East Lansing

Copyright © 1995 Don L. Hofsommer

All Michigan State University Press books are produced on paper which meets the requirements of the American National Standard of Information Sciences—Permanence of paper for printed materials ANSI Z23.48-1984.

Michigan State University Press
East Lansing, Michigan 48823-5202

03 02 01 00 99 98 97 96 95 1 2 3 4 5 6 7 8 9 10

Hofsommer, Donovan L.
    Grand Trunk Corporation : Canadian national railways in the United States, 1971-1992 / Don L. Hofsommer.
        p.   cm.
    Includes biliographical references and index.
    ISBN 0-87013-406-x
    1. Grand Trunk Corporation. 2. Canadian National Railways.
    3. Railroads—United States. I. Title.
TF25.G66H64   1995
385'.06'571—dc20

Cover painting by Gil Reid

TF
25
G66
H6A
1995

For
Sandra
and for
Kathryn, Kristine, and Knute

CONTENTS

LIST OF ACRONYMS

ACI	Automatic Car Identification
AT&SF	Atchison, Topeka & Santa Fe Railway
B&O	Baltimore & Ohio Railroad
B&M	Boston & Maine Corporation
BLE	Brotherhood of Locomotive Engineers
BN	Burlington Northern
CN	Canadian National
CP	Canadian Pacific Railway
C&O	Chesapeake & Ohio Railway
C&NW	Chicago & North Western Transportation Company
C&WI	Chicago & Western Indiana Railroad
Chessie	Chesapeake & Ohio Railway
CMStP&P	Chicago, Milwaukee, St. Paul & Pacific Railroad
CTC	Centralized Traffic Control
CV	Central Vermont Railway
CSXT	CSX Transportation
Conrail	Consolidated Rail Corporation
CWR	Continuous Welded Rail
DART	Dedicated Automobile Rapid Transit
D&H	Delaware & Hudson Railroad
D&TSL	Detroit & Toledo Shore Line Railroad
DM&IR	Duluth, Missabe & Iron Range Railway
DT&I	Detroit, Toledo & Ironton Railroad
DW&P	Duluth, Winnipeg & Pacific Railway
FELA	Federal Employers' Liability Act
GM	General Motors
GTC	Grand Trunk Corporation
GTL	Grand Trunk Leasing
GTW	Grand Trunk Western Railroad

IC	Illinois Central Railroad
ICG	Illinois Central Gulf
ICC	Interstate Commerce Commission
L&N	Louisville & Nashville Railroad
Milwaukee Road	Chicago, Milwaukee, St. Paul & Pacific Railroad
MN&S	Minneapolis, Northfield & Southern Railway
MD&W	Minnesota, Dakota & Western Railway
N&W	Norfolk & Western Railway
NS	Norfolk Southern
P&LE	Pittsburgh & Lake Erie Railroad
Santa Fe	Atchison, Topeka & Santa Fe Railway
SCAT	Short Crew Automobile Train
Shore Line	Detroit & Toledo Shore Line Railroad
Soo	Soo Line Railroad
SEMTA	Southeastern Michigan Transportation Authority
TOFC	Trailer-on-flat-car
USRA	United States Railway Association
UTU	United Transportation Union
VCA	Voluntary Coordination Agreement

PREFACE

"We think there is an important and interesting story in Grand Trunk Corporation." The voice on the other end of the telephone line was that of John H. Burdakin, retired president. "Would you be interested in looking at what we have done?" I would. But, I warned, if I were retained to evaluate the historical significance of Grand Trunk Corporation (GTC), the story would have to be unvarnished—told with warts, if any, and all. "Exactly," said Gerald L. Maas, Burdakin's successor in Detroit. "Tell it like it is."

A deal was struck. I would have full access to GTC records and personnel. The manuscript would be read by top managers although I retained full editorial control. In the event of a serious disagreement in interpretation, the company could exercise its right to present a contrary view; there are no such passages in the book. We agreed that this would not be a view of Grand Trunk or its railroad subsidiaries from windows of country stations or from the cabs of swift-moving locomotives. Rather, this would be a story of Grand Trunk Corporation as a business. Thus, I have concerned myself with management decisions, how these decisions were made, and the results of them.

John Burdakin was correct, I discovered. The GTC story is both important and interesting.

The story is also complex—made so in part by the curious ownership arrangement (GTC is owned by Canadian National [CN], which in turn is owned by the people of Canada as a Crown Corporation); by a rapidly evolving and explosive business climate throughout North America and, for that matter, the world; and by equally fluid and explosive currents among all modes of transportation. Complexity also springs from GTC's experimental nature. Born in 1971 as a precipitous departure from Canadian National conventions, GTC's senior managers inevitably found themselves as respondents to change and as agents of change—often simultaneously. To be sure, change is the overriding constant throughout this story. Tension is another important theme. Sometimes creative and other times not, this tension ebbed and flowed in strategic and tactical relations between the parent in Montreal and the offspring in Detroit. Such tension is predictable, of course, but in the case of GTC and CN, it proved broader and deeper than expected—reflecting a difference of customs and principles in the United States and Canada and differences in the theories and practices of private enterprise railroads (from whence came most GTC managers) versus publicly held Canadian National (from whence most CN managers derived).

The Grand Trunk Corporation failed to live a long life in its original form; an agent of change in its own right, GTC succumbed to change during the early 1990s. Yet the experiment was at least modestly successful from a financial point of view and, more important by far, it was a stunning success in buying time for Canadian National to sort out options regarding its railroad operations in the United States. GTC lives on, of course, its franchises intact, but without independent management in Detroit. That need was obviated when the parent unveiled CN North America, a bold attempt to meet changed and changing strategic and competitive realities two decades after birth of the Grand Trunk Corporation experiment.

This study would not have been possible without the sincere interest and assistance of scores of persons within and outside of the company.

Almost all of the primary sources come from internal records and oral history, but some archival materials have also been used. W. Thomas White at the James J. Hill Reference Library in St. Paul and Mark Cedeck at the Barriger Collection of the St. Louis Mercantile Library answered every request in a cheery and professional manner.

Among others outside the GTC family who provided information, illustration material, or otherwise helped me were Isabel Benham, Paul Trap, Robert A. Sharp, Sam Breck, Gil Reid, John Gruber, Charles Bohi, David Korkhouse, J. E. Lancaster, John J. Baisley, John W. Flanigan, Richard Haupt, Robert S. Onacki, Thomas J. Lamphier, Charles F. Wilkins, John David Williams, David DeBoer, and Janice Schlangen.

From dispatchers at Pontiac to enginemen at Battle Creek, I was warmly received by all hands in every department, at every subsidiary, and at the parent company. Those who assisted me in one way or another included Ernest B. Novak, John P. Baukus, W. Fred Anderson, Douglas G. Low, James R. Krikau, Jacqueline Matusko, Donald P. Mackinnon, William K. Smith, Kenneth L. Murphy, Karen Terrace, Nola Brunelle, Connie Romani, James W. Aldrich, Harry E. Beeson, D. Garry Boyd, Thomas Brady, Don A. Caster, Peter A. Clarke, Gloria R. Combe, Thomas J. Costello, Robert D. Cox, Graham Dallas, Jack E. Dodd, Thomas M. Dooley, Brant E. Ducey, Thomas J. Faucett, Earl G. Fontaine, Harry D. Gibson, Karen Golicz, Kenneth E. Haugen, Marc H. Higginbotham, Donald A. Johnson, Gary R. Jones, the late Andrew J. Kalabus, Ray W. Kelly, Paul K. Larner, Yvon H. Masse, Annette Mily, Howard D. Nicholas, Earl C. Opperthauser, George S. Pearson, Ray J. Prokopp, Robert L. Rixon, Mark A. Schoenhals, Peter L. Schwartz, Edward J. Stasio, John H.D. Sturgess, Neil M. Wiechman, William P. Willingham, Robert A. Yeager, and Robert M. Zaleta.

The operating department at Grand Trunk Western (GTW) and the general managers of Central Vermont Railway (CV) and Duluth, Winnipeg & Pacific Railway (DW&P) saw to it that I got a firsthand look at their railroads. Those who assisted in this way included Phillip C. Larson, Ernest E. Lamb, Christopher J. Burger, George D. Collins, William H. Dempsey, J. David Hathaway, Robert T. Holmstrom, James R. Hurd, Richard L. Neumann, William B. Porter, Thomas L. Schlosser, David L. Wilson, and Larry T. Wizauer.

Several persons within the company and others in the railroad industry or elsewhere read all or parts of the manuscript and offered their special insights and criticisms. In this, special thanks goes to Francis M. Carroll, Stuart F. Gassner, Robert W. Downing, Kenneth S. Mackenzie, Robert A. Bandeen, Byron D. Olsen, Thomas F. Powers, Dennis M. Cavanaugh, Robert H. Wheeler, Donald G. Wooden, the late Paul E. Tatro, Walter E. Rich, John H. Burdakin, Basil Cole, Jerome F. Corcoran, Walter H. Cramer, Lorne C. Perry, Robert I. Schellig, Robert P. vom Eigen, Robert A. Walker, Richard L. Neumann, Christopher J. Burger, and Robert L. Rixon.

During the course of research and writing I was favored with materials, encouragement, wise counsel, and assisted in a host of other ways by several persons who went far beyond the call of duty. I could always depend on John Burdakin for useful, candid, and detailed comment; it was much the same with Gerald Maas whose door was always open to me. To William J. McKnight fell the chores of liaison, and he handled those duties with wit, charm, and grace. Not to be forgotten is Robert Sexsmith Sr., who squired me endlessly—at all times of the day and night—to places near and far at GTW.

Finally, I am grateful to my wife and children who have alternately supported or tolerated my interest in railroads and railroad history—depending on tonnage of the train, length of ruling grade, degree of curvature, and my willingness to meet requirements of feed, water, and rest.

To all of the above, and to any others whom I might regrettably have overlooked, I am indebted. For errors of fact and for infelicities of style that remain, I alone am responsible.

Don L. Hofsommer
St. Cloud, Minnesota
17 October 1994

1  BANDEEN'S EXPERIMENT

Our objective is to turn the Grand Trunk around as soon as possible, and then try to take advantages of the tax shelter.

Robert A. Bandeen, *Chicago Tribune*, 7 November 1971.

Robert Bandeen fixed his suddenly steely eyes on the man. "That's right," the fellow repeated, "we never promote an American above a certain level." Was it a true bill? Bandeen mulled the words, studied the man's expression, looked deeply into his eyes, and reflected on the hard edge in the man's voice. Yes, he reluctantly concluded, it was all too true—another in a long list of festering problems he had discovered at the Grand Trunk Western Railroad (GTW). Yet it was one thing to uncover and puzzle over problems, Bandeen knew, and quite another thing to conceive means of redressing those problems. Nevertheless, his charge was clear enough: he was to change from red to black the color of ink on financial reports flowing from the company's accounting office in Detroit. Despite the clarity of his orders, Bandeen would find GTW's road to profitability serpentine at best.[1]

Bandeen's orders emanated from Canadian National (CN)—the government-owned colossus that operated everything from hotels and railroads to an airline and an express company in Canada as well as Grand Trunk Western and other rail entities in the United States. Not surprisingly, senior management at Canadian National focused on "home properties" which were, after all, the core operation and were, at the same time, more likely to be scrutinized by members of Canada's Parliament. Consequently, Grand Trunk Western and other U.S. holdings were viewed as comparatively insignificant and received attention accordingly. Indeed, the thought persisted at GTW that CN sent it only transient managers who were either on their way up at the parent company or on their way to oblivion. There were clues that CN looked on U.S. holdings as poor relatives unworthy of adequate and proper paternal attention. For instance, there was the nettlesome matter of rate divisions which appeared to favor CN over its properties in the United States. And when GTW turned in a net annual deficit—which was usually the case—CN simply shrugged and covered the shortage. Small wonder that all of this was reflected on Grand Trunk Western in a general lack of cohesion, stability, and direction; in the categoric lack of incentive; and in low morale among middle managers who saw no hope of promotion or reward for innovation. This, in turn, was reflected by the road's dreary income statement. The report of GTW's

CN's senior management concentrated on "home properties." Quebec Belœil Bridge. Photograph courtesy of Canadian National.

corporate secretary in 1960 was typical: " . . . it appears that the year 1960 will probably show a net deficit of $11,483,000, which reflects a reduction of $238,322 from the deficit suffered in 1959." The pattern changed not at all. The secretary dispassionately projected deficits in 1961 of $12,500,000; of $8,717,000 in 1962; of $8,500,000 in 1963; of $10,000,000 in 1964; and of $8,800,00 in 1965.[2]

These staggering and seemingly endless shortfalls finally shook Montreal out of its lethargy. During the summer of 1966, directors of GTW were told that "the Canadian National has been giving serious thought to various approaches that have been made . . . about the possibility of divesting its ownership of the Grand Trunk Western." To that end, CN had received or would receive "indications of interest in either a merger or a purchase" from major American carriers—Atchison, Topeka & Santa Fe, Penn Central, and Illinois Central—as well as from bit players—Monon and Chicago & Eastern Illinois. CN publicly stated that "the Grand Trunk Western is not for sale" but privately concluded that "a deal with either Santa Fe or Illinois Central . . .

because of the geography and traffic patterns" might prove attractive.[3]

CN managers were further jolted out of complacency by vociferous complaints from powerful General Motors Corporation (GM), which correctly argued that Grand Trunk Western's service had reached intolerably low levels—especially at Pontiac, Michigan, site of important GM plants whose rail transportation was supplied solely by GTW. Montreal's immediate response was to direct that such problems should be handled locally. This response followed predictable staff meetings, vague promises, added expenditures, and general paper shuffling at GTW. General Motors, however, was not to be put off. S. J. Moore, traffic director of GM's Pontiac Motor Division, wrote to GTW each working day of February 1969 detailing his assessment of the railroad's performance at Pontiac for the previous 24-hour period. That was noteworthy in its own right. It is even more notable that GM's Moore sent copies to Norman John MacMillan, president and chairman of Canadian National, as well as to ten other senior managers at CN, GTW, and his own company. In the end,

MacMillan himself was forced to meet with General Motors personnel at Pontiac. MacMillan was embarrassed—nay, humiliated—but the meeting proved fruitful. After he returned to the safety of Montreal, MacMillan ordered that a thorough study be completed to "effect immediate improvements" and, more important, to "define longer term activities which will enable Grand Trunk Western to achieve financial viability."[4]

CN's motivations were clear. Substantial annual deficits at GTW were no longer tolerable. Sale of the road was a possible avenue of resolution but negotiations to date suggested that prospective purchasers would not pay adequately for CN to recapture capital invested in GTW or even to meet "opportunity value" of the property. Another alternative had to be found.

The study ordered by MacMillan offered little comfort, however. "Continued CN operation of GTW has to be seriously considered," wrote CN analysts; but, they continued ominously, "it is indeed difficult to be optimistic about GTW's future." Improvement in performance would "take many years to achieve." Was this "Herculean task" worth the effort? CN's analysts seemed to doubt it. They hedged their bets, though, counseling "further study." Meanwhile, they pointed to three "available courses": merger of GTW with another railway; sale of GTW to a non-railway company; or voluntary bankruptcy and sale of assets to other railways. Meanwhile, they asserted, "capital spending on GTW should be limited to those projects absolutely essential to continued operations, or projects exhibiting a rapid payback in investment (2 or 3 years)."[5]

CN analysts continued with their depressing report. GTW, they observed, is "a short-haul carrier which principally originates and terminates traffic . . . with consequent small divisions of total revenue, with high per diem equipment" and forced to operate in "an intensely rail-competitive environment." In addition, they pointed to GTW's dependence on the automobile industry with its cyclical "boom and bust" traffic patterns, to "the general lack of natural resources in [GTW's service area] for outbound shipments," and to the fact that "inbound shipments tend to move by water." These inherent weaknesses loomed even larger when mirrored against the great merger movement just beginning to blossom in the United States and against increasingly fierce competition from the trucking industry.[6]

Certain aspects of GTW's modus operandi came under particularly close scrutiny. CN analysts were harshly critical of the absence of "an adequate management information system" at GTW as well as the absence "of marketing, analytical, and industrial engineering staff support." This "general lack of information has led to a 'seat of the pants' type management" that was reflected, for instance, in GTW's "failure to understand fully and manage the [automobile] car pool" which, in turn, "led to inflated equipment needs." The investigators from Montreal also called GTW's industrial development efforts "very ineffective."[7]

Was there any hope for Grand Trunk Western? What could be done? CN's team was skeptical that GTW had any long-term place in CN's world. "CN has, in part, justified continued ownership of the GTW on the basis of its 'feeder value,'" they noted. Indeed, belief in the feeder value of GTW was perhaps even a sacred cow at CN headquarters. But, said the analysts, "it is quite possible that the feeder value [to CN] of GTW could increase with sale." Dump this American property was the veiled message. Failing that, CN's team concluded, "the objective should be that GTW become totally autonomous within the Financial Objectives and General Policy set by System H.Q."[8]

Expansive internal debate followed. The options were frightfully few and mostly unattractive. Eventually, however, MacMillan agreed to a concept of autonomy and Robert A. Bandeen became the "point man" in developing an acceptable plan. Bandeen relished the opportunity. Outside attorneys urged creation of a holding company "in order to diversify into other business activities without the necessity of seeking Interstate Commerce Commission [ICC] approval." Why diversify? Bandeen knew that question was sure to surface internally and might even become a political question in Canada. Bankers were brought in. Kuhn Loeb advisors explained that the "choice is very significantly influenced by provisions of the U.S. federal income tax laws which permit an enterprise with tax losses to acquire profitable concerns and, in effect, to operate them on a tax-free basis [in this case] until railroad-generated tax losses cease to be available." This approach, they added, had been embraced earlier by Penn Central, Chicago & North Western, and Missouri-Kansas-Texas. Turning again to potential tax advantages, the bankers pointed out that CN might usefully choose to include another of its U.S. holdings—the increasingly prosperous Duluth, Winnipeg & Pacific Railway (DW&P), for example—as a part of the holding company package. This could occur without ICC approval and would make it possible to utilize GTW's accumulated losses to offset DW&P profits. Creating a holding company

simply for the purpose of evasion or avoidance of taxes could not be done, of course; CN's ultimate goal had to be creation of an affiliated group that would eventually generate a profit.[9]

N. J. MacMillan brought the matter to a head late in 1969 through discussions with Canadian National directors, and on 6 February 1970, he asked the board's approval "for the diversification of CN's subsidiaries in the United States" and for authority to "create a holding company [Grand Trunk Industries] in the United States . . . to hold the Grand Trunk Western Railroad Company and other of CN's American subsidiaries as a first step in this diversification effort." MacMillan's view was that a holding company would enable "the consolidation, for income tax purposes, of the operating profits and losses for these American operations." This, he added, was "not currently possible since CN, as a foreign-owned corporation, is unable to consolidate its U.S. tax returns." Whether such an approach would prove to be the ultimate solution remained in doubt. GTW, MacMillan warned, "makes more economic sense as part of a U.S. road where its traffic generation capability could be fully exploited." Nevertheless, under the holding company arrangement, "CN's assets [at least GTW] would be converted from a deficit railroad operation to a profitable conglomerate" and, as a consequence, give CN the option of selling its shares in the holding company and repatriating its resources for use in Canada."[10]

To that end, Grand Trunk Industries was incorporated under the laws of Delaware on 22 September 1970. Bandeen then suggested that "the name Grand Trunk Corporation [GTC] would be more appropriate and cause fewer problems in Washington and Ottawa." The change was made effective 20 November. An Order-in-Council would be required from the Canadian Privy Council for the entire matter, but meanwhile plans went forward under Bandeen's

GTW suffered from high costs of gathering and distribution without the offsetting benefit of long line haul. Kalamazoo Yard. Photograph courtesy of Canadian National.

Robert A. Bandeen, left, and Norman J. MacMillan, right, would agree to bold plans for CN's rail operations in the United States. Photograph courtesy of Canadian National.

leadership to flesh out the holding company. Bandeen urged that Grand Trunk Corporation issue shares to acquire Grand Trunk Western as well as the Duluth, Winnipeg & Pacific and another CN property in the United States, Central Vermont Railway (CV). In addition, Bandeen suggested that CN's line to Portland, Maine—the so-called Grand Trunk Eastern—eventually be reincorporated in the U.S. and then be acquired by GTC. Beyond that Bandeen counseled creation under the holding company's banner of Grand Trunk Leasing Company "to take over equipment currently owned by CN and leased to GTW" and Grand Trunk Real Estate Company "to take over the non-rail assets of the rail subsidiaries." Bandeen was emphatic that the new holding company and "its various subsidiary companies will be separated from direct CN management" and that "American executives take over [management of] the various subsidiary corporations" and eventually the holding company itself.[11]

Events moved toward full fruition. MacMillan resigned as president of Grand Trunk Western in June 1971, and was succeeded by Bandeen (who continued as vice president of CN's important Great Lakes Region to which GTW was physically connected). MacMillan became chairman of GTW. Then, on 13 July 1971, the necessary Order-in-Council was issued and GTC quickly issued its capital stock to Canadian National in exchange for the parent's Grand Trunk Western securities. The entire package was completed on 31 July when GTW, DW&P, and CV passed to ownership of Grand Trunk Corporation—a wholly owned subsidiary of Canadian National.[12]

In a very real way Grand Trunk Corporation was the offspring of Robert A. Bandeen. His success or failure in bringing this child to maturity would be scrutinized carefully not only within the confines of CN's Montreal headquarters but from far afield as well. All he had at this point was a flashing yellow signal. But that was adequate for Bandeen. At least for the present.

NOTES

1. Robert A. Bandeen, interview, 3 November 1989.
2. On the Canadian National, see Henry Eldon Hewetson, *The Financial History of the Canadian National Railway* (Chicago: University of Chicago Press, 1946); George R. Stevens, *Canadian National Railways,* 2 vols. (Toronto: Clarke, Irwin & Co., 1960) and *History of the Canadian National Railways* (New York: The Macmillan Company, 1973); Yvon H. Masse, interview, 24 May 1989; John H. Burdakin, interview, 24 May 1989, and 4 November 1989; Robert A. Bandeen, interview, 3 November 1989; Earl C. Opperthauser, interview, 6 November 1989; GTW, Minute Book No. 4: 17, 29, 45, 59, 69, 79.
3. GTW, Minute Book No. 4: 85.
4. Peter Ellimica to D. R. Bell, 13 February 1969;

unsigned memo to J. W. Demcoe, 13 February 1969; S. J. Moore to E. T. Rose, 2 February 1969; N. J. MacMillan to M. J. Caseio, 4 March 1969. All in President's File 750. A. H. Hart to W. D. Piggott, 31 March 1969, Secretary's Files [hereafter SF].

5. L. C. Durning et al., to A. H. Hart, 21 July 1969, (SF).

6. *Overview—Grand Trunk Western* (Montreal: CN, 1969), 18, 26, 28 (SF).

7. Ibid., 4, 21, 22, 61.

8. Ibid., 11, 76.

9. Merrill Shepard telex to R. A. Bandeen, undated [November 1969]; John Guest telex to CNR, 8 December 1969, (SF).

10. N. J. MacMillan to Directors of Canadian National, 6 February1970; National, 6 February 1970, with memorandum of same date, Vice President Files [hereafter VPF].

11. GTW minutes of the Executive Committee, 30 November 1970; R. A. Bandeen, 11 November 1970, and memorandum of same date, to N. J. MacMillan, (SF).

12. GTW Executive Minute No. 531; G. M. Cooper to J. W. G. Macdougall, 4 August 1971, (SF).

2  OUT OF CANADA

Precisely because CN has a history—a long and distinguished one, I hasten to add—changes in the structure and role of the company may be viewed, initially at least, with nostalgia for the comforts of a world of certainty. In fact, such a world has never existed and Canadian National's history has been one of change, adaptation, renewal and growth.

J. Maurice LeClair,
CN Annual Report (1985): 7.

What was the background and nature of Grand Trunk Corporation's constituent elements? It seemed at first blush that the only common thread among Grand Trunk Western, Central Vermont, and Duluth, Winnipeg & Pacific was the gauge of their track. After all, none was physically connected to the other, and traffic patterns for each were disparate in the extreme. On the other hand, all had direct physical attachment to the Canadian National. Moreover, Grand Trunk Western and Central Vermont were twin antecedents of an early and important strategic plan to link Western Europe with the heartland of North America through East Coast ports in the United States and southeastern Canada. Indeed, Central Vermont and the Grand Trunk Railway of Canada were principal players in the evolution of modern transportation in New England as well as in the Dominion.

Grand Trunk! Could there be a more fitting name for a transportation enterprise having gloriously expansive aspirations? Deriving from the Roman Empire, the trunk road or highway was an imperial tool—not just for military purposes, but a crucial device for political, economic, and social influence. The concept was all the more powerful after steam was harnessed for overland locomotion during the early nineteenth century. Small wonder that those who saw in the new railway technology a means of holding and maturing the vast and forbidding British North American provinces enthusiastically embraced the designation "Grand Trunk" for the organization they would employ in that task. What, these proponents asked, could be more effective in breaching dense forests and providing the glue of empire? Canals, replied naysayers, but there was no gainsaying that both the bountiful natural highways and man-made canals of the northlands were frozen and thus unusable for up to five months per year. Railways were the answer, no doubt about it.

Events north of the St. Lawrence River, as always, were inextricably linked to those south thereof. Shortly after Upper Canada and Lower Canada became the Province of Canada in 1841, the Webster-Ashburton Treaty defined the boundary of Maine in a way that drove a painful wedge of land owned by the United States into the Maritimes and precluded an all-Canada, short-mile rail route from tidewater ports such as Halifax or Saint John to Quebec City or Montreal. At the same time, American port cities from Boston and New York to Baltimore and Savannah were engaged in a free-for-all campaign of urban economic imperialism designed to hold hinterlands subservient to their respective urges. Would this be repeated in Maine? Would Portland have the same impulses? Yes. But there was precious little American land to the west that could be tapped. The mercantile class of Portland would have to look west *and* north—to Canada—to satisfy its economic imperialism. It was not an irrational idea. An airline route from Portland to Montreal, after all, was little more than one-half the distance from Montreal to Saint John and one-third the distance from Montreal to Halifax.[1]

Other Americans were equally alert to the prospects of alliance with the West through Canada. Business and political leaders of Vermont and New Hampshire urged Boston interests to take this view. But leaders in Boston held that their primary path to the interior lay directly over the Berkshire Mountains and placed early faith in a road that eventually became the Boston & Albany. Nevertheless, pamphleteers in Vermont and New Hampshire continued to rain a flood of proposals for rail links northwestward through their states from Boston to Lake Champlain—bringing Boston, they pointed out, twice as close to Montreal in transit time as it was from New York City to Montreal while at the same time allowing Boston to bid fair for the "commerce of the great lakes, a world within itself." With an enlarged Welland Canal, this route would provide a tantalizing alternative to the New York canals, would extend low-cost lake tariffs eastward beyond Buffalo and Oswego, and would thus allow Boston to attack New York City's primacy in a way that the Boston & Albany would not. There was merit to the idea. The eyes of Boston capitalists grew large as they dreamed of growing oceanic traffic passing through their port to and from an expansive American hinterland as far distant as the western waters of the Great Lakes—and Canada, too, incidentally.[2]

A great contest ensued. One force promoted a line from Portland, the other backed a line through Vermont. Both looked to the West. Both looked to Canada. Both solicited funds in Boston.

In Maine, the chief proponent was John A. Poor, an attorney who zealously and endlessly propounded on the utility of railroad technology. During a trip to Canada in 1844, Poor won the mind of Alexander Tilloch Galt whose influence was crucial. Events then moved swiftly. On 17 March 1845, the legislative assembly gave charter to the St. Lawrence and Atlantic Railroad which was authorized to build from a point opposite Montreal to the U.S. boundary. Meanwhile, Poor—on 10 February 1845—had smiled when the Maine legislature rushed to charter the Atlantic and St. Lawrence Railroad for the purpose of effecting a through route in connection with its Canadian counterpart.[3]

The Vermont venture, however, proved rather more complicated. On 31 October 1844, the Vermont legislature passed a special act authorizing the Vermont Central Railroad and giving it the right to link Lake Champlain on the northwest with the Connecticut River on the southeast. Another road gained rights of construction from Boston to the Connecticut River.[4]

The Vermont legislature also passed collateral legislation authorizing the Champlain and Connecticut River Railroad—later rechristened the Rutland and Burlington Railroad and clearly rival to Vermont Central—as well as still another new company, the Vermont and Canada Railroad. This latter company—a brainchild of St. Albans forces—was to extend from Burlington (and a junction there with both Rutland and Burlington and Vermont Central) through St. Albans to the Canadian boundary (and to an implied junction at that point with a Canadian road to Montreal). Majordomos in the St. Albans enterprise were John Smith, an attorney and politician, and Lawrence Brainerd, merchant and lake shipper.[5]

The Portland and Vermont ventures, if completed, would aid the interests of Boston—the Portland artery by stealing traffic from arch-rival New York City and the Vermont roads by encouraging oceanic traffic via Boston. What Portland and Vermont promoters offered in each case were a plan and a charter. What they each needed was money. Hesitant Boston bankers had anxiously watched the fortunes of the new road inching west to Albany (the future Boston & Albany). For them, that road represented a crucial test of whether steam locomotives could actually conquer heavy grades and whether railroad companies could be profitable. They were predictably pleased when the road over the Berkshires proved successful on both counts. Purse strings were loosed accordingly, and Boston money flowed to each of the projects.[6]

But it would take a lot of money to bring all of these plans to fruition. The problem was no less acute in Canada where great effort was required to breathe life into St. Lawrence and Atlantic. Alexander Tilloch Galt canvassed England but found competition for capital quite intense. Would Canada fail in its share of the joint enterprise? It was a matter of honor and ego, but it was also a matter of economics. Railroads had quickly become the prevailing symbol of progress and prosperity. Yet for Canada, there was an abundance of internal difficulty—Upper Canada remained suspicious of Lower Canada and Montreal worried about the potential of Toronto—and there was concern about the growing power of the United States in determining trade patterns with Canada West. The matter was further complicated by assumptions regarding intentions of the United States toward Canada, the circumstance of the British Empire at the moment, and the unintegrated nature of the British North American holdings. Nevertheless, the Canadian government in 1849 committed itself, in a momentous decision, to guarantee railroad bonds "on certain conditions" and at the same time agreed in principle to the idea of a trunk railroad or main line. The St. Lawrence and Atlantic, opened to Island Pond, Vermont, on 18 July 1853, was a most impressive step in reaching those strategic goals.[7]

In Maine, John A. Poor, writer, attorney, and railroad proponent extraordinaire, continued his evangelical campaign on behalf of Portland and the Atlantic and St. Lawrence. It was far from certain, however, whether Poor's dream would be fulfilled. The line would traverse a difficult terrain and an area that implied limited potential traffic. Investors and speculators understood this and Poor found solicitations among them a very hard sell. But the same men—and local politicians, too—understood the road's potential for through or overhead traffic that would arrive in Portland on a year-round basis and move to

Canada or through Canada to the burgeoning American Midwest. So money came forward, grudgingly to be sure, but adequate. Work began in 1846 and the road was opened to Island Pond, Vermont, in January of 1853. Impressive through business developed, just as Poor had predicted. Indeed, the Canadian government subsidized weekly steamship service to Liverpool, at least during the winter months when the St. Lawrence River was iced over, and through bills of lading from Great Britain to Canada diverted bonded business to Portland from Boston.[8]

In Vermont, meanwhile, progress was halting and always had a curious flavor. Construction started on Vermont Central in 1848 and by the end of 1849 the road was open to business from just south of White River Junction to Burlington, 117 miles. Connecting traffic from Boston arrived over what would become an artery of Boston & Maine and, after 1 June 1851, went forward above Burlington over rails of the Vermont and Canada Railroad through St. Albans to the New York-Vermont border just east of Rouses Point. The link between Rouses Point and navigation on the St. Lawrence River below Lake Ontario was filled by the Northern Railroad Company, later renamed the Ogdensburg and Lake Champlain Railroad. Service between Rouses Point and Ogdensburg commenced in 1850 but its utility, insofar as Boston was concerned, did not flower until the Vermont and Canada arrived from the east in the following season. Lying between the two rail lines was Lake Champlain where navigation interests and allied forces complained at any prospect of bridging. Nevertheless, the Vermont and Canada sent crews to drive piling from the east bank, and its counterpart did likewise on the west. At center channel the roads employed an ingenious 300-foot floating bridge, arduously removed and replaced to accommodate navigation and rail requirements. In this way Boston, late in 1851, secured another major outlet to the American West. Not to be forgotten in all of this was Montreal. On the Vermont and Canada, a bit of additional construction in 1864 from Swanton, Vermont, to the international boundary plus 24 miles of new line in Canada provided a connection with existing trackage leading to Montreal—which now boasted a direct route to and from Boston and another leading to and from Portland.[9]

VERMONT CENTRAL RAILROAD.
TIME CARD.

	1st Pas. Train.				2d Pas. Train.				Dist. bet. St
	DOWN.		UP.		DOWN.		UP.		
	ARR. H. M.	DEP. H. M.	ARR. H. M.	DEP. H. M.	ARR. H. M.	DEP. H. M.	ARR. H. M.	DEP. H. M.	Miles.
Montpelier,	—	4.20	4.55	—	—	10.40	9.30	—	—
Northfield,	5.00	5.45	4.15	4.25	11.10	11.20	8.40	8.50	9.8
Roxbury,	—	6.03	—	3.56	—	11.39	—	8.20	7.1
Braintree,	—	6.25	—	3.36	—	12.01	—	8.00	8.5
Randolph,	—	6.39	—	3.22	—	12.15	—	7.46	5.6
Bethel,	6.54	7.00	3.00	3.05	12.30	12.35	7.24	7.29	7.1
North Royalton,	—	7.08	—	2.52	—	12.43	—	7.16	3.8
Royalton,	—	7.12	—	2.48	—	12.47	—	7.13	1.1
South Royalton,	—	7.18	—	2.42	—	12.53	—	7.08	1.8
Sharon,	—	7.30	—	2.29	—	1.05	—	6.55	4.9
West Hartford,	—	7.43	—	2.16	—	1.18	—	6.42	5.6
White River Vil.	7.55	8.01	1.58	2.03	1.30	1.36	6.23	6.30	5.8
White River Junc.	8.05	8.10	1.47	1.55	1.40	1.55	6.13	6.20	1.5
North Hartland,	—	8.23	—	1.35	—	2.08	—	6.00	5.6
Hartland,	—	8.33	—	1.25	—	2.18	—	5.50	4.1
Windsor,	8.43	—	—	1.15	2.28	—	—	5.40	4.3
									76.6

Service as of 23 July 1849.

Before this, however, Canadian leaders and British investors had formed a much broader vision of the Canadian rail web. To that end, on 10 November 1852, the Province of Canada provided for the incorporation of the Grand Trunk Railway of Canada (Grand Trunk) investing it with broad powers to acquire earlier charters and to prosecute the notion of a "main line." A board of directors was elected in mid-1853. The purpose of Grand Trunk, they quickly announced, was a grandiose rail operation beginning at Portland, Maine, and running through Montreal, Toronto, and Sarnia to Detroit—but with Chicago as its ultimate destination. For that purpose, the St. Lawrence and Atlantic—linking Montreal with Island Pond, Vermont—was amalgamated with Grand Trunk in 1853 and in the following year Grand Trunk took a 999-year lease on Atlantic and St. Lawrence, the American cousin emanating from tidewater at Portland and reaching northwestward to Island Pond. With these established lines and others plus impressive additional construction, Grand Trunk quickly moved to implement the overall strategy.[10]

The government of Canada was a willing participant in all of this to an extent utterly foreign in the American experience. State and local funds were used extensively to foster railroad development in the United States, true enough, and the federal government gave generously of the western public domain and issued bonds in temporary support of strategic western lines. Yet the degree of governmental support and involvement in the United States was, on balance, much less than in Canada. The United States, when in doubt, embraced a laissez-faire approach, a more capitalistic tradition. Canada, on the other hand, took the position that its circumstance was different— that private enterprise alone was inadequate to the task because Canada's "distances were too great, its population too sparse, its commitments too heavy, the British North American possessions too unintegrated, the times too uncertain. . . ." Likely so. In any event, the Canadian and American experience in railroad development were strikingly different from early on.[11]

British capital and overt support for Grand Trunk from the Canadian government proved effective. The company continued to expand its theater of operation and to improve its plant. The great Victoria Bridge at Montreal, opened in 1859, seemed the perfect symbol. Yet an even more profound symbol was the incorporation of the explicitly styled Chicago, Detroit and Canada Grand Trunk Junction Railroad on 16 March 1858. This road, born under a well-defined understanding that it would eventually be part of the Grand Trunk Railway of Canada, was to build from Port Huron to Detroit and thereby link Grand Trunk with two roads to Chicago— the Michigan Central and the Michigan Southern—via Detroit. Even before the 60-mile Port Huron-Detroit line was placed in revenue service on 21 November 1859, it had been leased by Grand Trunk for 999 years. Until the St. Clair Tunnel would be opened in 1891, traffic between Sarnia and Port Huron was handled by ferry. All

This impressionistic view of the Toronto station in 1857 suggests the growing view of empire—empire in the West. Photograph courtesy of Canadian National.

of this reflected calculated corporate policy. "I am convinced," general manager S. R. Bidder wrote in 1854, "that a large amount of the breadstuffs of Michigan, Iowa, Wisconsin and a portion of Illinois, which now find their way to the Seaboard by water and by United States lines of road, must pass over the Grand Trunk, not only on account of its being the cheaper and more direct route, but also because of the less number of handlings these goods would have, and the consequent extra rapidity with which they would be conveyed."[12]

Traffic did flow as Bidder had forecast and Grand Trunk bid fair to increase its volume. But there were problems. The government had determined early on that the gauge of Canadian railroads should be 5' 6" (a wise decision from a long-range technological point of view), but that quickly proved a very serious disadvantage since roads in the United States adopted 4' 8 1/2" as standard gauge. Traffic to and from Grand Trunk, as a consequence, had to be transloaded— a procedure that was both time-consuming and expensive. That problem was obviated at great expense in 1873 and 1874 when Grand Trunk

changed to standard gauge. There were other problems. The eastern seaboard-Chicago market, however vibrant, was extremely competitive—a circumstance exacerbated when Vanderbilt interests gained control of Canada Southern (between Niagara Falls and Windsor, effectively Buffalo to Detroit) and the crucial Michigan Central, upon which Grand Trunk relied, between Detroit and Chicago. Vanderbilt's New York Central, with a marvelous main line from New York City to Chicago—with a lucrative feeder in Boston & Albany—had been hurt by Grand Trunk. It was unlikely that the Vanderbilt roads would continue to provide Grand Trunk with a friendly outlet at Detroit.[13]

There followed a most interesting interlude of intrigue. Vanderbilt forces correctly calculated that Grand Trunk would seek a direct route to Chicago from Port Huron and laid a trap accordingly. There were already bits and pieces of railroad that with additional trackage could be cobbled together into a through route. To preclude that, William Vanderbilt, son of the redoubtable Cornelius, in 1876 quietly acquired bonds of the Chicago and North Eastern, a short

The Chicago, Detroit, and Canada Grand Trunk Junction would link the Grand Trunk Railway of Canada with roads leading to Chicago. Here a construction train pauses a mile west of Mt. Clemens in the fall of 1859. Photograph courtesy of Grand Trunk Western Railroad.

The railroad implied permanence and prosperity. The new depot was a clear and perfect statement to that effect. The year is 1859. Photograph courtesy of Grand Trunk Western Railroad.

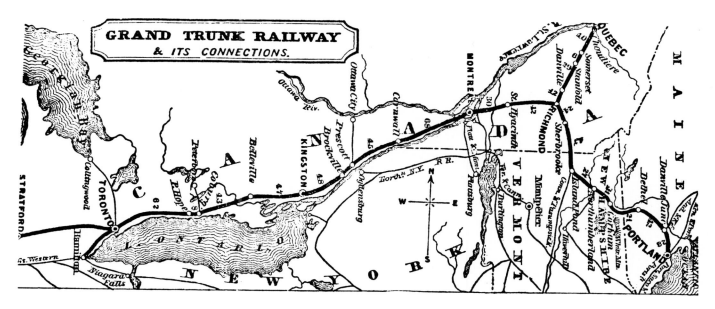

but—for Grand Trunk, at least—strategically located pike between Flint and Lansing, Michigan. Grand Trunk countered, in 1879, by picking up the Port Huron and Lake Michigan Railroad (Port Huron to Flint, 66 miles) and the Peninsular Railways of Michigan and Indiana (Lansing to Valparaiso, Indiana, 165 miles). Vanderbilt's Chicago and North Eastern then found itself in a vise, caught without friendly exits on either side of its line. The shrewd Canadians offered to take Chicago and North Eastern off Vanderbilt's hands but the wily New Yorker demurred until Grand Trunk threatened to stitch its disconnected properties together with a new line between Flint and Lansing to the north through the coal fields around Owosso. William Vanderbilt came to heel; Chicago and North Eastern came to the Grand Trunk. An additional acquisition and a modest construction campaign carried the Chicago and Grand Trunk Railway, holder of these several properties, to Elsdon, on the outskirts of Chicago. Vanderbilt made one last-ditch effort to prevent Grand Trunk from reaching downtown Chicago; for a while he was successful, but in the end other carriers sided with Grand Trunk to defeat Vanderbilt. Through service between Port Huron and Chicago began on 8 February 1880. The great dream was realized; the Grand Trunk Railway of Canada had, indeed, its own "grand trunk" rail line from Portland, Maine, to Chicago, Illinois, by way of Montreal and Toronto.[14]

For a moment, at least, Grand Trunk was the toast of Chicago. It was similarly true that Chicago was the toast of Grand Trunk. With good reason. About 40 percent of the company's receipts came from Chicago during the early 1880s; Grand Trunk eagerly billed grain to eastern destinations and the company instituted combined "rail-and-ocean bills of lading to United Kingdom ports at reduced rates." In addition, it was the flagship handler of dressed meat from the Chicago packers. Numbers told the story: Grand Trunk's business to and from the United States was more profitable than its Canadian business.[15]

More lines of railroad in the United States came under the flag when Canada's Great Western Railway was amalgamated with Grand Trunk on 12 August 1882. The Great Western, as part of its own imperial strategy, had gained control of the Detroit, Grand Haven and Milwaukee Railway—a successor to various predecessors that had built from Detroit to Pontiac (1838-1844) and on to Grand Rapids and the eastern shores of Lake Michigan at Grand Haven (1855-1870). This 191-mile route crossed the newly opened Port Huron-Chicago line (Chicago and Grand Trunk) at Durand and afforded Grand Trunk a doglegged but nevertheless important means of competing for Detroit-Chicago business. Another spur, this one off the Grand Haven line, the Toledo, Saginaw and Muskegon Railway (96 miles, from Ashley to Muskegon) came into the fold in 1888, and yet another appendage, heading north from Durand—

(No. 7 C. & M.) Corrected to April 20th, 1891.

TIME TABLE
—OF—
THE OLD RELIABLE

DETROIT, GRAND HAVEN AND MILWAUKEE RAILWAY.

TO AND FROM

Northern Michigan

ALL POINTS ON

GRAND RAPIDS & INDIANA RY.

AND

DULUTH, SOUTH SHORE & ATLANTIC R'Y,

TO THE

→ EAST ←

New England

Canada,

And the PROVINCES.

characterized it, had become a "perpetual bankrupt and debtor." The road had defaulted on bonds in the 1850s and thus earned the dubious distinction of becoming the earliest large-scale receivership in the United States. And the property remained under the continuous management of receivers until 30 June 1884. Nevertheless, Vermont Central continued as a valuable feeder of westbound traffic for Grand Trunk. At one time it owned or controlled more than 500 miles of track in Canada and the United States including, for example, the Rutland Railroad (successor to Rutland and Burlington), the Ogdensburg and Lake Champlain, and the New London Northern Railroad. In the process, Vermont Central—restyled as Central Vermont Railroad (CV) on 21 May 1873—was the largest railroad in New England. Masters of ceremonies, as always, were the Smiths of St. Albans—John and his sons John Gregory and Worthington C.—and associated relatives and friends, most of whom were sometime politicians, attorneys, and businessmen.[17]

All of this must have perplexed Grand Trunk's management. On the other hand, Central Vermont represented an important peripheral defense and a friendly connection. Indeed, by 1883, Central Vermont carried one-third of westbound traffic from New England and, with an outlet on Long Island Sound at New London, Connecticut, CV even entered into arrangements with steam vessels (and later would own such vessels) for carriage to and from New York City. But, CV's continuing litigation was discomforting and the road might eventually fall into unfriendly hands. Moreover, CV was in arrears on traffic balance agreements with Grand Trunk. Consequently, for several reasons—defensive, strategic, traffic, and financial—Grand Trunk in 1883 began buying into Central Vermont with the idea of controlling the company. Two years later, it held a majority of CV securities—stocks and bonds alike.[18]

CV at its apex was strategically impressive. The jury-rigged system that the Smiths had put together gradually came unglued. Leases were surrendered one by one. The Ogdensburg and Lake Champlain went back to its owners as did Rutland and several others. What remained when reorganized as the Central Vermont *Railway* on 16 November 1898, was a combination of owned and leased lines that collectively made up CV's main line from St. Albans, Vermont, to New London, Connecticut, plus a few branches. That

the Cincinnati, Saginaw and Mackinaw, 54 miles, served Saginaw and Bay City. It entered the family in 1890.[16]

On the eastern flank, the affairs of Vermont Central were ever more confusing. That road, as one Canadian historian saw it, had become "a statutory monkey puzzle of contractual entanglements, interlocking alliances and vague understandings," and, as an American historian

Durand became Grand Trunk's major crossroads. Photograph courtesy of the collections of Sam Breck.

For a while Vermont Central even owned the Rutland Railroad. Here a VC train is shown in the yards of Rutland in the company's namesake city. Photograph courtesy of Canadian National.

CENTRAL VERMONT RAILROAD

THE BEST AND MOST DIRECT ROUTE
BETWEEN THE

EAST and WEST

CLOSE CONNECTIONS
MADE WITH ALL THE PRINCIPAL

Railroad and Steamboat Lines
in NEW ENGLAND and

NEW YORK and CANADA

THROUGH TICKETS
Can be obtained at all the Principal Railroad Stations
and Ticket Offices in the United States and Canada.

S. W. CUMMINGS,   CHAS. A. BROWN,   L. MILLIS,
    Gen. Pass. Agt.   Trav. Agt.   Gen. Supt. Traffic.
                ST. ALBANS, VERMONT.

was fine insofar as Grand Trunk was concerned, for Central Vermont remained the Trunk's primary connection with New England states and represented the eastern arm of its fast freight line—the National Dispatch, famous for handling dairy products, dressed meat, and other time-sensitive commodities. In addition, tremendous amounts of Boston-bound corn and wheat moved over the Grand Trunk-Central Vermont route and eastern connections. Grand Trunk and Central Vermont also provided through passenger service between Montreal and New York City in conjunction with the Norwich & Worcester Line, operator of "splendid steamers."[19]

Competition, not an issue earlier, grew exponentially as the United States and Canada witnessed the growth of huge systems that built not only main routes but a plethora of branches and feeders. And for Grand Trunk and its counterpart in the United States, Chicago and Grand Trunk, there was the omnipresent reality of waterway competition. Yet the primary competitors were other railroads, especially for traffic moving to and or from the American Midwest through northeastern ports—Portland, Boston, and New York among others. During the last quarter of the nineteenth century, Vanderbilt interests skillfully fashioned a most impressive system including New York Central & Hudson River—"the Great Four-Track Trunk Line" from New York City through Albany to Buffalo; Lake Shore & Michigan Southern with a superbly located route from Buffalo along the south shore of Lake Erie to Cleveland, Toledo, and Chicago—with principal branches in Michigan to Detroit, Jackson, Lansing, and Grand Rapids; and Michigan Central with a line from Buffalo on the north side of Lake Erie in Canada to Detroit and on to Jackson and Chicago with a web of additional lines in Michigan. All of these, plus Boston & Albany, Cleveland, Cincinnati, Chicago & St. Louis, and others would eventually combine in the New York Central colossus. The powerful Pennsylvania Railroad would also be a prime player in this contest as would other roads such as Baltimore & Ohio; New York, Chicago & St. Louis (Nickel Plate); Pere Marquette; and Wabash.[20]

The competitive circumstance in Canada was different but no less intense and rather more complex. The Grand Trunk Railway, with its early and impressive 800-mile main line from Portland, Maine, through Montreal and Toronto to Sarnia was, in a real way, the godfather of Canadian railroads but it was hardly the only contender. The mood of Grand Trunk's executive officers remained expectant when the Canadian Pacific Railway (CP) completed its fabled route to Pacific tidewater. Yet when CP came galloping to raid Grand Trunk's service area, when other pretenders threatened similarly—well, that was another story. The mood in Grand Trunk's London office at 9 New Broad Street grew pensive. To expand was to threaten stability; to stand pat was to invite strangulation. What approach to take? The board summoned an American. Charles

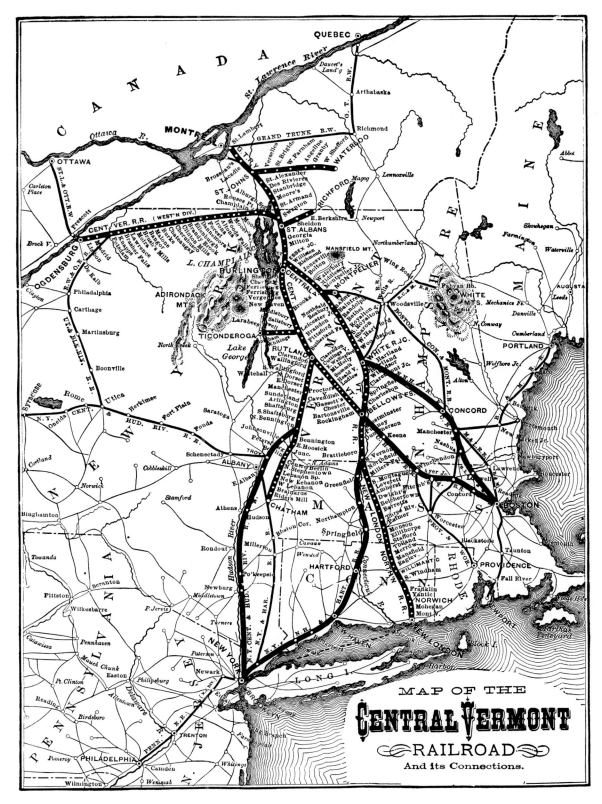

MAP OF THE
CENTRAL VERMONT
RAILROAD
And Its Connections.

Courtesy of Central Vermont.

U. S. MAIL ROUTE

Pullman Palace Drawing-Room and Sleeping Cars

ON ALL EXPRESS TRAINS BETWEEN

BOSTON, ST. ALBANS and SPRINGFIELD.

Wagner's Silver Palace Sleeping Cars

RUN THROUGH BETWEEN

St. Albans and New York

☞ Without Change. ☜

Passengers Leaving St. Albans at **6.00 P.M.** arrive in New York at **6.30** next morning,

5 hours earlier than ever before.

FIRST-CLASS DINING ROOMS

At convenient points, where ample time is given for Meals, and passengers always notified of departure of trains.

Don't Forget This :

ASK FOR TICKETS VIA ST. ALBANS.

SPEED, SAFETY AND COMFORT, **AND SURE CONNECTIONS.**

Courtesy of Central Vermont.

An American, Charles Melville Hays, would lead Grand Trunk. Photograph courtesy of Canadian National.

Melville Hays would chart a future course for the Grand Trunk Railway of Canada.[21]

Hays was a logical choice. He owned a firm reputation as a skillful operating man and much of his experience had been on a friendly American road—Wabash, which, with the Grand Trunk, offered what was labeled "Chicago, Detroit and Niagara Falls Short Line" service between Chicago and Buffalo through southern Ontario. Hays improved Grand Trunk's efficiency and paid dividends. He also promised a continuing stable performance. It was not to be. Canada was awak-

ening to its potential—a promise that only railroads, ever more railroads, could deliver. Who should build them? In the West the refrain was constant: not Canadian Pacific, which had a monopoly there. But who? Grand Trunk hesitated. Into the breach leapt a new player, Canadian Northern, which spewed lines in the West and talked of aggressive expansion in the East. At the same time, Canadian Pacific talked little and did much, building right into the Grand Trunk's domain. Flanked on the south by a host of strong American roads eager to siphon off Grand Trunk's lucrative Michigan-Ontario business and threatened on the West and even on its own turf by other Canadian rail carriers, Hays determined that Grand Trunk had to expand or expire.[22]

Expansion, however, was fraught with risk. Canada—its potential notwithstanding—remained tyrannized by great distances, sparse population, difficult terrain, and harsh climes. Was there adequate justification for massive expenditures to expand the country's rail net ahead of demand? No. Hays and Grand Trunk had properly hesitated. But powerful forces—bankers, promoters, the government, and the Canadian people themselves—decreed otherwise.

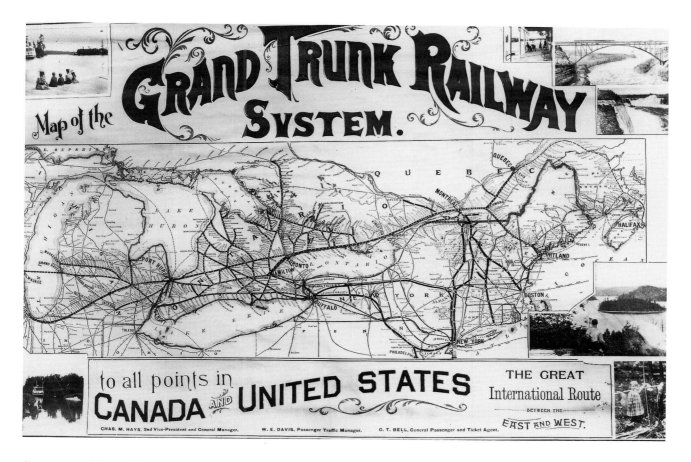

Courtesy of Canadian National.

The prevailing mood favored expansion—massive expansion, regardless of cost, for there were social ends to be met as well as transportation needs. Hays and Grand Trunk were swept up in it.[23]

The march to abyss was halting, however. Even before Hays arrived, Grand Trunk strategists studied a route west from Sault St. Marie along the south shore of Lake Superior to Duluth and northwestward to Winnipeg. Such a route, had it been executed, would have preempted Canadian Pacific clients which did adopt the route, but prevailing wisdom at Grand Trunk maintained that the right and proper route of transportation flowing from eastern to western Canada was through Chicago. After Hays arrived, he approached Canadian Pacific with proposals for cooperative undertakings, but he was spurned. Indeed, the rival established harsh rates that discriminated against trans-Canada shipments over routes to Winnipeg via Chicago and St. Paul. Hays felt he

was badly treated and was forced to seek alternatives. Some counseled collaboration with the free-spirited Canadian Northern. Hays demurred, feeling that Grand Trunk would eventually swallow up that western renegade. He was wrong.[24]

The Grand Trunk Railway and the Canadian government soon brewed an alliance of monumental importance. On 24 October 1903, the Dominion Government entered into an agreement whereby a new company, the Grand Trunk Pacific Railway, would build and operate a transcontinental railway "wholly upon Canadian territory" from Moncton, New Brunswick to the Pacific Ocean with several important branches. Collateral agreements called for the government, in fact, to build the eastern portion—Moncton to Winnipeg—and lease it to Grand Trunk Pacific while the western part was to be built by Grand Trunk Pacific with generous governmental assistance. Some questioned the need for a third major player in the West. After all, they observed, Canadian Pacific was already in place and Canadian Northern was pledged to its own trans-Canada campaign. They were shouted down. Work on the eastern leg was completed late in 1913; the western leg entered service in April 1914. Canadians now boasted three pretenders for transcontinental business.[25]

Canadians soon would realize that they also had an outsize financial embarrassment. Canada's total population was a bit over six million, giving the Dominion one mile of railway for every 185 persons. (By comparison, the United States at the same time had one mile of rail line per 400 persons.) Moreover, a great portion of Canadian trackage ran through unpopulated regions and construction costs, in virtually all cases, had far exceeded predictions. All of this aggravated existing problems. The Grand Trunk, parent and guarantor of Grand Trunk Pacific, was itself malnourished. Its major sources of revenues, Michigan and Ontario, were under competitive attack and its historic eastern seaboard-American Midwest route was long-mile and thus less efficient than others, especially the Vanderbilt lines. Consequently, Grand Trunk and Central Vermont managers, while admittedly innovative and aggressive, frequently were compelled to lower rates to ruinous levels in order to attract or retain traffic. Of problems there was an abundance.[26]

Yet for Grand Trunk there were also glimmers of hope. Hays knew well the American landscape and he labored to make the Grand Trunk's holdings in the United States more efficient and thus more valuable to the parent. In some cases his attention turned to strategic considerations; in other moments, he made tactical changes. In

Grand Trunk profoundly improved service through Sarnia and Port Huron with the St. Clair Tunnel. Photograph courtesy of the collections of Sam Breck.

1897, Hays took a more personal interest in the Michigan lines by closing the Detroit headquarters and moving managerial functions to Montreal. In the same year he also authorized further acquisitions of Central Vermont securities—increasing Grand Trunk's ownership of common shares to 70 percent. Then, in 1900, when first mortgage bonds of Chicago and Grand Trunk matured, that company was placed in friendly foreclosure; on 22 November, the Grand Trunk Western Railway (GTW) was formed to receive—in a financial sense, if not a managerial sense—the several Michigan properties. Earlier, in 1891, Grand Trunk profoundly improved service through Sarnia and Port Huron by opening the famous St. Clair Tunnel. Hays authorized additional improvements in the tunnel by replacing steam locomotives with electrical. These collective changes spelled improvement in service, in efficiency, and in financial performance. The Michigan lines gradually began to pull their weight, to repay advances made to them by the parent, and by midpoint of the first decade in the new century were even prospering.[27]

Hays was less than successful in the important strategic game, however. In 1899, he studied the possibility of extending northwestward from Chicago into Manitoba with the further idea of throwing branches over the prairies. Nothing happened, but the dream stayed alive. A decade later Hays entertained similar aspirations. Nor did his eyes rest solely on the West. In 1904, Hays laid tentative plans to connect the Michigan lines (Grand Trunk Western) directly with Central Vermont by way of a route along the south shores of Lakes Erie and Ontario. The banking firm of J. P. Morgan, closely allied with the Vanderbilt roads, thwarted this because, as Morgan correctly perceived, Hays had a secondary agenda: he wanted to reach New York City. Frustrated in this venture, Hays took another approach. In 1909, he announced bold plans to lengthen Central Vermont from Palmer, Massachusetts, to Providence, Rhode Island, 76 miles. Construction began in 1912 on the 58-mile section in Massachusetts. Why expand in an area already well served by an abundance of carriers, including, as always, powerful roads of the Vanderbilt heritage? The answer, Hays affirmed, was simple: move Canadian export grain to New England and manufactured goods to the Canadian West—loads in both directions. Moreover, steamship service might easily be established from Providence to New York City. It was not to be. Hays held tickets on the *Titanic* and died at sea on 14 April 1912. So, too, did the

Sir Henry W. Thornton would head the sprawling Canadian National. Photograph courtesy of Canadian National.

Providence venture which subsequently was called off although nearly $2 million had already been expended on it. One is left to speculate what might have been if Hays had been successful in his strategic aspirations on behalf of Grand Trunk Western and Central Vermont.[28]

There is no reason to believe that Charles M. Hays could have prevented the "Titanic" course of Canadian railroads as they steamed into the second decade of the twentieth century. At best they had been overbuilt. There were simply too

many miles of line built through difficult terrain serving an inadequate traffic base. Hays understood as much, especially in terms of Grand Trunk Pacific, and felt the only way of saving the Grand Trunk Railway of Canada—the parent— from disaster was to abrogate Grand Trunk's 1903 National Transcontinental agreement with the government. There were additional problems. The Panic of 1907 had proved particularly difficult in Canada; Grand Trunk had suffered a devastating strike in 1910; the Board of Railway

Commissioners would not raise rates to compensatory levels and, in some cases, actually lowered them; and there were crop failures. The knockout punch came, however, with World War I. Traffic levels escalated, but costs of delivering transportation soared. The burden proved overwhelming. On 4 March 1919, Grand Trunk Pacific somberly announced that its financial condition precluded continued operation "after present funds were exhausted." The Grand Trunk of Canada was also in difficulty, as were many other Canadian railroad companies. The government, which had encouraged the enterprise with monies and in other ways, was confronted with a crisis. A few days later the minister of railways and canals was appointed receiver for Grand Trunk Pacific.[29]

There followed a long and arduous process which finally gave birth to Canadian National Railway Company (CN) on 6 June 1919. Eventually, into it were poured all properties held by Grand Trunk Railway of Canada, Canadian Northern Railway, and sundry others. Conspicuous by its absence was Canadian Pacific, which remained privately held. Bold were the purposes of the new Canadian National: to consolidate these several diverse lines and to operate them as a national system. Directors were to be nominated by the governor in council and stock vested in the minister of finance. The board convened for the first time on 10 October 1922; Sir Henry W. Thornton was appointed president and chairman. Thornton, an American by birth, had started his career on the Pennsylvania Railroad and quickly established at Long Island Railroad a reputation as a skillful leader before moving in 1914 to London's Great Eastern Railway—a huge commuter system—as general manager. During World War I the British War Office tapped him to serve in France as inspector-general of transportation. After the conflict he returned to England and in March 1919 was knighted. Thornton now had the awesome responsibility of presiding over the management of nearly 22,000 miles of rail lines and almost 110,000 employees spread across the incredible breadth of Canada.[30]

Thornton faced a daunting task. Canadian National was a Crown Corporation—a quasi-independent body that was to be, ostensibly at least, free from political influence. Thornton and the CN board of directors were to answer to the minister of railways and in that way to the federal government and ultimately to the Canadian people. Thornton made it clear that he would tolerate no untoward political pressure, but Canadian traditions and circumstances made that impossible. After all, government involvement of one sort or another had typified Canadian railroad experience from the beginning and some government-sponsored lines had been specifically designed for social, political, or strategic reasons and not for the purpose of profits from operation. Against this heritage was the mirrored image of reality. Canada was changing. Yes, its population was still fleshing out, but it tended toward a thin strip just north of the U.S. boundary and was increasingly urban; before the end of the 1930s, only one-third of Canadians lived in the countryside. At the same time, the economic axis tilted evermore to a north-south orientation, in other words, linking increasingly to the United States as opposed to an east-west or cross-Canada direction. Thornton would have his hands full trying to consolidate the strange amalgam of lines then at work under the Canadian National canopy, trying to satisfy the parochial and often conflicting needs of the various provinces and constituencies, trying to ward off snoopy and often petulant politicians, trying to lift an inordinate interest debt, and trying to run an efficient and coordinated operation under the shadow of the strong and privately held Canadian Pacific. To this list of difficult problems would soon be added another: modal competition in the form of motorized vehicles.[31]

Vehicular competition had its ironic side, however, for as the North American automobile industry evolved, Detroit—located as it was on Grand Trunk Western—became the center of motor vehicle manufacturing and would produce monumental revenues for GTW and Canadian National as well. Several factors militated in Detroit's favor. It proved beautifully located to receive bulk commodities such as coal and iron ore by way of the Great Lakes; nearby hardwood forests provided essential materials for the early carriage industry that evolved into automobile manufacturing; its early managerial and technological talent as well as its financial resource base was diverse and not tied to a single industry; and, most important if accidentally, a remarkable group of entrepreneurs entered the business almost simultaneously in Detroit and elsewhere close by. Names such as Ford, Durant,

Automobiles typically moved in boxcars such as this one, but in 1923 Buick dispatched nine set up machines on one flat. GTW did the honors. Photographs courtesy of Grand Trunk Western Railroad.

Dodge, and Olds—among many others—collectively labored to make Detroit the principal motor vehicle production center of North America and, really, for the world. The impact, particularly in the United States and Canada, was quick and acute; the steam car civilization passed in favor of the auto age. Indeed, as one writer put it: "A train was a service. A motor car was a servant." For Grand Trunk Western and its parent, the Michigan-based automobile industry provided nothing less than love and hate. Total production of passenger autos in the United States rose from 199,000 in 1911 to 3,915,889 in 1937. Most of these and an appreciable proportion of the parts and/or raw materials necessary to manufacture them moved by rail. But once sold to eager customers these same automobiles immediately became deadly threats to rail passenger revenue. More crucial by far, however, was the threat posed by motor trucks which imperiled freight revenues. Bittersweet would be the motor vehicle industry for Grand Trunk Western and the railroad industry at large.[32]

Henry Thornton proved an able and personable manager for the Canadian National experiment. In 1922, he had started with a jury-rigged assortment of lines and traditions. By the end of the decade Thornton had confounded many a naysayer: CN was a viable property. Management had expanded CN's web of lines, had coordinated operations, and had improved services and gained a modicum of harmony with labor even while modestly trimming employment. Yet there was an abundance of difficulty. CN's operating ratio (ratio of operating expenses to operating revenues) from 1923 through 1929 averaged a marginally adequate 86.22 and the company ran up a staggering aggregate debt of $281,259,000.[33]

Contributing to Canadian National's financial woes during the 1920s was the Grand Trunk Western Railway. GTW and its constituent roads seemed a constant drain on Canadian National. By the end of 1927, capital advances to these subsidiaries reached a breathtaking $25,889,259. This nonnegotiable indebtedness represented cash advances necessary to cover operating deficits and arrearage in bond interest. The case of the Detroit, Grand Haven & Milwaukee, one of the GTW roads, was typical. That company advertised itself as "The Old Reliable . . . To and

From Northern Michigan," but CN accountants had reason to consider it "The Old Reliable" only in suckling at the parent's breast. In any event, the Grand Trunk Western *Railroad* was incorporated on 1 November 1928, to consolidate almost all of CN's holdings west of the St. Clair and Detroit rivers under one wing. The idea was to attain more efficient operation and to place finances on a sound basis, "independent," as far as possible of the parent company.[34]

The consolidation was straightforward. Capital stock of the former American companies owned by Canadian National was exchanged for 422,400 shares of Grand Trunk Western common stock of non-par value but upon which was placed a value of $25 per share. Important codicils dealt with the Grand Trunk-Milwaukee Car Ferry Company, the Cincinnati, Saginaw & Mackinaw Railroad, and companies which CN or the American predecessor roads leased or owned in proportion. For instance, the car ferry company remained an independent but now wholly-owned subsidiary of Grand Trunk Western, while Cincinnati, Saginaw & Mackinaw would not be merged into GTW until 1 January 1943. Proportional ownership held by predecessors in the Belt Railway Company of Chicago, Chicago & Western Indiana Railroad, and Detroit & Toledo Shore Line passed to Grand Trunk Western. The

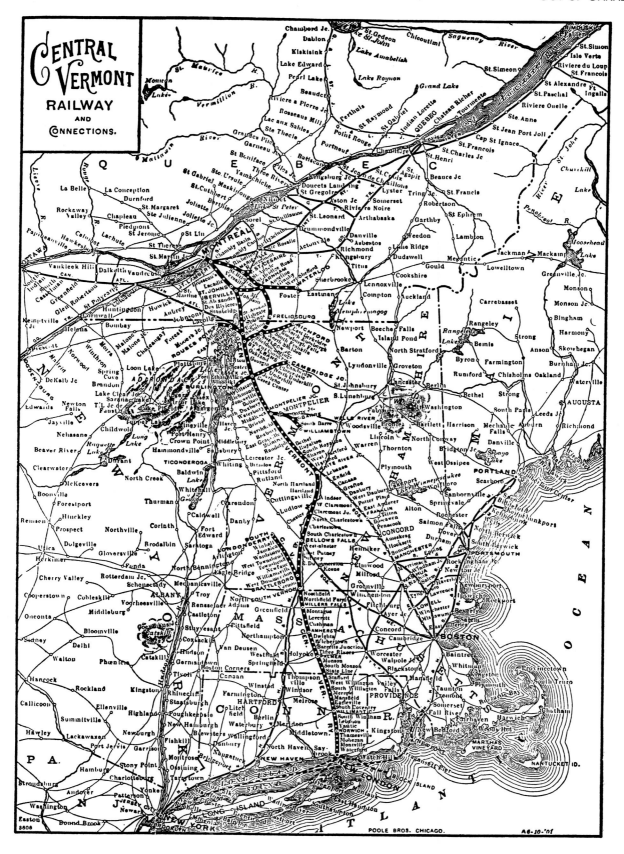

Interstate Commerce Commission gave its nod to all of this on 8 November 1929. That hardly meant managerial prerogatives passed to GTW. Only nominal decisions would be made in Detroit; major decisions, as always, were to be rendered in Montreal.[35]

The circumstance of CN's holdings in New England remained mixed. The great promise of traffic to and from Portland's year-round, ice-free harbor never materialized. Neither had the promise of Central Vermont been fully achieved. The CN line to Portland and CV's route remained strategically important, however, even though New England was overbuilt with rail lines and now faced growing threats from modal competition. The Central Vermont experience proved especially vexing in the late 1920s. More than two-thirds of its common stock had been acquired by the former Grand Trunk Railway of Canada and these securities passed with Grand Trunk to Canadian National in 1923. In addition, CN held Central Vermont's Refunding Mortgage Bonds and had advanced CV, over time, nearly $21 million for the purpose of improvements to property and to meet operating deficits. CV acted as an important intermediary in handling heavy shipments of packing house products, cattle, and grain from the American Midwest to the Boston area via White River Junction, traffic to and from break bulk steamers at New London, Connecticut, as well as outbound consignments of Barre and Bethel granite. These shipments and through passenger movements on "The Green Mountain Route" were severely affected early in November 1927, however, when torrential rains resulted in devastating floods that damaged the Central Vermont Railway Company so badly that on 12 December it went into receivership.[36]

Canadian National managers worriedly studied options regarding Central Vermont. True, there was the historic and important flow of business from the American Midwest through Canada to Boston. CV was also a long-haul conduit for Canadian newsprint, lumber, and Christmas trees in season to the thickly populated eastern American seaboard as well as a useful funnel for manufactured products and fresh fruits and vegetables moving north. There was also the matter of strategy: Central Vermont was CN's chip in maintaining competitive balance in the important Montreal-New York/New

England corridor as against Delaware & Hudson via Rouses Point, New York, and New York Central via Huntingdon, Quebec. Finally, though Central Vermont might be marginal in its own right, it did have the attractive means to give Canadian National—as a system—long hauls and presumably attractive overall revenues. In the end, money flowed again from the parent to New England to repair some 290 miles of damaged roadway. It was not simply a matter of renewing, though; it was also a matter of upgrading. New rails were installed, passing tracks were added, bridges were strengthened, ten new powerful freight locomotives were acquired as were 1,000 automobile cars. In addition, obsolete equipment was scrapped and the balance sheet tidied. CN was clearly positioning Central Vermont to play an important part in the system's strategy. Moreover, said CV's comptroller, "Central Vermont should in the future be able to finance its own Addition and Betterment projects thereby eliminating the necessity of Canadian National making further advances to this company." That must have been music to Henry Thornton's ear. Out of Central Vermont Railway *Company* emerged, on 12 August 1929, Central Vermont Railway *Incorporated*, a wholly owned subsidiary of Canadian National.[37]

Other lines of Canadian National in the United States earned less attention than Grand Trunk Western and Central Vermont, were more humble in their origins, and led more prosaic—and often more profitable—existences. One of these was the former Minnesota and Manitoba Railroad, chartered on 12 April 1899, for the purpose of building a line in Minnesota south of Lake of the Woods, from near Warroad to Baudette, about 44 miles. At Baudette, the Minnesota and Manitoba was linked to its cousin, the Minnesota and Ontario Bridge Company, incorporated, on 21 December 1899, to build a bridge over the Rainy River between Baudette and Rainy River, Ontario. The two properties were opened for business in 1900 and 1901, respectively, and were integral parts of Canadian Northern Railway, linking its Manitoba and Ontario lines. The Minnesota properties passed with Canadian Northern to Canadian National and eventually became wholly owned subsidiaries.[38]

Other holdings in Minnesota took shape more slowly. The North Star State boasted some of the

CN recommitted to CV, acquiring ten 2-10-4 locomotives for expedited freight service. Photograph courtesy of Canadian National.

finest white pine anywhere, and shortly after the turn of the century lumbermen turned their attention to the largest remaining stand of such timber—several billion board feet extending southeastward from the Canadian border on the Rainy River to the Mesabi Range. Wirt H. Cook and others who owned impressive holdings northwest of Virginia, Minnesota, presently undertook to build milling and transportation facilities to harvest these white pine forests. To this end, they formed the Duluth, Virginia & Rainy Lake Railway on 15 August 1901. Initial construction was modest in character and in strategic design. In 1905, however, Cook projected extensive plans to carry the road to additional timber holdings nearer the Canadian boundary. In the same year, the corporate designation was changed to the Duluth, Rainy Lake & Winnipeg Railway. Its line was extended substantially in 1908, from the Canadian boundary at Ranier, near International Falls and opposite Fort Frances, Ontario, to Cook and existing trackage there into Virginia.[39]

Not surprisingly, this activity caught the fancy of those behind the expansive Canadian Northern. On 18 November 1908, they purchased the capital stock of Duluth, Rainy Lake & Winnipeg. Not satisfied with a stub of railroad and lured by the extensive port facilities at Duluth, they formed the Duluth, Winnipeg & Pacific Railway (DW&P) on 19 March 1909. In 1910, DW&P received the capital stock of Duluth, Rainy Lake & Winnipeg and late in 1912 bridged the gap between the Lakehead and Virginia with a 78-mile line. The whole was operated as one system from Duluth to a connection with Canadian Northern at Ranier. The road was predictably dependent on billings from the Virginia and Rainy Lake mills at Virginia. Those facilities, with combined capacity of 300 million board feet annually, dispatched a seemingly endless flow of product to the docks or connecting carriers at Duluth.[40]

All capital stock, assets, debt, and leases of the Duluth, Winnipeg & Pacific moved with Canadian Northern to Canadian National. Henry

In 1908, the line was completed to Ranier, across from International Falls. Terminal facilities are shown here. Photograph courtesy of Duluth, Winnipeg & Pacific Railway.

An inspection train, at right, has crossed from International Falls to Ranier before completing its trip to the Lakehead at Duluth. Photograph courtesy of Duluth, Winnipeg & Pacific Railway.

Some way station facilities, such as that at Ellsmere, were quite impressive, but others like that at Orr, were more prosaic. Photographs courtesy of Duluth, Winnipeg & Pacific Railway.

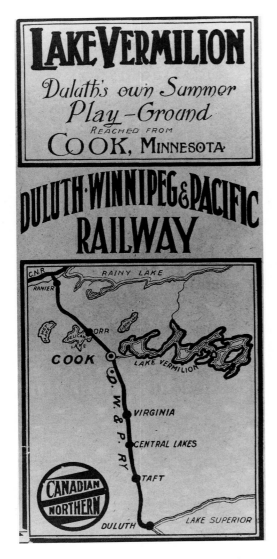

Thornton may have foreseen DW&P's long-term strategic value, but he had good reason to be perplexed by its immediate financial performance. For the years 1923-29, inclusive, DW&P earned a surplus from operation only in 1927 and 1928 and rolled up a total operating deficit for the period of $590,976. And the future looked worse. Minnesota's magnificent white pine forests were nearly exhausted. The closing of the huge mills at Virginia on 9 October 1929 reflected that sad reality. A few days later came an unrelated but even more ominous development: the great Wall Street crash. Over the next six years, Duluth, Winnipeg & Pacific would suffer nearly $5 million in operating losses.[41]

DW&P's frightening financial performance mirrored, albeit in microcosm, the financial results of the Canadian National during the Great Depression. CN's mounting deficits as hard times deepened were reflected politically as forces aligned themselves against the Crown Corporation and Henry Thornton as its leader. Thornton had, in fact, inherited a bewildering array of properties laded with an equally bewildering array of problems. He had molded them into a functioning, viable whole, but profits for the most part had eluded him. But profits alone, said Starr W. Fairweather, one of Thornton's subordinates, should not be the sole measure of Canadian National's value; rather, overall contribution to the Canadian community should be the ultimate test. Perhaps so, but Henry Thornton was forced to resign in 1932, the victim of shabby treatment by politicians and, in a sense, a victim of the raging depression. Samuel J. Hungerford had the unenviable task of following Thornton and of steering CN through perilous times. CN's employee numbers dropped by a startling 25 percent from 1930 to 1936 before turning upward, and the road's aggregate debt for the 1930s totaled a disheartening $739,071,000. The operating ratio for the decade was a dreary 93.64.[42]

The war years brought CN a new president, R. C. Vaughan, a huge surge in business, higher employee numbers, higher average salaries and wages, and revenues adequate to cover operating expenses and interest as well. For the period 1941-45, CN earned a surplus of $116,142,000 and its managers pointed with pride to an operating ratio that averaged 78.55. CN's properties in the United States—Central Vermont, Duluth, Winnipeg & Pacific and, especially, Grand Trunk Western which profited from war-related industries—gleefully contributed to its financial happiness.[43]

But what did the postwar era portend? For Canadian National, there were historic hazards—heavy debt and the mixed blessing of being a Crown Corporation—to which were added increasing modal competition from water, vehicular, and air transport. Would the war years prove an aberration? Would auditors again post their reports in red ink? How would the elevation of the United States to the rank of superpower affect Canada? Would Canada, with its huge land mass configured on an east-west axis, tilt evermore to a north-south orientation? If so, what meaning was there for CN in its properties south of the border?

Early results were mixed. Canadian National came out of the war years with its physical property in rather good shape but its car supply and car condition were little better than adequate. Its motive power was essentially steam of modest repute. Passenger numbers were about what they had been in the 1920s—higher than the 1930s and lower than the war years—and revenue ton miles were impressive. But wages and salaries were high relative to rate increases and employment was disproportionately high, a fact reflected in the operating ratio: 92.49 for the years 1946-49. Cumulative deficits for the same years amounted to $100,423,000.[44]

How would CN meet challenges of the 1950s and beyond? Those strategic decisions would not be rendered by R. C. Vaughan, who retired on 11 October 1949. He was succeeded by a most unlikely man—a banker who freely admitted his ignorance of all things ferrorail. But Donald Gordon, born in Scotland in 1901, was a most marvelous choice to solidly position Canadian National in an increasingly hostile competitive environment. He promised "leadership, imagination and energy" in building CN into a stronger system. He delivered on all accounts, but progress came along a bumpy path. His banker's eye predictably watered over the condition of CN's income statement. Gordon knew that starving the property into prosperity was impossible; neither was it probable that the road could gain adequate and proper rate increases. Laboring in the shadow of CN's well-publicized deficit, Gordon determined to spend expansively to replace steam power with diesel; to modernize rolling stock; to improve productivity; to advance CN's analytical capacity; and to exploit new markets. He also attacked CN's legacy of inherited debt. The federal government grudgingly agreed to lift much funded indebtedness, but Gordon

Wartime traffic was both heavy and time sensitive. But Mother Nature occasionally held the trump card. DW&P crews battled snow at milepost 14 on 16 March 1943. Photographs courtesy of Duluth, Winnipeg & Pacific Railway.

Detroit had grown up with the auto industry and by the end of World War II was a substantial city. Windsor, Ontario lies across the Detroit River. Photograph courtesy of Grand Trunk Western Railroad.

was less successful in the field of labor productivity. Indeed, employment rose during the 1950s and numbers did not show an appreciable decrease until 1960—reflecting, in part, CN's conversion to diesel power. Meanwhile, average hourly earnings per employee rose steadily. CN earned surplus in four years of the 1950s, but for the decade accumulated a debt of $171,803,000. The operating ratio averaged 94.53. Would the 1960s see a better financial result? The experience of 1960 augured ill. The deficit for that year alone was $61,497,000 and the operating ratio climbed to an abysmal 98.94.[45]

There was no denying that Canadian National was a more vibrant, modern enterprise after ten years under Donald Gordon who continued to preach that CN should be operated on a business basis. But that was not always possible, for as a Crown Corporation CN was open to political

pressure from a wide and often parochial constituency. Employee productivity was an obvious case, as was the "passenger problem." Gordon was pessimistic about the future of the passenger carrying trade, but public sentiment—if not public ridership—was emphatic in support of the trains. Gordon had to reverse field on that issue. CN spent heavily to upgrade passenger equipment and service. Boardings stabilized, rose, and then declined again. By 1960, passenger numbers were slightly above depression levels although the Canadian population had increased in the meantime.[46]

The circumstance of CN's American roads was not entirely analogous. All of them—GTW, DW&P, and CV—had boasted passenger operations that, while serving local needs, were strategically linked to the parent. Central Vermont, for example, prided itself in forwarding name trains to and from Montreal, Boston, and New York City, and for some years handled a Boston-Chicago Pullman sleeper in conjunction with the Grand Trunk Railway of Canada and its Chicago & Grand Trunk Railway. As late as 1960, CV still handled name trains and offered a local north of White River Junction, Vermont, but in 1966 it dropped all passenger offerings. Passenger service at DW&P was never as grand, although in 1913 it handled "Through Coaches, Standard Sleeping Cars and Diner on Trains 1 and 2. Cafe Observation Cars on Trains 3 and 4." The road solicited business especially from outdoorsmen, pointing out that "the country traversed by the Duluth, Winnipeg & Pacific is one singularly attractive to the sportsmen." Patrons could transact business at the Duluth city office, conveniently located at 430 West Superior Street. For a while DW&P even participated in through service from Chicago to Vancouver in conjunction with Chicago & North Western and Canadian National. In 1950, the road still advertised coach service on daily-except-Sunday Duluth-Fort Frances-Winnipeg trains with a buffet sleeping car available on a tri-weekly basis. A decade later only "Railiner" (RDC) service remained, and that ended on 1 July 1961.[47]

Of CN's properties south of the border, Grand Trunk Western was the leader in passenger offerings. "The 'Limiteds' of the Grand Trunk Railway . . . are the equal of any railway system in the world," boasted the company in 1913. One of these trains, *The International Limited*, served Chicago from Montreal via Detroit beginning in 1900. The road handled an astonishing number of through trains of cars to and from Montreal, Boston, and New York City by way of Detroit or Port Huron. In 1893, a half-dozen trains in each direction served Chicago. That pattern obtained into the depression, but by 1950 service had been trimmed to three trains on the Chicago route and three trains to Detroit. The service was good, and the equipment reflected Gordon's campaign of modernization. The flagships were the *International Limited* (Montreal-Chicago), the *Inter-City Limited* (Montreal-Detroit-Chicago), and the *Maple Leaf* (Montreal-Detroit); each featured coaches, diners, parlor cars, and sleepers. Such service levels extended into the 1960s, although demand softened as passengers turned to jet air service or took to the new interstate highway system.[48]

The "passenger problem" and CN's other liabilities, assets, and opportunities were increas-

The *Ambassador* was CV's pride and joy. Shown here, it is departing the historic station at St. Albans. Photograph courtesy of Canadian National.

THE *New* AMBASSADOR

FASTEST DAY TRAIN
Montreal - Vermont - Boston

ingly the province of a small but lively cadre of managers headed by Starr Fairweather, the venerable if "erratic genius and autocrat at the head of [CN's] Research and Development." Donald Gordon had been shocked at the stodgy "chief clerk mentality" and the outmoded apprenticeship system that governed training and promotion at CN. Merit and broadening were given short shrift. At CN, Gordon discovered, the military style was writ large; one questioned not one's superior; one learned the way the boss did his work so that in time one could replace the boss. All of it represented and perpetuated the status quo, the "this is the way we have always done it" syndrome. The Staff Training College, instituted in 1952, was designed to broaden managerial viewpoints and improve morale. It was a good start, Gordon chafed, but inadequate. He cast about for new talent—outside the company, and frequently outside the industry. To CN came Robert Tarr, Pierre Taschereau, Ralph Vaughan, Omand Solandt, and Robert A. Bandeen among others. Most were placed with Fairweather, who had a volatile if productive relationship with Gordon. CN's reputation for analytical studies, testing, research, and innovative methods grew as Fairweather's men poked and prodded in all of the company's closets. Not everybody was happy with the activity; there were, after all, turfs and traditions to be pro-

tected, egos to be guarded. But none believed there would be turning back.[49]

By 1960, Gordon's impact on CN was unmistakable. He had persons whom he respected running the operation while he himself acted increasingly as the head of a holding company. His trusted executive vice president was an attorney, Norman J. MacMillan; the two made a good team. Meanwhile, for more than five years Parliament had been wrestling with the role of railways in Canada. The first volume of the so-called MacPherson Royal Commission was scheduled for release early in 1961 and Gordon was frankly apprehensive as to its intent and impact. One of the new recruits, Robert A. Bandeen, had labored hard before the MacPherson Commission on behalf of CN and the Canadian rail industry and had reason to expect much of it. Bandeen was correct. The government would finally recognize that the railroad industry's near modal monopoly was a thing of the past, that rates should meet or surpass costs of providing service, that service rendered on behalf of the public should be compensated by the government, and that while an era of competitive coexistence had dawned, the railroads remained Canada's transportation backbone. Gordon came to embrace the MacPherson report and with it Bandeen, who had defended it to him.[50]

Gordon, however, was increasingly under fire. His efforts to modernize and generate more rev-

The *Inter-City Limited* has made its daily westbound calling at Durand and now heads for Lansing, Battle Creek, South Bend, and Chicago. Summer 1953. Courtesy of the Cleland B. Wylie collection.

Dieselization had been a priority during the Gordon years. Here new power heads a long train at Chicago's Elsdon Yard. Photograph courtesy of Grand Trunk Western Railroad.

enues (especially freight) were duly recognized but, frankly, the financial condition of CN was not materially improved. And there was the man himself; he acted as a lightning rod on some. Most of all there was a change in government with predictable political whipsawing. Gordon made his departure on 31 December 1966. To his successor, Norman J. MacMillan, Gordon bequeathed a modernized property with a strong management team. Moreover, payments of inherited indebtedness had been pared to a mere 2.2 percent of annual revenues.[51]

MacMillan did not find himself in a bed of roses, however. Profitability remained elusive and there was the always nettlesome matter of trying to balance the east-west Canadian axis with overwhelming economic impulses from the United States. Such impulses and channels could not be ignored, even if they threatened CN's coast-to-coast or all-Canada routes and responsibilities. What policies should govern between the Canadian National and its American properties, especially the increasingly debt-producing Grand Trunk Western? What strategic roles would CN's American roads play in a rapidly changing and fiercely competitive market? What should be the administrative linkage between parent and siblings? What of profitability? These proved troublesome issues for N. J. MacMillan. They were troublesome issues for Robert A. Bandeen as well. They were also opportunities.

NOTES

1. Edward C. Kirkland, *A History of American Economic Life,* 4th ed. (New York: Appleton-Century-Crofts, 1969), 131-70.
2. James Hayward, *Report on the Proposed Railroad between Boston and Ogdensburg* (Boston: Hendee & Babcock, 1831), quoted in Edward Chase Kirkland, *Men, Cities and Transportation: A Study of New York History, 1820-1900,* 2 vols. (Cambridge: Harvard University Press, 1948), 1: 159-60.
3. G. R. Stevens, *Canadian National Railways: Sixty Years of Trial and Error* (Toronto: Clarke, Irwin & Co., 1960), 52-54 [Hereinafter cited as Stevens I]; A. B. Hopper and T. Kearney, compls, *Canadian National Railways: Synoptical History of Organization, Capital Stock, Funded Debt and Other General Information as of December 31, 1960* (Montreal: Canadian National, Accounting Department, 1962), 2-6, 719-20 [Hereinafter cited as *Synoptical History*]; On Poor, see Alfred D. Chandler, *Henry Varnum Poor: Business Editor, Analyst, and Reformer* (Cambridge: Harvard University Press, 1965), and Matthew A. Redinger, "Henry Varnum Poor," *Railways in the Nineteenth Century,* Robert L. Frey, editor (New York: Facts on File, 1988), 330-32.
4. *Synoptical History,* 247; Stevens I, 54.
5. Ibid., 708; Kirkland, *Men . . . Transportation,* 169; William E. Navin, "The Founding of the Rutland Railroad," *Vermont Quarterly* 14 (July 1946): 91-94.
6. Kirkland, *Men . . . Transportation,* 164.
7. Stevens, I, 56-62; *Synoptical History,* 719.
8. Kirkland, *Men . . . Transportation,* 206-14; *Synoptical History,* 2.
9. *Synoptical History,* 247-48, 653; Kirkland, *Men . . . Transportation,* 1: 171-75.
10. Ibid., 3, 363-64, 719; Stevens I, 81-89.
11. Stevens I, 67.
12. *Synoptical History,* 365, 369, 713-15.
13. Ibid., 367-69, 389; Stevens I, 333.
14. *Synoptical History,* 340, 363, 371.
15. Stevens I, 340, 363, 371.
16. *Synoptical History,* 296-97, 740-41; Stevens I, 368-69; Paul Trap, "Foreign Railroads in Michigan, 1857-1893," *The Old Northwest: A Journal of Regional Life and Letters* 13 (Winter 1986): 371-98.
17. Stevens I, 351; Kirkland, *Men . . . Transportation,* 1: 351; *Synoptical History,* 251-52, 653, 708 ; On the Rutland, see Jim Shaughnessy, *The Rutland Road* (Berkeley: Howell-North Books, 1964); Lawrence Doherty, "General History of the Ogdensburg & Lake Champlain Railroad," *Bulletin, Railway & Locomotive Historical Society* (August 1942): 91-95; Charles J. Kennedy, "The Rutland Railroad," *Railroads in the Nineteenth Century,* Robert L. Frey, editor (New York: Facts on File, 1988), 355-57: J. Kevin Graffagnino, "John Gregory Smith," *Railroads in the Nineteenth Century,* Robert L. Frey, editor (New York: Facts on File, 1988), 365-66.
18. Stevens I, 351-52; Kirkland, *Men . . . Transportation,* 1: 436-46.
19. *Synoptical History,* 251-52; Kirkland, *Men . . . Transportation,* 1: 438, 439, 444-46, 464-65; *Official Guide of the Railways* (June 1893): 76-77, 157.
20. John F. Stover, *American Railroads* (Chicago: University of Chicago Press, 1961), 110-11, 117-18, 135.

21. G. R. Stevens, *Canadian National Railways: Towards the Inevitable, 1896-1922* (Toronto: Clarke, Irwin & Company, Ltd., 1962), 125 [Hereinafter cited as Stevens II]. On the Canadian Pacific, see Omer LaValle, *Van Horne's Road* (Montreal: Railfare, 1975), Pierre Berton, *The Impossible Railway: The Building of the Canadian Pacific—A Triumphant Saga of Exploration, Politics, High Finance and Adventure* (New York: Alfred A. Knopf, 1972), and W. K. Lamb, *History of the Canadian Pacific* (New York: Macmillan, 1976).

22. Stevens II, 125; *The Biographical Directory of the Railway Officials America* (Chicago: The Railway Age, 1896), 211-12.

23. Stevens I, 241-58.

24. Stevens II, 127.

25. *Synoptical History*, 346-49; Donald Mackay, *The Asian Dream: The Pacific Rim and Canada's National Railway* (Vancouver: Douglas & McIntyre, 1986), 53-83, 99-103.

26. MacKay, *The Asian Dream,* 101; Kirkland, *Men . . . Transportation,* 465, 502-13.

27. Stevens II, 235, 237, 245, 248; *Synoptical History,* 44, 713-14.

28. Stevens II, 242, 253, 251-53; Gregg M. Turner and Melancthon W. Jacobus, *Connecticut Railroads . . . an Illustrated History* (Hartford: Connecticut Historical Society, 1989), 229-30.

29. Stevens I, 253; *Synoptical History,* 348-49.

30. *Synoptical History,* 82-83; On the amalgamation of Canadian National, see Stevens II, 455-523; Kenneth S. Mackenzie, "Term of Convenience to Legal Entity: The Canadian National Railways, 1918-1923," *Canadian Rail* (May-June 1983): 76-87; John Eagle, "Monopoly or Competition: The Nationalization of the Grand Trunk Railway," *Canadian Historical Review* 62, no. 1 (1981): 3-30.

31. G. R. Stevens, *History of the Canadian National Railways* (New York: Macmillan Company, 1973), 307-10, 447, 449 [Hereinafter cited as Stevens III]; Kenneth S. Mackenzie, J. Norman Lowe, with Bill Palmer, "A Legacy Transformed," *CN Movin* 21 (February 1989): 9-10; S. W. Fairweather, "A New View of the C. N. R.," *The Railroad Telegrapher* 56 (April 1939): 246-49.

32. Stevens II, 256; John B. Rae, *The Automobile Industry* (Boston: Twayne Publishers, 1984), 29-30; James J. Flink, *The Automobile Age* (Cambridge: MIT Press, 1988), 56-72, 86-111, 135-57; Stevens III, 396; Alfred D. Chandler, compl. and ed., *Giant Enterprise: Ford, General Motors, and the Automobile Industry* (New York: Harcourt, Brace & World, 1964), xi-xii, 3, 9-20.

33. Stevens III, 311-44; *Synoptical History,* 90, 120-21.

34. Ibid., 333; Grand Trunk Western Railroad Company, Agreement of Consolidation (9 May 1928), Secretary's file; *Synoptical History,* 429-37; Detroit, Grand Haven & Milwaukee Railway, Time Table (20 April 1891), front page; 158 ICC, 117-43, 239-53.

35. *Synoptical History,* 429-33; 258 ICC, 239-53.

36. Ibid., 254-57; Central Vermont Railway, "Report Prepared for Hon. W. C. Kennedy, Minister of Railways and Canals" (1 March 1922).

37. Central Vermont Railway, Inc., "A Brief Resume as to the Central Vermont Railway, Inc., and the Territory Served," E. Deschenes to George A. Gaston and J. W. Richmond, receivers of the Central Vermont Railway Co., undated [1930]; *Synoptical History,* 254-57; Charles Spooner Forbes and Jack B. Wood, "History of the Vermont Central—Central Vermont Railway System, 1843-1933," *The Vermonter* 37 (1932): 265; *Railway Age* 84 (21 January 1928): 207; *Railway Age* 84 (11 February 1928): 352-54; *Railway Age* 87 (5 October 1929): 815-16; St. Albans (Vermont) *Daily Messenger,* 29 July 1929.

38. *Synoptical History,* 547-50; Richard S. Prosser, *Rails to the North Star* (Minneapolis: Dillon Press, 1966), 148.

39. Prosser, *Rails,* 43, 48-49, 131, 133; *Synoptical History,* 303-4; Frank A. King, *Minnesota's Logging Railroads* (San Marino: Golden West Books, 1981), 119-20.

40. *Synoptical History,* 304-8; King, *Minnesota's,* 121-23; 141 ICC, 503; Stevens II, 64.

41. King, *Minnesota's,* 127.

42. *Synoptical History,* 120-21; Stevens III, 343, 347, 348-78.

43. Ibid., 120-21; Stevens III, 379-414.

44. Ibid.

45. Stevens III, 415-36; *Synoptical History,* 120-21.

46. Ibid., 436-40; *Synoptical History,* 121.

47. William L. Rohde, "Border Line," *Railroad Magazine* 43 (August 1947): 8-33; *Official Guide of the Railways* (June 1893): 96-97, 104 and (October 1960): 966; Scott Hartley, "Central Vermont . . . A Survivor," *Trains* 56 (February 1991): 30-42; Canadian Northern/DW&P, *Time Table* (2 November 1913), back cover; DW&P, *Time Table* (1 October 1923), front cover; *Official Guide of the Railways* (January 1930): 1200, (November 1950):

1141, and (October 1960): 995; Prosser, *Rails,* 74, 79; Patrick C. Dorin, *The Canadian National Railways' Story* (Seattle: Superior Publishing Co., 1975), 164.

48. Arthur D. Dubin, *Some Classic Trains* (Milwaukee: Kalmbach Publishing Co., 1964), 334-45; *Official Guide of the Railways,* (June 1893): 96-97, 103-4; Ibid., (January 1930): 1204-5, 1225-26; Ibid., (November 1950): 1114-15, 1131-32; Ibid., (October 1960): 968-69, 985-86.

49. Joseph Schull, *The Great Scot: A Biography of Donald Gordon* (Montreal: McGill-Queen's University Press, 1979), 152-55, 173-74.

50. Ibid., 142, 175, 196, 209.

51. Ibid., 209; Stevens III, 449, 451, 456-58.

3  GRAND BEGINNINGS

At the senior level, I would like your officers, as well as yourself, to regard the Grand Trunk as an integral part of the Canadian National family. This being so, I expect there will be instances where the System interests may outweigh more parochial considerations.

N. J. MacMillan to R. A. Bandeen,
18 November 1971

As Robert A. Bandeen saw it, the constituent members of Grand Trunk Corporation represented a very mixed bag but, taken together under a holding company, they represented a monumental opportunity. And he said as much. Doubters, of whom there were many, may have snickered that Bandeen's assessment was itself a monumental cliché. It was. When a newcomer arrived in Detroit at Bandeen's invitation he asked an old hand from Canadian National "if we have a chance of success?" Responded the old hand: "No chance whatsoever, but you'll have a good time trying." Such dire predictions notwithstanding, Grand Trunk Corporation was a model that Bandeen could shape and form—a model which he could tinker with and test.[1]

Among other immediate problems and opportunities was the necessity of forging a senior management team that would be made up,

Bandeen reminded Montreal, of railroaders from the United States. The focus would be on Grand Trunk Western; Central Vermont and Duluth, Winnipeg & Pacific would continue temporarily under the management aegis of Canadian National. Bandeen considered three areas to be of crucial importance: operating, marketing, and finance. He chose for these John H. Burdakin, Walter H. Cramer, and Donald G. Wooden, respectively.

A career railroader, John Burdakin came from Penn Central where he had been vice president and general manager of the Lakes and Northern regions. He was born on 11 August 1922 at Milton, Massachusetts, and graduated in civil engineering from Massachusetts Institute of Technology after a three-and-one-half-year interruption for service as an officer in the army during World War II. Burdakin's father was a manager for a small manufacturing firm that perished during the Great Depression. This event made an indelible impression on the younger Burdakin who resolved never to work for a small company. Thus when the mighty Pennsylvania Railroad offered him a position in 1947, he was receptive. After all, the size and heritage of the Pennsylvania implied stability, and the company's well-established training program implied rapid promotion. He rose rapidly

John H. Burdakin. Photograph courtesy of Grand Trunk Western Railroad.

cate of marketing as opposed to the well-ingrained "traffic" or "have a cigar" sales traditions of the railroad industry. This stood him in good stead with Bandeen who viewed the world similarly.[3]

Donald Wooden's assignment was at once well defined and amorphous. He was placed in charge of finance and corporate planning. Wooden was born in Baltimore on 5 November 1925 and graduated from George Washington University before serving with the U.S. Department of Commerce as a business economist. Previous railroad experience came at Baltimore & Ohio and Chesapeake & Ohio where he dealt with cost research and financial planning—areas akin to Bandeen's own interests.[4]

It was on these three men—Burdakin, Cramer, and Wooden—that Bandeen pinned his hopes for a successful Grand Trunk Corporation. In Burdakin, Bandeen had found a "hardnosed operating guy," as one fellow-railroader called him, and "down to earth; an engineer," as defined by another. To Burdakin fell the responsibility of markedly improving GTW's productivity and shaking up its "this is the way we have always done it, and Montreal likes it that way" operating tradition. Cramer's responsibility called for creating a true marketing approach, carving out a clear identity for GTW in the mind of the shipping community, and in interfacing with CN's tradition-bound traffic department which might be expected to look at Cramer and his marketing group as upstart poachers. Wooden's task was easily as taxing. He was to set up the books so they could be audited, to provide useful and timely planning, budgeting, and reporting systems, and to explore

through the chairs at the Pennsylvania and its successor, Penn Central, with one brief sabbatical leave to head the Panama Canal's railroad operation. He was predictably frustrated at ill-fated Penn Central and eagerly accepted Bandeen's invitation to become GTW's vice president of operations.[2]

The marketing responsibility fell to Walter Cramer who moved to GTW from the St. Louis-San Francisco Railway where he had been assistant vice president for traffic development and planning. Born in Philadelphia on 8 June 1928, Cramer was educated at Pennsylvania State University and the University of Pittsburgh. His career included positions inside and apart from the railroad industry. Cramer was an early advo-

Walter H. Cramer. Photograph courtesy of Grand Trunk Western Railroad.

Donald G. Wooden. Photograph courtesy of Grand Trunk Western Railroad.

all means by which to make GTW—and to an extent Grand Trunk Corporation—a financially viable operation.[5]

All three men, in one fashion or another, labored to create a new image—and self-image—of Grand Trunk Western. For example, GTW officers began to participate in the affairs of the Association of American Railroads and Bandeen would sit on its board of directors. In addition, part of Cramer's marketing task was to advertise GTW as part of the much larger Canadian National and at the same time as a freestanding entity in the United States. Burdakin had the opportunity to physically change GTW's image. CN a decade earlier had abandoned its delightful and famous maple leaf logo in favor of an "elision of the letters CN into an attractive monogram that swam endlessly forward." GTW had reflected this change with its own GT logo which Burdakin understood was not negotiable. But by employing approved CN colors in a new admixture, Burdakin reasoned that motive power and rolling stock could be adorned in a way to imply independence. Bandeen agreed. Locomotives quickly appeared in a striking combination of blue, white, red/orange, and black; rolling stock showed up in blue. Wooden took up the essential task of creating new departments—accounting, finance, budgets and analysis, real estate and tax—as well as fashioning appropriate procedures for each. He also set up a computer system adequate to the needs of GTW independent of CN.[6]

Burdakin, Cramer, and Wooden also turned to the business of establishing new practices and traditions. This would prove difficult. Burdakin, for example, was astonished and dismayed to find steam locomotive parts stocked at the Battle Creek shops—a decade after the demise of steam. It reflected a deeper problem. Absentee or remote management had resulted in the absence of incentive across GTW. Montreal had not encouraged or rewarded innovation. As Don Wooden candidly observed: "Absentee management was no management." The new team constantly confronted profound cases of lethargy and suspicion. Its chore was nothing less than transforming GTW's corporate culture.[7]

In that endeavor, the team of three would require talented and enthusiastic lieutenants. Wooden brought in Jerome F. Corcoran as director of budget and cost analysis, Paul E. Tatro as controller, and Howard M. Tischler as assistant

Burdakin reasoned that motive power and rolling stock could be adorned in a way that implied independence. Bandeen agreed. Photographs courtesy of Canadian National.

Burdakin, Cramer, and Wooden set about to transform the culture of Grand Trunk Western. They would have their hands full. Photograph courtesy of Grand Trunk Western Railroad.

vice president-information and control systems. In marketing, Cramer recruited Robert A. Walker as general manager of marketing, and R. Franklin Unger and then William J. McKnight as director of automotive marketing; he also promoted Robert M. Zaleta from within to director of pricing services. For his part, Burdakin selected E. Robert Adams as general superintendent of transportation and, a bit later, William Glavin as general manager. As aide-de-camp and eventual corporate secretary, Bandeen tapped Earl G. Fontaine. Except for McKnight, who came from Ford, all had experience in the railroad industry.

Bandeen supported Burdakin and the others in their campaign of independence for it reflected his "Americanization" philosophy. There was at least tacit support from Montreal since Norman MacMillan had agreed to the idea of an American team that would be more autonomous and

responsible for its own affairs. Moreover, senior officers at CN ultimately recognized that GTW had not been managed as a business and now agreed to give Bandeen and the Grand Trunk Corporation idea a try. "Get it up and running, and we'll see what the options are," said an important officer in Montreal. One very real option, Bandeen sternly reminded his new team in Detroit, was to get rid of Grand Trunk Western "if it [the GTC experiment] did not work out." He was not jesting.[8]

Canadian National's public position regarding the Grand Trunk Corporation was opaque. As stated by CN in 1971: "An important objective is to improve the financial position of the subsidiaries by giving them greater ability to formulate and implement marketing and operating strategies in close relations to U.S. conditions." Small wonder. CN had posted deficits of

Earl G. Fontaine, GTW.

E. Robert Adams, GTW.

Robert M. Zaleta, GTW.

William Glavin, GTW.

Howard M. Tischler, GTW.

William J. McKnight, GTW.

$413,164,000 for the decade of the 1960s, but in some seasons the net deficit for Grand Trunk Western alone was greater than for the parent. The new decade started no better. GTW losses in 1970 were $30 million; for CN in the same year the deficit was $29.7 million. Small wonder indeed that the very deliberate and cautious MacMillan was willing to give Bandeen his head. "You will be responsible for ensuring that the best possible advantage will flow from the consolidation of the American companies," MacMillan told Bandeen.[9]

Bandeen took this as a mandate and promised support for a broad pattern of change. The shift to American managers was not, he affirmed, a paper change. "The Grand Trunk will be run like a separate corporation, including an active board of directors." Advanced marketing techniques and firm cost control would be hallmarks of the new style. "We've been operating [GTW] like a branch line, picking up freight business for the CN in Canada—business we would probably get anyway." Now, Bandeen asserted, "we will go after freight traffic in the productive southern Michigan market, bound for the West, through Chicago." Eventually he would even look to the South and to the East and go head-to-head with powerful competitors there. Meanwhile, unproductive branches would be shorn as the property slimmed down.[10]

Reviews were mixed. Principal shippers which had long chafed because "everything had to be referred to CN and it took a long time to get a decision" appreciated Walter Cramer's fresh style, especially in regard to rates and equipment. They also appreciated GTW's businesslike approach. "Setting up the railroad on a stand alone basis was a good step," enthused one impressed shipper's representative. Competing railroads took another view. They had often chided shippers, asking: "Why are you using a railroad owned by foreigners? Why are you subsidizing a foreign country?" That xenophobic challenge often had been a disadvantage to GTW, but with Bandeen's "Americanization" program, Burdakin and Cramer had a new and powerful tool to hold or possibly increase business.[11]

The new team made progress, if slowly. Walter Cramer identified and "de-solicited" unprofitable business such as livestock and less-than-carload

Bandeen would focus on Chicago, hoping to drive more traffic through that crucial gateway. Photograph courtesy of Grand Trunk Western Railroad.

Bandeen authored and fully supported the Americanization plan for GTW. Major shippers, including the great automakers, approved. Photograph courtesy of Grand Trunk Western Railroad.

commodities while probing for new and profitable lading. Donald Wooden labored to formulate immediate as well as long term financial plans. John Burdakin conducted "clean-up" programs and safety campaigns and sought to improve train performance and plant while trimming employee numbers. It was a delicate balancing act.[12]

Robert Bandeen was cautious in appraising the first full year of Grand Trunk Corporation's existence. He recalled that on 1 January 1972, the amounts payable to Canadian National by the constituent roads—GTW, CV, DW&P—as well as locomotives and cars on lease to these properties had been transferred to GTC in exchange for capital stock. During the full calendar year GTC recorded a $6.6 million deficit, compared to losses of $10 million for the "same operations under other companies for 1971." Among benefits of consolidation was the amalgamation of the tax loss position of Grand Trunk Western, both past and current, against the profitable DW&P and CV. At the end of 1972, GTC had $123.7 million in remaining previous tax losses.[13]

Of this $123.7 million, $14 million in tax losses would expire in 1973 and other amounts in succeeding years. With this in mind, Bandeen urged acquisition by GTC of operating companies related to transportation with good profits but with heavy tax liabilities that could be sheltered with GTC losses. Bandeen hoped that at least one such company would be listed on the stock exchange so that Grand Trunk Corporation could be merged into it and thus acquire a stock listing. MacMillan predictably thought the plan daring but went along, feeling that it offered the best hope for getting back some of the monies that CN had poured into Grand Trunk Western. Thus was laid the foundation for GTC's eventual diversification program.[14]

The first annual report issued by GTC for the public was in 1972. It did not contain the opinion of an independent accountant, but the 1973 issue did, which was of considerable importance. Indeed, because of this imprimatur Wooden was

Employees at the Port Huron Shops decorate the annual Santa Train. Photograph courtesy of Grand Trunk Western Railroad.

able to arrange lease financing of a microwave network and a teleprocessing system—the former the first of its kind to be so financed.

John Burdakin recalled that "Bandeen was willing to wait as long as the current year was better than the last." The current year, 1973, proved immensely better than 1972. Indeed, GTC posted a net income of $3.9 million. Unfortunately, the future looked much less promising and, in fact, the United States slid into a severe recession with curtailed demand for automobiles, durable goods, and housing materials—traffic staples of GTC's railroads. The recession was exacerbated by an energy crisis and severe inflation.[15]

All of these circumstances put great pressure on Grand Trunk Western and on John Burdakin who by then was the company's executive vice president. The new team had succeeded in driving down GTW's operating ratio from 90.3 in 1971 to 82.2 in 1973. This had been accomplished in part by cutting jobs which, predictably, had gone down badly with labor leaders. To be sure, Burdakin had crossed swords with labor shortly after he arrived in 1971 when he abolished yard assignments at Christmas time. That had

resulted in pickets at 131 West Lafayette Boulevard, GTW's general office building in downtown Detroit, and headlines in one newspaper that read, "BURDAKIN KILLS SANTA CLAUS." In fact, the automobile industry routinely shut down from Christmas Eve until the day after New Years leaving several GTW yard crews without meaningful work. The tradition under Canadian managers had been to call these crews anyway, but Burdakin saw in it only waste and unnecessary expense— intolerable given GTW's awful financial performance. The Christmas incident simply reflected a deeper problem. Labor leaders had long since learned that GTW, managed at a distance and dependent as it had become on the automobile industry, would cave in if workers slowed service to and from General Motors plants. The tradition was firm: upon interruption of service or even a slowdown, GM officials contacted Montreal and GTW managers were told to yield. By 1971, however, competitive pressures were so intense and GTW's financial position so precarious, that Burdakin—with Bandeen's clear support—determined that this tradition had to go. The problem, in many ways, was one of communication. "We might argue how to carve up the pie," Burdakin said of contract forces at GTW, "but we had to find agreement on how to make a good pie." Burdakin sent a strong message that he intended to be firm, but he also promised to be candid and fair. He joined with Bandeen, Cramer, and Wooden in touring the property and in meeting with the various crafts. He also authorized expenditures for corporate communications as well as an annual "Santa Train," designed to open avenues of communication among all hands. Burdakin insisted that "business as usual" was not good enough. To cling to old ways, if those old ways were unproductive, was to invite extinction.

Change was painful, but change was essential. It came, if grudgingly, and was typified by closer relations with employees and their unions.[16]

One major drain on GTW had passed. The "passenger problem" ended with the establishment of the National Railway Passenger Corporation (Amtrak) on 1 May 1971. GTW's out-of-pocket losses for passenger service in 1962 had come to $1.17 million but had risen to $2.038 million in 1968. Two years later GTW managers studied the possibility of ending all intercity service, but the issue became moot when Amtrak determined to omit GTW routes (Port Huron-Chicago, Detroit-Chicago) from its national network. Final runs were made on 30 April 1971. GTW was obliged to purchase $2.1 million of Amtrak stock and $2.5 million in expenses were charged against 1971 income as extraordinary items. Passenger equipment leased from CN was returned and, significantly, twenty locomotives were converted to freight service—

GTW ended passenger train service on 30 April 1971. The last westbound *International* is shown here departing South Bend. Photograph courtesy of David G. Korkhouse.

negating for the time-being the need to order new freight power. If the intercity passenger service ended, the commuter problem—three daily-except-Saturday-and-Sunday trains in each direction between Detroit and Pontiac—persisted.[17]

A corollary issue was the matter of properties held by Chicago & Western Indiana Railroad (C&WI) of which GTW was part owner. CW&I dated from 2 June 1879. It had been purchased

The commuter problem remained. Photograph courtesy of Grand Trunk Western Railroad.

48

GTW had no operating interest in Dearborn Station after the end of intercity passenger operations, but it was still an owner of Chicago & Western Indiana. Photograph courtesy of Canadian National.

shortly thereafter by a consortium of roads that had equal rights to common property in and about Chicago. Included was Dearborn Station, made redundant by Amtrak's decision to centralize its Chicago operations at Union Station. Dearborn and other nearby C&WI properties had great real estate potential encumbered by collective ownership that was not overcome until late 1975. Remaining C&WI operations were conducted on a user-shared-cost basis.[18]

The May 1971 issue of *GT Reporter* stated that with the inception of Amtrak, "GT communities—Detroit, Pontiac, Durand, Lansing, Battle Creek, South Bend, and Valparaiso—saw the last intercity passenger train rumble through, pick up passengers, and head for the terminal." The writer was only partially correct. Michigan politicians soon pressured Amtrak to expand service and on 15 September 1974, Port Huron-Chicago service was reestablished via GTW to Battle Creek and Penn Central beyond. In that way, intercity passenger service returned to GTW communities of Port Huron, Lansing, Durand, and Battle Creek. (Amtrak and VIA would combine to offer Toronto-Chicago service over this route on 31 October 1982.) The contract called for GTW to be reimbursed for avoidable costs plus incentive payments for on-time performance.[19]

Passenger service over GTW rails was reestablished amidst band, bunting, and speeches when Amtrak began service between Port Huron and Chicago effective 15 September 1974. Photograph courtesy of Grand Trunk Western Railroad.

Robert A. Bandeen became president and chief executive officer of CN on 1 May 1974. Photograph courtesy of Canadian National.

rumored to be in the running as MacMillan's replacement was Robert A. Bandeen, who on 1 May 1972 had moved back to Montreal as executive vice president—remaining as president of Grand Trunk Corporation and firmly in control of that experiment. The early positive results from GTC likely prompted Canadian Prime Minister Pierre Trudeau to appoint the 43-year-old Bandeen as president and chief executive officer of CN effective 1 May 1974.[21]

What ramifications, if any, did this development have for GTC and its constituent properties? Most of all, it implied continuing and even greater support for the holding company. It also implied managerial alterations. In 1971, Bandeen had pledged that an American would head GTC once it was on its feet. During the months and years following he had watched the "little group" of senior managers in Detroit—"not all sweetness and light among the members"—with a keen eye. Which one among them would be the best choice to advance up the ladder? Bandeen bet on John Burdakin who was named to head Grand Trunk Western effective 1 October 1974.[22]

Matters shifted by degree. Grand Trunk Corporation had been formed "to place under one American corporation all separately incorporated U.S. rail operations of Canadian National Railway Company." On that basis, CN's line from Portland, Maine, to Island Pond, Vermont (the old Atlantic and St. Lawrence Railroad, part of the historic main line from Portland to

Grand Trunk Corporation came through the 1973-74 recession surprisingly well. Car loadings were down but revenues turned upward because of Interstate Commerce Commission (ICC)-approved rate increases. At GTW, John Burdakin diligently labored to control costs by way of extended shop closings, force reductions, and operating efficiencies. GTW's deficits were reduced annually from 1971 through 1975; in the latter year the shortfall was $7.2 million, the lowest in nineteen years. GTC showed net profits of $6.65 million in 1974 and $4.251 million in 1975.[20]

Meanwhile, Canadian National's Norman J. MacMillan faced retirement. Among those

DW&P was no longer a sleepy branch or logging road. Photograph courtesy of Duluth, Winnipeg & Pacific Railway.

DW&P motive power was tenderly cared for at the engine facility in West Duluth. Photograph courtesy of Canadian National.

CV remained a colorful, if sometimes financial, performer. Photograph courtesy of Canadian National.

Chicago via Montreal and Toronto), although initially contemplated as part of GTC, was not included since it owned no separate corporate identity under CN's umbrella. Neither was CN's line from Thunder Bay to Winnipeg included, although it ran for 44 miles in northern Minnesota. Separately organized companies—GTW, DW&P, and CV with their subsidiaries—were included although the early focus was solely on GTW. "Present plans," Norman MacMillan had told Bandeen late in 1971, "do

not contemplate any change in organization of the Central Vermont . . . and the Duluth, Winnipeg and Pacific, which will continue under the guidance of the St. Lawrence and Prairie Regions' Vice Presidents respectively." On the other hand, "operating and capital budgets and accounts" of the two roads were to be included in GTC reports. In that sense, GTC was, as Bandeen said, "a shell operation without much substance," except that as a holding company it could file a consolidated tax return sheltering income from profitable properties with losses from Grand Trunk Western.[23]

One of the profitable properties was Duluth, Winnipeg & Pacific—no longer a logging road or a sleepy branch but now a funnel for increasingly heavy traffic moving from central and western Canada into the United States. CN managers designed a calculated campaign to improve DW&P's track structure, but not in a way that would deny net profit so necessary to Bandeen's holding company strategy. This was often difficult. For instance, maintenance engineers found it necessary on DW&P to go beyond approved standards for ballast, track anchors, and ties per mile on trackage through swampy areas. This obviously added capital and/or operating cost, but was essential if DW&P was to shoulder growing volumes. Net income for the period 1971-75, inclusive, averaged $3,146,000 annually. Principal commodities handled included lumber, potash, and paper and wood pulp.[24]

Central Vermont, by comparison, was a sometimes performer. It had turned in net losses from 1968 through 1970, but from 1971 to 1974, inclusive, boasted average annual net income of $699,250. Red ink returned in 1975, however. CV found itself serving a region that was overbuilt with rail lines given modal competition, that was losing its industrial base, and that increasingly embraced an antibusiness climate. Gross-ton miles reflected this—dropping from over one billion in 1968 to 642 million in 1975. On the other hand, average tons per train remained constant; no efficiencies were produced in that important category. The number of employees fell from 680 in 1968 to 439 in 1975, a number easily adequate to handle CV's business, but the rapid decline caused consternation among employees who recalled a more robust era of prestige passenger trains and fast freights not so long ago. The new age, they agreed, suffered by comparison. Amtrak did reinstitute passenger service on 30 September 1972 above White River Junction as part of a New York City-Montreal route, but now more freight moved inbound from Canada than outbound. The future of Central Vermont looked distressingly problematic, but Bandeen wondered if a shake-up similar to that under way at GTW would produce similar results for CV. With that in mind, and to reestablish executive authority in St. Albans, Bandeen dispatched Donald Wooden as executive vice president in March 1974. His responsibilities included all nonoperating functions, as well as internal and external corporate affairs. Wooden also retained financial duties on behalf of GTC.[25]

Another if quite unheralded subsidiary of Grand Trunk Corporation was Grand Trunk Leasing Corporation (GTL), to which rolling stock leased by GTW was transferred on 1 January 1972. Thereafter all interest, principal, or rental payments were rendered to Grand Trunk Leasing. DW&P and CV later became parties and GTL also expanded into leases of motive power. The arrangement was profitable from the start. GTL offered additional advantages. As an example, GTL could raise capital from financing its lien-free rolling stock. Additionally, GTL provided a means of separating rolling stock from the constituent railroads if any or all were disposed of.[26]

In announcing Robert Bandeen's appointment as president of Canadian National, the *GT Reporter* asserted that the "separately incorporated Canadian National properties in the United States" had been "revitalized." That overstated reality. But Bandeen's concept of a holding company had been validated and a strong management team had been established for Grand Trunk Western. Bandeen clearly had constructed a firm foundation. And a crucial lesson had been learned: change was necessary to survive in a changed and changing world. If Grand Trunk Corporation was to survive—let alone prosper—its managers would have to be nimble. And Montreal must allow them to be nimble—nay, Montreal must demand it.[27]

NOTES

1. Walter H. Cramer, interview, 9 October 1991.
2. *Who's Who in Railroading and Rail Transit,* 17th ed. (New York: Simmons-Boardman, 1971), 60-61; John H. Burdakin, interview, 4 November 1989.
3. Ibid., 91.
4. Ibid., 449.
5. Ron Lawless, interview, 7 August 1989; G. B. Aydelott, interview, 9 February 1990; James R. Sullivan, interview, 9 February 1990.
6. G. R. Stevens, *History of the Canadian National Railways* (New York: The Macmillan Company, 1973), 455; Charles R. Foss, *Evening Before the Diesel: A Pictorial History of Steam and First Generation Diesel Motive Power on the Grand*

Trunk Western Railroad, 1938-1961 (Boulder: Pruett Publishing Company, 1980), 377; John H. Burdakin, interview, 21 February 1991.

7. John H. Burdakin, interview, 6 December 1988, 4 November 1989.

8. *Chicago Tribune*, 2 November 1971; Ron Lawless, interview, 7 August 1989, Yvon H. Masse, interview, 24 May 1989; John H. Burdakin, interview, 21 February 1991.

9. CN, Annual Report (1971): 23; Ibid., (1974): 24; N. J. MacMillan to R. A. Bandeen, 18 November 1971, President's File 105 [hereinafter PF].

10. *Detroit News*, 6 October 1971; *Chicago Tribune*, 7 November 1971.

11. John J. Baisley, interview, 6 March 1990; Richard Haupt, interview, 6 March 1990; Earl C. Opperthauser, interview, 6 March 1990.

12. GTW, Minute Book No. 5, 145, 150, 153.

13. GTC, Annual Report (1972): 2, 3, 5.

14. GTC, Minute Book No. 1, 26-27.

15. John H. Burdakin, interview, 4 November 1989; GTC, Annual Report (1973): 2-3; Jonathan Hughes, *American Economic History*, 3d ed. (Glenview, Ill.: Scott, Foresman/Little Brown, 1990), 589-92; John F. Willis and Martin L. Primack, *An Economic History of the United States*, 2d ed. (Englewood Cliffs, N. J.: Prentice Hall, 1989), 417-19.

16. *GT Reporter* (March/April 1973): 1; John H. Burdakin, interview, 4 November 1989.

17. CN, Overview—Grand Trunk Western (Montreal: July 1969), 64-65; GTW, Minute Book No. 4, 122; Patrick C. Dorin, *The Grand Trunk Railroad: A Canadian National Railway* (Seattle: Superior Publishing, 1977), 36-37, 57; *GT Reporter* (May 1971): 1; GTW, Minute Book No. 5, 1971 Financial Results, 6; GTC, Annual Report (1972): 29.

18. CN, *Synoptical History*, 275-78; GTW, Minute Book No. 6, Executive Minute No. 539; GTW, Minute Book No. 5, 195-96; GTW, Minute Book No. 5, 1972 Financial Results, 8.

19. *GT Reporter* (May 1971): 1; GTW, Minute Book No. 5, 172, 192-93; *GT Reporter* (September/October 1974): 5; GTC, Annual Report (1974): 4, 6; GTW, Minute Book No. 6, 199; GTC, Annual Report (1975): 4.

20. Tabular data from GTC annual reports, 1972-75.

21. Robert A. Bandeen, interview, 3 November 1989; *GT Reporter* (March/April 1974): 1; CN, Annual Report (1974): 15.

22. *Chicago Tribune*, 7 November 1971; *GT Reporter* (September/October 1974), 1; Robert A. Bandeen, interview, 3 November 1989.

23. GTC, Annual Report (1972): 2; Norman J. MacMillan to R. A. Bandeen, 18 November 1971; Robert A. Bandeen, interview, 7 March 1990; Earl C. Opperthauser, interview, 6 November 1989.

24. Patrick C. Dorin, *The Canadian National Railways' Story* (Seattle: Superior Publishing Company, 1975), 162-69; Stanley H. Mailer, "In Minnesota CN is Spelled DW&P," *Trains* 34 (March 1974): 20-28; GTC, Annual Report (1972): 2; Ibid., (1973): 2; Ibid., (1974): 17, 21; DW&P, Corporate Records Book No. 3, Executive Minute No. 15; GTC, Annual Report (1974): 10.

25. GTC, Annual Report (1972): 9-15; Ibid., (1973): 8-15; Ibid., (1974): 13-16; Ibid., (1975): 13-16.

26. GTW, Minute Book No. 5, 1971 Financial Results, 8; GTC, Annual Report (1972): 3; GTW, Executive Committee Book No. 7, Executive Minute No. 565; GTC, Annual Report (1973): 3; Ibid., (1974): 25.

27. *GT Reporter* (March/April 1974): 1.

A PATIENT APPROACH

For the first time, our three operating railroads, Grand Trunk Western, Central Vermont, and Duluth, Winnipeg & Pacific, all recorded profits for the year.

Robert A. Bandeen, GTC, Annual Report (1977): 3.

Robert A. Bandeen made bold plans for Canadian National; he enunciated those plans with equal vigor and directness. A new management organization went into effect on 1 January 1976. "Underlying current corporate planning," said Bandeen, "is the conviction that the best interests of Canada are served when the Company is able to conduct its operations on a commercial basis." Bandeen recognized that CN was altogether too conservative and traditional in its business posture and modus operandi, and that its organizational structure and traditional orientation resembled a stodgy government bureaucracy. His alterations were designed to give CN "the flexibility to adapt to changing market demands and financial conditions." The new plan was based on the profit center concept and included five operating divisions to manage CN's major revenue-producing activities. The object, said Bandeen, was to "simplify the administration of CN and improve the efficiency and profitability of its various divisions."[1]

Bandeen warmed to his subject. "In the economic and political climate of today, the role of CN as a profit-seeking business corporation is by no means incompatible with acknowledged public service obligations of the Company. Indeed, business efficiency enhances CN's ability to supply any public service required of it fully and well and as economically as possible." That meant, Bandeen said bluntly, that CN would have to reduce costs, increase productivity, and generate more revenues. The entire package mirrored Bandeen's philosophy and his experience with Grand Trunk Corporation.[2]

Bandeen was the right man for CN at the right time. Canada was increasingly willing to acknowledge that the transportation climate had changed and with it CN's role. CN, of course, had been positioned for change by Donald Gordon and was ready for an aggressive leader following the caretaker style of Norman MacMillan. Bandeen liked to find solutions to problems; he was imaginative, aggressive, and ambitious; and he had fixed ideas about what he wanted to do and how to do it—fast. Within the headquarters building and abroad, Bandeen set a dynamic tone. While he understood CN's roots and would be informed by the company's history, he would not be controlled by it. For example, CN was dominated by the operating department, hardly

**Bandeen demanded that CN "adapt to changing market demands and financial conditions."
Photograph courtesy of Canadian National.**

unusual in the North American rail industry at the time, but pronounced at CN. Bandeen recognized this domination, saw its shortcomings, and challenged the tradition. He was similarly put off by arrogance in the traffic department, the mentality of which he sarcastically summarized as: "If it doesn't go in a boxcar, carry it yourself." Those who craved constancy were uncomfortable with Bandeen for change would typify his watch.[3]

Bandeen would have his hands full. In the 1960s CN had produced more than $413 million in deficits and had earned surplus before interest charges only in 1960 and 1961. Employment had been pared from 104,155 in 1960 to 84,388 in 1969, but the company's operating ratio averaged a dismal 99.43 for the decade. CN's performance

during the early part of the 1970s was little better. Deficits for the years 1970-75 were more than $47 million, and the operating ratio averaged 99.62.[4]

As Robert Bandeen labored to redefine the way Canadian National addressed its business, he increasingly trusted John H. Burdakin to do the same at Grand Trunk Western. Bandeen reminded Burdakin that the circumstance at GTW was very much like that of its parent: GTW, like CN, had to reduce costs, increase productivity, and generate more revenue. Yet there were differences; CN had much longer average hauls and relatively less competition. For GTW there remained the uncompromising demand to maintain a high-speed, high-capacity plant in the short Chicago-Port Huron/Chicago-Detroit corridor while supplying very demanding on-line customers with saturated gathering and distribution services—all of it in a fiercely competitive environment featuring multiple modes, especially in Michigan, a state that never saw a roadway or a multiple-axle truck it did not admire.

Burdakin's charge from Bandeen was to effect change at GTW. Change, however, meant alteration of the status quo—disruptive, painful, and emotional. Such, for example, was the case with line abandonments. Earlier pruning had occurred in Michigan between Green-

The car ferry agreement with Pennsylvania Railroad ended in 1954 with GTW surviving on the route. Photograph courtesy of Canadian National.

ville and Moorland (on the Muskegon line) and on 1 May 1951 between Cass City and Bad Axe (a branch off the Caseville line). A CN team in 1969 urged scrutiny of a full 240 miles of line, branches or segments of branches, all in Michigan. Internal studies were initiated before Burdakin arrived and abandonments were prosecuted by him as data showed clear deficit from operation and as the political climate allowed. First to go was a portion of the Jackson line (Jackson to Lakeland, 35 miles). More wrenching was a decision in 1974 to seek termination of the westernmost section of the Grand Haven line which handled a mere 176 cars in fiscal 1974. The final runs came on 20 July 1977, between Coopersville and Grand Haven, 15 miles. Burdakin took no pleasure in abandonments, neither did he apologize: "We have an obligation to the people of Michigan and our customers not to waste our resources on continued maintenance and operation of lines which, despite our best efforts, produce net deficits."[5]

Line abandonment was an issue that always charged emotions and carried political risk. GTW's deficit-ridden car ferry operation on Lake Michigan was even more difficult. Ferry service to Milwaukee from Grand Haven and later Muskegon dated from the nineteenth century. Subsequent to 15 January 1937, Grand Trunk-

Milwaukee Car Ferry Company, a wholly owned subsidiary of GTW, served the joint needs of GTW and Pennsylvania Railroad, but that arrangement ended on 1 January 1954, with GTW surviving on the route. Ferry service on Lake Michigan was also offered by Ann Arbor Railroad and Chesapeake & Ohio Railway (C&O), but among them only C&O forcefully advertised the fact. Ferrying rail cars had the very real advantages of avoiding the congested Chicago gateway, of saving ton miles, and of expediting time sensitive shipments. Unfortunately, ferrying operations were also extremely labor intensive—a vexing problem exacerbated by escalating wage scales and expanded modal competition.[6]

By the late 1960s, CN analysts predicted a savings of at least $1 million annually if GTW dropped service. These same analysts recognized, however, that the issue was complex. Cross-lake tonnage for GTW aggregated 833,000 in 1967 and 800,000 in 1968 and included significant blocks of autoframes and beer moving eastbound, Canadian newsprint moving westbound, and local movements of industrial sand and coke between Milwaukee and Muskegon. GTW's actual presence in Milwaukee was minimal; it served no industry and relied on Chicago & North Western, Milwaukee Road, and Soo Line

Unfortunately, ferrying was extremely labor intensive. Photograph courtesy of Grand Trunk Western Railroad.

The *Madison* dated from 1927. Photograph courtesy of Canadian National.

Would retaining car ferry operations give GTW an edge over competition? Photograph courtesy of Grand Trunk Western Railroad.

for interchange. Integral to ferrying was GTW's 129-mile rail line from Durand to Muskegon, but that line, sad to say, produced only marginal local traffic. Any cost-benefit analysis was obligated to consider water operations plus terminal costs in Milwaukee as well as the lengthy branch to Muskegon against system benefits to GTW and CN.[7]

GTW managers looked for options. The company's three vessels—*Grand Rapids* (1926), *Madison* (1927), and *City of Milwaukee* (1931)—could be modernized to make them less labor-intensive or new vessels could be acquired. Neither alternative could be justified, however, on a capital-reward basis. Focus turned to the rail line. Perhaps running rights over C&O could be arranged between Lansing and Grand Rapids and the GTW line from Durand to Grand Rapids abandoned. Burdakin ordered further study, pointing out the need to protect, as much as possible, important traffic emanating from Milwaukee or passing overhead.[8]

James L. Elliott, general manager of the car ferry company, prepared an impressive proposal for survival late in 1972. Elliott noted that car ferry operations historically had made money for owners, but that trend had been reversed in more recent years by inflationary trends, increasingly obsolete fleets, higher labor costs, and intense modal competition. Nevertheless, the Interstate Commerce Commission (ICC) felt strongly that cross-lake service was a public necessity and therefore must be maintained. Thus, Elliott concluded, GTW was obligated to increase benefits and revenue by way of vastly improved service— the type of which could only be provided by a new vessel. What he proposed was a 390-foot, diesel-powered craft capable of making two round trips daily and costing $12 million. Elliott argued that Grand Trunk Western enjoyed "no particular geographic or service advantage . . . [and was] . . . just another of several carriers that can be utilized in routes eastward from Chicago." Thus, retaining cross-lake service and improving that

Car ferry operation steamed into heavy seas . . .

. . . and, in fact, into oblivion on 31 October 1978. Photographs courtesy of Canadian National.

service would give GTW "an edge." Long-term profit was likely, too, predicted Elliott, since revenues would derive from the carriage of rail cars, private automobiles and trucks, and passengers.[9]

Elliott's proposal might have been implemented had GTW been flush; it was not flush. Loaded cars handled by ferry in 1971 dropped to 10,900, requiring only one round trip daily. The sharp recession and fuel crisis of 1973 and 1974 hastened a decision. On 21 May 1974, GTW's board authorized "whatever action . . . deemed necessary and prudent to relieve the Company of the economic burden of continuing operation of the Grand Trunk-Milwaukee Car Ferry Company." Papers were filed with the ICC on 14 February 1975. Said the plainspoken Burdakin: "The use of a 2,942-ton ferry manned by a 34-man crew to move 22 rail cars across Lake Michigan is now too costly to meet the competition." While the ICC dallied, losses increased: $1.1 million in 1974, $1.3 million in 1975, $1.5 million in 1976. John C. Danielson of GTW's legal department pressed the case with vigor and skill; eventually no shippers but only state transportation authorities and the seafarer's union objected. Authorization for termination of service finally arrived, and when the *City of Milwaukee* tied up in Muskegon at 1:08 A.M. on 31 October 1978, Grand Trunk Western wrote finis to an important chapter of its history. Even earlier, the *Grand Rapids*, long out of service, had been sold and, in 1977, the Coast Guard condemned the *Madison*. Only the *City of Milwaukee* survived in service, briefly, under Ann Arbor's flag. The Grand Trunk Milwaukee Car Ferry Company was dissolved in 1980.[10]

Burdakin realized that it was not enough to trim; prosperity for Grand Trunk Western could not be achieved simply by reducing operations. It was, as always, necessary to spend money to make money. Conservative by nature, Burdakin weighed his monetary resources, husbanded them, and spent only when and where he was convinced there was promise of return. Track structure, he firmly believed, required constant attention and upgrading to provide the thoroughfare adequate to high-speed needs of GTW customers. The road had less than 75 miles of continuous welded rail (CWR) when he arrived in 1971, but over the next nine years GTW installed 161 miles of CWR, averaging 17.9 miles in good years and bad.

Additional impressive expenditures went for mechanized track machines, steel bridges, extended passing tracks, lengthened yard tracks, power switches and heaters, ties and anchors, hot box detectors, and centralized traffic control (CTC). Burdakin was properly pleased by the campaign. In 1975, GTW—with Burdakin's enthusiastic blessing—began to advertise itself as the "Good Track Road." The motto was hardly whimsical. "It is a challenge to everyone on the railroad," said Burdakin, "because any shortcomings in track maintenance, or employee performance, or customer service can mar the reputation gained." The "Good Track" concept derived in part from Burdakin's engineering background and his experience at Penn Central where property conditions had rapidly deteriorated and in part from Walter Cramer's knowledge that nervous customers were moving away from rail transport because of poor track conditions and correspondingly poor service on many eastern and midwestern carriers. Shippers and other railroads quickly took note of GTW's "Good Track" pledge and applauded. GTW, said Denver & Rio Grande Western's G. B. Aydelott, "is a hell of a good railroad; they have a good piece of track and they work at it."[11]

An adequate and well-maintained stable of motive power was similarly required to move freight on demanding schedules. Diesel power came to GTW as early as 1929, but the era of

The official end of steam on GTW was in 1960, but in September 1961, the road pulled one of its 4-8-4s from storage to handle a special train for the National Railway Historical Society. It is shown here taking water at Valparaiso, Indiana. Photograph by Don L. Hofsommer.

Most photogenic of GTW's motive power was a unit renumbered 1776 for the Bicentennial. John Burdakin is on the locomotive, nearest the cab, in this view made at Royal Oak. Photograph courtesy of Grand Trunk Western Railroad.

steam did not end until 29 March 1960. The motive power fleet when Burdakin arrived was made up mostly of models from General Motor's Electro Motive Division (EMD), with some switchers from American Locomotive Company (Alco). The end of passenger service freed units which were regeared for freight service and allowed Burdakin to put off acquisition of expensive second-generation units. When eventually ordered they came from EMD in high-horsepower models and later in the form of utilitarian 2,000-horsepower GP-38s. The Battle Creek shops also rebuilt four Alco switchers in the late 1970s. Most

The shops at Port Huron turned out impressive work in all seasons. Photograph courtesy of Grand Trunk Western Railroad.

photogenic of GTW's motive power was a unit renumbered 1776 and repainted in patriotic colors for the Bicentennial celebration of 1976.[12]

Equipment needs were constant and varied to reflect the demanding needs of GTW's largest customers. New boxcars, flats, tri-level auto racks, airslide covered hoppers, and cabooses were procured by lease, leveraged lease, and conditional sales agreement. Shop forces at Port Huron repeatedly proved their mettle by "stretching" boxcars, by converting auto racks into trailer-on-flat-car (TOFC) flats, by making ballast cars out of covered hoppers, and by maintaining the entire 10,000-car fleet. Ownership of rolling stock held by Grand Trunk Leasing passed to GTW on 1 January 1976, and GTW then entered into informal lease arrangements with Central Vermont and Duluth, Winnipeg & Pacific for the same equipment. This resulted in increased depreciation and interest expense but was offset by reduced rental costs. Grand Trunk Leasing was then dissolved by merging it into Grand Trunk Corporation.[13]

Beginning in 1973, John Burdakin launched GTW on a path that he hoped would turn the company into "a 21st century railroad in 1975."

What he referred to was Automatic Car Identification (ACI), an electronic information system designed to locate and identify all of the company's freight cars and trains at a moment's notice—a plan that would provide the most comprehensive network in the North American railroad industry. The cost would be a staggering $7.5 million, but the system—said Howard M. Tischler, general manager of information systems—would provide a database of revenue statistics linked to car movements and thereby establish a reservoir of information for marketing and accounting purposes. Functionally, information would be gathered by trackside electronic scanners that "read" color-coded plates on rolling stock and locomotives and feed data to the company's new IBM Central Processor in Detroit. Wheel sensors would provide additional data from principal yards. Employment among clerks would be lowered through the reduction of car checking in the field and elimination of the punch card process. Tischler predicted a direct 11.32 percent return on investment over 84 months. Burdakin became a passionate advocate of ACI and preached its gospel to the entire industry.[14]

63

The Association of American Railroads took note of GTW's experiment with ACI and, in 1975, initiated intensive assessment of the concept. A buoyant Burdakin pointed out that GTW was receiving 99.9 percent accurate data from its label scanner-wheel sensor-computer system. This resulted, he said, in the reduction of mishandled cars, cars delayed by lack of proper paperwork, errors in car movements, and per diem payments. "We believe our system . . . clearly pioneers a way for other railroads," said Burdakin. The Association of American Railroads eventually mandated that all rail cars in the country be applied with bar-code plates but, after great expenditures were made, powerful forces in the industry complained of imperfections and, rightly or wrongly, ACI as an industry standard perished late in 1977 before total results had been tabulated and

John Burdakin preached the virtues of Automatic Car Identification; perhaps he was ahead of his time. Photograph courtesy of Grand Trunk Western Railroad.

without providing a substitute system. Burdakin shook his head in dismay. Ironically, the industry in the early 1990s would consider a similar program—Automatic Equipment Identification.[15]

Events surrounding the Pontiac-Detroit commuter operation proved more palatable. The three trains in each direction daily-except-Saturday-and-Sunday were a constant financial drain. Any attempt to discontinue them was bound to arouse public hostility, but Burdakin stated emphatically that "the deficit operation must be eliminated." Fortunately, GTW avoided a public relations disaster when a bargain was struck for the Southeastern Michigan Transportation Authority (SEMTA) to assume responsibility for the service effective 19 December 1973.[16]

GTW's suburban service, begun in 1931, shared terminal facilities with the road's intercity passenger trains at Brush

GTW exited the commuter business when SEMTA took over on 19 December 1973. Photograph courtesy of Grand Trunk Western Railroad.

GTW's Brush Street Station had served the company's passenger-carrying needs since a fire in 1866 consumed another facility at the same location. Photograph courtesy of Grand Trunk Western Railroad.

riverfront. There was no question about acceding to "requests" from Ford. GTW would vacate the historic passenger station and move the commuter stop two blocks upriver. The 107-year-old building closed on 29 June 1973 and fell to the wrecking ball shortly thereafter.[17]

The entire package that Ford Motor Land Development Corporation required of GTW for its magnificent Renaissance Center was approximately 29 acres including, of course, the depot site. More important from an operational standpoint was the company's car ferry slip and support tracks used to facilitate interchange with Canadian National at Windsor. Those properties, too, would be sold to Ford. GTW, however, could not give up the essential interchange with CN, yet its options were few. GTW could relocate to another site, build another

Street Station, hard by the Detroit River in downtown Detroit. That property had less equity for the railroad after intercity service ended in 1971, but it took on greater potential value when Henry Ford II disclosed plans for a large commercial and residential project along the central

Ford would require the Brush Street facility and additional GTW properties including the car slip—in this view about to receive CN's *Lansdowne*. Photograph courtesy of Canadian National.

Car ferry operations over the Detroit River between Detroit, on the far side in this view, and Windsor provided the crucial connection between GTW and CN. All of that ended when rail traffic was diverted via Penn Central's tunnel. Photograph courtesy of Canadian National.

The first GTW train to use the Penn Central tunnel between Detroit and Windsor plunged into the bore on 20 February 1975. Photograph courtesy of Grand Trunk Western Railroad.

slip, and continue ferry operations, or it could ask Penn Central to grant trackage rights through its Detroit-Windsor tunnel. Penn Central had nothing to gain from that kind of arrangement and, in fact, much to lose in granting GTW—a head-to-head competitor—such advantage. With energetic pressure from Ford, however, Penn Central grudgingly agreed; GTW trains began use of the tunnel on 20 February 1975. This procedure resulted in expedited service for lading in conventional equipment, but the tunnel could not accommodate high or wide loads including tri-level auto racks which moved exclusively via Port Huron and the ferries there. In the end, several agreements between GTW and Ford Land Development involved sale of land for cash and/or exchange of Ford-acquired land elsewhere that could be employed by the railroad for industrial development.[18]

Other property in the Detroit area came under close scrutiny. The Detroit Terminal Railroad Company, organized in 1905 as a switching operation and owned in equal shares by GTW and Penn Central, suffered progressive losses—$118,000 in 1971 and $102,000 in 1972. These were only the most recent in an unbroken string from 1956. Bandeen sought to sell GTW's interest to Penn Central and negotiations to that end ebbed and flowed until Penn Central disappeared. Consolidated Rail Corporation (Conrail), successor to many Penn Central properties, including one-half interest in Detroit Terminal, renewed negotiations. For GTW, Detroit Terminal's primary value derived from a connection it provided with the Detroit, Toledo & Ironton Railroad (DT&I), but GTW—under provisions of the final system plan defining Conrail—gained a new and more direct connection with DT&I through Conrail itself. Consequently, for GTW, Detroit Terminal was a cash drain and became operationally redundant. GTW finally dumped its interest in 1981.[19]

Robert Bandeen, who had "wanted to take a whole new look at things" when he was appointed president of Grand Trunk Corporation, took the same approach to his presidency at Canadian National. Outsiders viewed him as an extroverted dynamic businessman who enjoyed a high profile. Insiders considered him a leader of men, a good communicator, reserved, and dispassionate. All hands saw him as an agent of change.[20]

Bandeen's philosophy was strikingly simple: "We are applying a commercial, private-entrepreneur

Henry Ford II, right, could take proper pride in plans for Detroit's riverfront development. Photograph courtesy of Grand Trunk Western Railroad.

approach to running a nationalized railroad." Bandeen did not ignore CN's social responsibilities but he warned that "nothing can waste public money faster than a railway which is run without concerns for profits and productivity and which has to be subsidized out of the public purse." CN's policy in regard to social responsibility would be defined as "providing the maximum amount of transportation at the minimum cost to the user and taxpayer." Parliament responded positively if reluctantly: substantial change in ratemaking came in 1967 with the National Transportation Act; CN's debt-equity ratio changed from 60-40 to 40-60 in 1978 when Parliament approved recapitalization by converting debt to common stock; the government agreed to finance grain car acquisitions; and the government agreed to consider relief of passenger losses. Bandeen took an active part in all of these negotiations; he was equally active internally. His profit center concept, introduced at GTC, was fully implemented at CN. And in a bold attempt to generate adequate data for interpretation and to develop an efficient car-handling policy, Bandeen authorized huge expenditures for a new on-line computer system styled after Southern Pacific's famous TOPS. Important indices reflected improvement. Freight car

The "passenger problem" remained to vex Bandeen. Photograph courtesy of Canadian National.

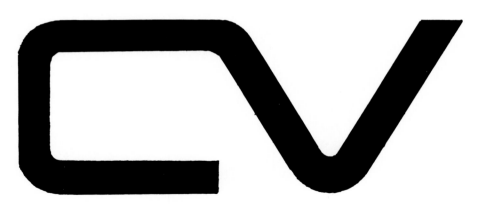

independent personalities. Neither man viewed integration and autonomy as contradictory. Rather, both agreed that most management decisions should be made locally—at St. Albans and Duluth, not at Detroit or Montreal. There would be oversight, to be sure, but they predicted that initiative and independence would result in greater productivity.

Donald Wooden had already done much to put a stamp of independence on Central Vermont. Maas, who followed Wooden, continued and expanded the process. Train dispatching, for example, returned to St. Albans from Montreal. This was more than symbolic. It reflected Maas's determination to make CV "a stand alone railroad." Run-through train operations were perfected between Washington and Montreal in cooperation with Conrail, Boston & Maine, and CN; CV's marketing arm was reorganized to aggressively seek new business; and the property was spruced up. The campaign was striking in its completeness and in its effectiveness.

productivity increased one-quarter from 1974 to 1978; gross tons per employee rose by 3.8 percent per year in the same period; and the operating ratio approached 90.0 by the end of the decade.[21]

As Bandeen struggled with the Canadian National labyrinth, he increasingly gave authority to John Burdakin for matters related to Grand Trunk Corporation. Indeed, Burdakin became president of the holding company on 1 January 1976. At the same time, Bandeen and Burdakin agreed that it was time to integrate Central Vermont and Duluth, Winnipeg & Pacific more fully into GTC's orbit. Consequently, management agreements with CN were dropped and Burdakin appointed Gerald L. Maas as general manager of CV and Phillip C. Larson as general manager for DW&P. Maas, a fourth-generation railroader, came to CV from Conrail where he had been superintendent at Cleveland. Larson began his career on the Nickel Plate and had joined DW&P in 1973 as superintendent of transportation.[22]

Integrating CV and DW&P more fully into GTC, Bandeen and Burdakin agreed, meant that the two roads—like GTW—needed to develop

The St. Albans enginehouse personnel took understandable pride in CV's bicentennial locomotive. It reflected the strong esprit de corps at CV. Photograph courtesy of Central Vermont.

68

Burdakin's pleasure was reflected when he promoted Maas to general manager of GTW. Larson moved from DW&P to CV as successor to Maas, and Jerome F. Corcoran—formerly director of budgets and cost analysis at GTW—moved to DW&P.[23]

Wooden, Maas and then Larson pumped vitality into Central Vermont. New sales offices were established in Toronto and at New London; CV eagerly solicited newsprint to Florida destinations and established impressive on-line distribution centers; trackmen installed the first welded rail on CV—and the first in Vermont; and, a new *Rocket* intermodal train entered service. Employment in 1976 was only 60 percent of 1968 but morale was strong; CV won the E. H. Harriman Bronze Medal for its safety record in 1976. And the road repainted one of its diesel units in a bold patriotic style to commemorate the nation's bicentennial.[24]

Such a happy face, however, belied reality. In fact, Central Vermont faced a very uncertain future. Its operating ratio for the last two years of the 1960s was an appalling 144.4 and Canadian National managers worried privately that CV might become redundant in the confused New England rail scene. CV turned in profits for the four-year period 1971-74 (mostly on the basis of net car rentals) but red ink reappeared in 1975 and 1976. Gross ton miles in 1976 were only 57 percent of 1968 and the road found itself increasingly dependent on products inbound from Canada as its traffic base. Forest products led all commodities. During the summer of 1976, Burdakin met with a senior CN executive who "agreed to review specifically the relationship of Central Vermont to CN Rail." CN's team of analysts went to work. The primary question was: What would be the impact on CN service quality if "the Central Vermont through main line connection ceased to exist?" Second, "would CP Rail improve its competitive advantage if the CV mainline route were severed and CN relied on its

Phillip Larson, center, took pride in accepting the Bronze Medal for safety in 1976. He is flanked here by Secretary of Transportation Brock Adams (left) and W. Averell Harriman (right). Photograph courtesy of Grand Trunk Western Railroad.

other connections to the U.S. (Penn Central and later Conrail via Huntingdon, Quebec and Delaware & Hudson via Rouses Point, N.Y.)?" CN's freight sales and marketing forces were strangely ambivalent, seemingly interested only in getting tonnage to the border. The operations department, on the other hand, doubted that the Huntingdon route would ever be competitive with Delaware & Hudson (D&H) or CV, but one of its officers did observe that if CV were not around D&H service might deteriorate since the "quality of competition for D&H on CN Rail traffic would have disappeared." CV earned $4.7 million in operating income for the period 1977-79 but behind the scenes discussions went forward with possible buyers such as neighboring Providence & Worcester. This thoroughly unnerved Boston & Maine (B&M), then in reorganization proceedings under Chapter 77. After all, reminded B&M's Alan G. Dustin, his company was a historic partner with CV in the Montreal-Boston trade, and CV and B&M shared trackage in the Connecticut Valley. Burdakin admitted that "there have been a number of inquiries regarding the availability of the CV." Still, he told Dustin, "the performance of the CV in recent years does not demand instant action.

CV clearly traverses a beautiful countryside—but one that requires sophisticated engineering and constant maintenance. Photograph courtesy of Central Vermont.

And consequently, transfer of ownership would not be contemplated unless residual benefit would result." Dustin must have found that a curious response. In reality, Burdakin was waffling because Montreal was having second thoughts about CV. Indeed, the matter would remain in limbo, unresolved, in a manner that was uncharacteristic of the Bandeen era.[25]

The record of Duluth, Winnipeg & Pacific was less complex and more profitable. As with CV, DW&P gained more autonomy in 1976 with accountability resting with managers appointed by GTC. Unlike CV, however, marketing and sales responsibilities remained with Canadian National; GTW would provide other "services, counsel, advice, and expertise" under management contract. DW&P's compact operation simply did not require "hiring and maintaining a large staff of its own for such purposes." With low overhead costs and with a narrow but lucrative

traffic base (lumber, pulpwood, paper, and potash as leading commodities), DW&P earned impressive profits during the last half of the 1970s—$3.67 million as low for the period in 1975 and $8 million for the high in 1978.[26]

DW&P's performance was impressive by most standards. In only one area was the road deficient—in local business, which in some years was less than 1 percent of total volume. Otherwise DW&P was enviable. Gross ton miles escalated as did average tons per train; at the same time, the operating ratio steadied at a most agreeable 65.9 average for the last half of the decade. Productivity improved perceptibly in 1976 when agreements with labor organizations allowed the company to eliminate Virginia as a crew change point. Subsequently, crews ran through from Duluth to Ranier, across from Fort Frances, Ontario. Running through was made possible by agreements with the unions and significant

An increased volume of traffic, especially inbound from Canada, moved through Ranier. Duluth, Winnipeg & Pacific Railway.

equipment with dependable high-speed service in a corridor always characterized by profound competition. Of challenges there were plenty.

Walter Cramer continued his campaign to seek, hold, and expand volume. His work gained respect for GTW in powerful quarters. At Burlington Northern, Thomas J. Lamphier said: "He is one of the first real marketers in the railroad industry, and he understands all concepts." James R. Sullivan at Conrail noted that GTW was not a leader in ratemaking because of its relatively small size, but he considered GTW "a responsible organization" and certainly "no patsy." Generally speaking, said Sullivan, "I am quite favorably impressed with GTW." Cramer insisted on a program designed to improve the road's penetration in key areas and to better respond to customer needs. Industrial

expenditures to upgrade track structure with heavy welded rail, deep ballast, and thousands of ties. By the end of 1976, a 45-mile-per-hour track speed was afforded over most of the line. Employee numbers sagged, but morale remained high; DW&P ranked high in safety among railroads of its size. The road's new motto, "DW&P—Delivered With Pride," was as much fact as long term aspiration.[27]

Of the Grand Trunk Corporation's railroad properties, DW&P might be the least remarked, but it had assuredly become the financial star; CV and GTW were the problematic financial performers. Yet because of its size and scope of operation, GTW always demanded greatest attention. Burdakin's formula for GTW was characteristically direct: advanced marketing and energetic sales coupled with aggressive cost control. Easily enough said. As always, however, GTW was pressured by powerful shippers that demanded a fleet of often expensive and specialized

DW&P's motto—Delivered With Pride—derived from a suggestion made by an employee in the mechanical department. Duluth, Winnipeg & Pacific Railway.

71

DW&P's 3605 heads the 19-car International Bicentennial Friendship Train out of Duluth on 7 August 1976. Duluth, Winnipeg & Pacific Railway.

development and automotive marketing sections were strengthened and pricing responsibility moved from CN's Chicago office to GTW in Detroit. Further refinement came in 1974 when Cramer departed from the traditional geographic or territorial assignment of his force by concentrating sales and service into three basic markets—automotive, merchandise, and intermodal. Each of the three divisions was assigned a director who became responsible for sales, marketing development, profitability, and overall direction. Cramer's efforts paid off. In 1974, GTW garnered the American Railway Development Association's outstanding marketing achievement designation by reclaiming shipments of iron and steel previously lost to truckers. Four years later GTW earned *Modern Railroads'* Silver Freight Car Award for its imaginative and aggressive "Tank Train" package to move residual oil on behalf of Michigan's Consumers Power Company.[28]

Like most railroaders of the time, Cramer chafed at the prescribed circumstance in which he found himself because of regulation under the Interstate Commerce Commission. Rates, divisions, and routes were essentially determined in

GTW's territory by the Traffic Executive Association of Eastern Railroads, a body made up mostly of vice presidents of traffic from the carriers. Personality was a major factor in gaining "favors" for one's road; dominant personalities simply "bulldozed" others. Rarely, if ever, Cramer complained, was there any cost analysis; salesmen, after all, were not responsible for profit but for soliciting maximum movements and tonnage. Tools available to salesmen were few given legal requirements on all carriers for uniform rates. They could hand out cigars and scratch pads and they could sell service—reliability, speedy transit, prompt settlement of claims and accurate tracing of cars. It was inadequate, Cramer believed, and GTW's emphasis on marketing as opposed to simple salesmanship reflected his philosophy. But the fullest application of marketing would await deregulation of the railroad industry.[29]

In all seasons, GTW's fortunes ebbed and flowed with the fortunes of the automobile industry. But Detroit had become arrogant, complacent, lazy, and bloated; the dominance of American manufacturers was threatened accordingly.

The automakers demanded expensive and specialized equipment. Photograph courtesy of Grand Trunk Western Railroad.

related directly or indirectly to that still vital manufacturing sector. Motor vehicle parts and set up automobiles and trucks represented nearly 40 percent of GTW's revenues for the 1970s. The year 1977 was representative. General Motors was clearly GTW's most important customer, contributing almost 47 percent of its revenue. GM, in fact, produced more than 30 percent of the holding company's operating revenues. For GTW, Ford Motor Company was in second place, Chrysler in sixth position among revenue producers. Handling, holding, or expanding this business required constant cooperation and coordination among all hands at GTW and with transportation officers and plant managers at the auto companies. It was also expensive: yard expansion at Flint to accommodate Chevrolet; acquisition of land at Lansing to provide a marshaling, storage, and shipping yard for Oldsmobile; and replacement of outdated equipment with enclosed

Volkswagen "Beetles" arrived in the 1950s and by 1967 the United States had become a net importer of automotive products. During the mid-1970s Volkswagen was surpassed as the major foreign exporter to the United States by Toyota and Nissan. Oil shocks in the 1970s, concern over automobile safety, urban sprawl, traffic congestion, and environment degradation added to Detroit's woes. The North American industry seemed at best hapless and at worst defensive. Market demands for higher quality, safer, more efficient, and more ecologically acceptable vehicles were well noted elsewhere if not in Detroit. The U.S. manufacturers were obdurate, yielding finally to federal legislation mandating change. Managers of automobile companies, it seems, would have profited from a close reading of American railroad history in the twentieth century.[30]

The North American auto industry's travail aside, GTW moved prodigious tonnage

In all seasons, GTW's fortunes ebbed and flowed with the fortunes of the automobile industry. Photograph courtesy of Grand Trunk Western Railroad.

73

At Lansing. Photograph courtesy of Grand Trunk Western Railroad.

connecting railroads—which collectively provided half of GTW revenues—were also important and easily worthy of attention.

One area of important potential growth was intermodal—piggybacking trailers and containers on flat cars. As volume grew, 35 acres of land was acquired in Chicago to provide a modern facility at that critical juncture. The $2.5 million "GT RailPort," opened in the fall of 1975, reflected expanded service to Detroit, Toronto, Montreal, and to and from Halifax in conjunction with trans-Atlantic steamship interests. The expenditure seemed justified given the 120 percent increase in intermodal business at Chicago in 1976 over 1975. Detroit's Ferndale Yard was also modified to handle expanded volumes. "MoTerm"—a 13-acre, $1.5 million facility—opened for business late in 1976 and was expanded in 1978. GTW claimed to offer the lowest ramp-to-ramp rates, an unmatched availability of equipment, and the fastest and most reliable service in the Detroit-Chicago corridor. Indeed, intermodal volume between those points increased by 96 percent in 1978, and a year later GTW operated two daily dedicated intermodal trains in each direction on that run. The financial reward from all of this was unclear, however.[32]

tri-level flat cars. The lesson was constant: It took money to make money.[31]

Cramer insisted that General Motors and the other motor vehicle customers receive adequate and proper attention, but he recognized that other industries, individual companies, and even

Cramer's forces looked elsewhere for business and found diverse opportunities—edible beans for export moving in containers from Saginaw, steel to Flint, oil in unit trains to a generating station at Essexville. Especially impressive was the establishment in 1975 of "FoodTerm," a modern facility in Detroit to handle bulk food products.[33]

GT RailPort opened with appropriate ceremony in the fall of 1975. Chicago's Richard J. Daley is shown here with an out-sized key to symbolize the opening. Burdakin is at left, Bandeen in the center. Photograph courtesy of Grand Trunk Western Railroad.

Early in 1975, John Burdakin enumerated GTW's objectives. The first goal, he said, was to "direct the activities of the company so as to achieve a long term profitable position reflecting adequate return on assets and to attain fiscal stability and independence in terms of cash for operating and capital expenditures." The statement was short and direct—characteristic of Burdakin. Yet GTW was, as Ron Lawless at Canadian National would say, "a high cost railroad with a limited revenue stream." Burdakin's aspiration would be difficult to achieve.[34]

The task of making Grand Trunk Western a more efficient property rested primarily with Burdakin and those who followed him in the operating department.

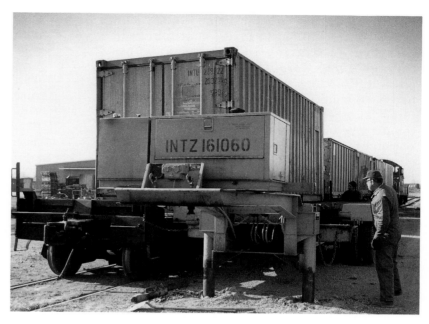

Edible beans for export moved by container from Saginaw. Photograph courtesy of Grand Trunk Western Railroad.

The road was small enough, as Gerald Maas was fond of pointing out, "to get your arms around." On the other hand, GTW was no "mom and pop operation." Its locomotive fleet during the 1970s averaged 191 units, its rolling stock for the same period averaged 10,278 cars, and the road produced prodigious ton miles—nearly nine billion for 1978, for example. Employment averaged 4,548 per year. The numbers were impressive. But so were the problems, especially GTW's vest pocket route structure which did not provide long hauls to offset staggering costs of gathering and distributing. GTW's operating ratio averaged a disappointing 109 for the 1970s. Nevertheless, Burdakin's nostrums—weight reduction with complementary body building exercises—were bearing fruit. GTW's losses in 1976 were $1.7 million, the lowest in twenty years. Moreover, GTW earned net profit of $18.6 million during the final three years of the decade.[35]

Such good news traveled rapidly, as might be expected. "It is not true that GTW is doomed to a succession of mounting deficits, service deterioration and eventual bankruptcy," wrote Gus Welty in *Railway Age*. Indeed, "GTW has come a long way toward a U.S. orientation in the way it's managed, compared with the way it was run (more or less as a CN afterthought) for the first 40-plus years of its existence." Tom Shedd, at

Modern Railroads, also took note of the "turn-around now underway at GTW" and concluded that "Canadian National made a wise decision in freeing its U.S. subsidiaries to do their own thing—and in bringing in American operating, financial and marketing officers to lead. . . ." Moreover, Shedd observed, "GTW has become a lively, competitive, full-fledged member of the U.S. railroad industry." Still another writer noted that "Burdakin has a management team that takes second place to nobody in its enthusiasm for the job at hand, with a work force that seems to take equal pride in what's happening." Burdakin properly shared such accolades. "My personal pride in the corporation comes from pride for the people within the company. Our improved financial picture reflects the activities of those employees."[36]

Nobody was happier than Robert A. Bandeen. Grand Trunk Corporation, he gleefully observed, produced net profit after the second year of existence and for the decade of the 1970s earned an admirable $53.8 million and, in some years, all three railroads—GTW, CV, and DW&P—were profitable on a stand-alone basis. Furthermore, Bandeen reminded, since its inception in 1971 GTC had filed a consolidated federal income tax return with its subsidiaries which took into account previous operating losses. As the corporation looked to the new decade, $16.4 million in investment tax credit carryovers, expiring in various amounts through 1986, were available to reduce tax payable. Bandeen's vision—his experiment—had been vindicated. But there were new problems, strategic in some cases, and a new competitive environment to understand and to respond to. Managers would have to be nimble of mind and fleet of foot if GTC was to bear full flower in the 1980s.[37]

NOTES

1. CN, Annual Report (1975): 7.
2. Ibid.
3. J. H. D. Sturgess, interview by author, 7 August 1989; Peter A. Clarke, interview by author, 7 August 1989; Peter L. Schwartz, interview by author, 7 August 1989; Yvon H. Masse, interview by author, 24 May 1989; Ron Lawless, interview by author, 7 August 1989; Robert L. Bandeen, interview by author, 3 November 1989.
4. CN, Annual Report (1970): 46; Tabular data from CN annual reports.
5. CN, *Synoptical History*, 291; CN, Overview—Grand Trunk Western (Montreal: 1969), 66-68; GTW, Minute Book No. 4, 122; GTW, Minute Book No. 5, 140, 187; *GT Reporter* (November-December 1974): 5; Ibid. (August-September 1977): 3.
6. On the century-old rail-marine operation on the Great Lakes, see George W. Hilton, *The Great Lakes Car Ferries* (Berkeley: Howell-North, 1962), and for that portion dealing with the Grand Trunk, see pages 169-86; Grand Trunk Milwaukee Car Ferry Company, Agreement, Grand Trunk Western Railroad (15 September 1954). Grand Trunk Milwaukee Car Ferry Company Minute book, n.p.; *Railway Age* 150 (27 March 1961): 30-31; CN, *Synoptical History*, 331-35, 432-33.
7. CN, Overivew—Grand Trunk Western, 68-69.
8. Ibid., 70-74.
9. J. A. Elliott, "A Proposal Concerning the Grand Trunk Western Car Ferry Service," n.d. [1972], 1-52.
10. GTW, Minute Book No. 5, 1971 Financial Results, 7; George W. Hilton, "Great Lakes Ferries: An Endangered Species," *Trains* 35 (January 1975): 42-51; Patrick C. Dorin, *The Grand Trunk Western Railroad: A Canadian National Railway* (Seattle: Superior Publishing, 1977), 140-41; GTW, Minute Book No. 5, 187; Grand Trunk Milwaukee Car Ferry Company, Minute Book, 206; *GT Reporter* (April 1975): 3 and (August 1978): 1; ICC, Certificate and Decision, Docket No. AB-31 (Sub. No. 5), 31 October 1978; *GT Reporter* (December 1978): 1; Grand Trunk Milwaukee Car Ferry Company, Minute Book, 209; GTC, Annual Report (1978): 2; GTC, Accounting Issues Manual 1, no. 5 (1978): 5; Grand Trunk Milwaukee Car Ferry Company, Minute Book, 221.
11. Earl. C. Opperthauser, interview, 6 November 1989; John David Williams, interview, 7 March 1990; GTC, Annual Report (1976): 4; Ibid. (1977): 7; *GT Reporter* (May-June 1975): 1; GTC, Annual Report (1975): 7; Ibid. (1976): 5; Ibid. (1977): 9; G. B. Aydelott, interview, 9 February 1990.
12. Charles R. Foss, *Evening Before the Diesel: A Pictorial History of Steam and First Generation Diesel Motive Power on the Grand Trunk Western Railroad, 1939-1961* (Boulder: Pruett Publishing Company, 1980), 267-68, 365-77; *GT Reporter* (December 1979): 3; GTW, Minute Book No. 7, 301, 323; GTC, Annual Report (1979): 8; *GT Reporter* (November-December 1975): 3.
13. GTW, Minute Book No. 6, 229, 237; GTW Minute Book No. 7, 301, 303; GTW, Executive Committee Minute Book No. 7, Executive Minute No. 602; *GT Reporter* (November-December), 2; GTC, Annual Report (1976): 22; GTC, Minute Book No. 2, 79-81.
14. *GT Reporter* (May-June 1973): 1-2; GTW, Minute Book No. 5, 159; GTC, Annual Report (1974): 7.
15. GTC, Annual Report (1975): 7; Ibid. (1976): 5; Ibid. (1977): 3; Ibid. (1979): 8; Gus Welty, "Mandatory AEI Tagging," *Railway Age* 192 (March 1991): 34-38.
16. GTW, Minute Book No. 5, 172, 178; *GT Reporter* (November-December 1973), 5; Dorin, *The Grand Trunk Western*, 61-67.
17. GTC, Annual Report (1972): 31; *GT Reporter* (September-October 1972): 2; Ibid. (May-June 1973): 5; Ibid. (July-August 1973): 4.
18. GTW, Minute Book No. 5, 1971 Financial Results, 7; GTW, Minute Book No. 5, 1972 Financial Results, 6; GTW, Minute Book No. 6, 248; GTW, Minute Book No. 7, 297; GTC, Annual Report (1978): 8; GTW, Corporate Planning and Finance Review of Accomplishments (November 1973), 15.
19. CN, *Synoptical History*, 298-99; GTW, Minute Book No. 5, 1971 Financial Results, 8; GTW, Minute Book No. 5, 1972 Financial Results, 7; GTW, Minute No. 5, 169, 188; GTW, Minute Book No. 6, 201; GTW, Minute Book No. 7, 284.

20. John David Williams, interview, 7 March 1990; Peter A. Clarke, interview, 7 August 1989; J. H. D. Sturgess, interview, 7 August 1989; Yvon H. Masse, interview, 24 May 1989.

21. Luther S. Miller, "CN: Productivity is the Road to Profits, and CN Rail is Showing the Way," *Railway Age* 179 (25 December 1978): 22-30.

22. *GT Reporter* (May 1977): 1.

23. Gerald L. Maas, interview, 9 February 1990; GTC, Annual Report (1977): 1, 13.

24. GTC, Annual Report (1977): 10-12; Ibid. (1978): 121; Ibid. (1980): 14.

25. CN, Overview—Grand Trunk Western (Montreal: July 1969), 37-38; D. P. MacKinnon to R. R. Latimer, 30 August 1976; A. J. Wilson to R. L. Lawless, 21 September 1976; Jack Cann to R. R. Latimer, 27 September 1976; *Journal of Commerce* (28 December 1978); Alan G. Dustin to John H. Burkakin, 8 January 1979; T. Brady to P. E. Tatro, 21 May 1979; John H. Burdakin to Robert H. Eder, 26 June 1979; John H. Burdakin to Alan G. Dustin, 31 May 1979, President's File 109.

26. GTC, Annual Report (1976): 1; DW&P, Executive Committee Book, Executive Minute No. 27.

27. GTC, Annual Report (1976): 9; Ibid. (1978): 10.

28. Thomas J. Lamphier, interview, 29 March 1989; James R. Sullivan, interview, 9 February 1990; GTC, Annual Report (1972): 26; *GT Reporter* (August-September 1977): 1; GTC, Annual Report (1977): 6; *GT Reporter* (May-June 1974): 1; Ibid. (August 1978): 1.

29. Walter E. Cramer, interview, 11 August 1989.

30. James J. Flink, *The Automobile Age* (Cambridge: MIT Press, 1988), 293, 327, 378.

31. GTC, Annual Report (1977): 19; GTW, Minute Book No. 5, 15; *GT Reporter* (July-August 1972): 1; Ibid. (April 1975): 5; GTC, Annual Report (1975): 6; GTW, Minute Book No. 6, 241.

32. *GT Reporter* (September-October 1973): 6; Ibid. (September-October 1975): 2; GTC, Annual Report (1976): 5; *GT Reporter* (October-November 1978), 2-3; GTW, Minute Book No. 7, 281; GTC, Annual Report (1978): 7; Ibid. (1979): 8.

33. GTC, Annual Report (1972): 32; *GT Reporter* (May-June 1974): 1; *Railway Age* 179 (25 December 1978): 50-51; GTC, Annual Report (1976): 5.

34. John H. Burdakin, "Grand Trunk Western Railroad Corporate Objectives," February 1975, (SF) 2-01; Ronald L. Lawless, interview, 7 August 1989.

35. Tabular data from GTC annual reports 1972-79.

36. Gus Welty, "Grand Trunk Western: Battling Toward Profitability," *Railway Age* 176 (8 September 1975): 30-32, 104; Tom Shedd, "Freedom Pays," *Modern Railroads* (July 1976): 20-23; *Railway Age* 179 (25 December 1978), 27; Bill Palmer, "CN's American Brother," *CN Movin'* (March-April 1977): 4-7.

37. GTC, Annual Report (1979): 8.

5 GT WHERE DO WE FIT IN?

The purpose of the proposed transition is to integrate the organizations and operations of the GTW, DT&I and DTSL so that the combined system will be more economical and efficient, provide better service, attract larger volumes of traffic, maintain competitive balance, and produce greater financial return than any or all of the three railroads independently operated.

GTW, Application, Finance Docket 28499, 4.

In summary, we submit that there are too many uncertainties, risks, and even perils about GTW's financial abilities to involve DT&I in them. The railroad industry has been and is going through perilous times. It is no time to take chances. The commission cannot accept GTW's inducement to gamble.

N&W/B&O-C&O, Brief of the Joint Applicants to Administrative Law Judge Richard H. Beddow, Jr., Finance Docket 28676, 49.

By the late 1970s, American railroads were the embodiment of a "mature industry," as economists and business historians liked to note. The designation was often one of derision, implying that the industry was past

its prime, that the steam car civilization was but a quaint and romantic particle of the misty past. There was no denying that much had changed; the creation of Amtrak in 1971, for instance, was a tacit admission on the part of the industry itself that the grand era of passenger carriage had passed in favor of rubber tires and jet aircraft. Nevertheless, perceptions yield reluctantly to reality; public policy still understood railroads as if they enjoyed a virtual modal monopoly. Eventually, however, even Congress came to a grudging and halting recognition that railroads—while still major players on the transportation stage—were under tremendous competitive pressure from modes that received a variety of public support and sustenance and that regulatory framework in place reflected a competitive environment long since vanished. Fresh breezes were blowing, driven by these realities and a recognition of them; they would result in modified public policy designed to upset the status quo. How would railroad managers—accustomed as they were to the ways of the old order, the ways of a mature industry—respond to the new order? Bandeen's experiment—Grand Trunk Corporation—had "earned its spurs" in the old environment. How well would Bandeen and Burdakin handle the new circumstances?

Railroad managers had long and properly complained that government regulations and bureaucratic inertia shackled them, restricting their ability to respond, to innovate, to—well, to manage. Their complaint was merited, as Albro Martin showed in his seminal study, *Enterprise Denied*. They recognized for example, irony in the Transportation Act of 1920 which, in part, proposed a national system of mergers that, if implemented, would forge a few strong regional carriers. This was exactly what railroad moguls such as James J. Hill and Edward H. Harriman earlier had argued for only to be shouted down by "reformers" who feared tyrannical monopoly as a consequence. What resulted from the new legislation of 1920, however, was considerable study, much creative posturing by academics, politicians, and railroad leaders themselves, but no grand consummation. The merger movement—as much a part of the American railroad landscape as spikes and ties, locomotives and cars—was subsequently retarded, a reality exacerbated by the Great Depression and then World War II. Thereafter, the movement for "super railroads," as advocated by John W. Barriger and others, gained steam—if slowly.[1]

The modern merger movement began humbly but accelerated in speed and escalated in scope as the public climate became more receptive. The merger of Alton into Gulf, Mobile & Ohio during 1947 set the stage. Ten years later Louisville & Nashville (L&N) absorbed Nashville, Chattanooga & St. Louis, and in 1959 Norfolk & Western swallowed Virginian. The campaign gained momentum during the next decade. In 1960, Erie combined with Delaware, Lackawanna & Western to form Erie Lackawanna, and Chicago & North Western bought Minneapolis & St. Louis. In the following year Canadian Pacific placed three of its American flags under one—Soo Line—while in 1963 Chesapeake & Ohio gained control of Baltimore & Ohio. Norfolk & Western moved boldly in 1964 to merge Nickel Plate, lease Wabash and Pittsburgh & West Virginia, and gain control of Akron, Canton & Youngstown. Seaboard Coast Line came about by merger of Atlantic Coast Line and Seaboard Air Line in 1967, and a year later Chicago & North Western further expanded by acquiring Chicago Great Western. But the real news in 1968 was combination in the East of arch rivals New York

Central and Pennsylvania to form Penn Central, which in turn was expanded later the same year when New York, New Haven & Hartford was added.[2]

Quickened merger activities in the East mirrored the general pattern of the industry, but with a difference, because the industry's woes, including money-draining passenger and commuter operations, marginal branch lines, high costs of gathering and distributing, counterproductive labor agreements and costly terminal and classification yards, were acute in the East. Few enough recognized the profound implications when Lehigh & New England ceased operation in 1961, when Wabash in 1962 handed over operation of malnourished Ann Arbor to Detroit, Toledo & Ironton, or when Rutland called it quits in 1963. All of this was small potatoes, however, compared to the spectacular collapse of Penn Central in 1970. Indeed, Penn Central's bankruptcy—the biggest business failure in history to that time—forced the issue. Public policy had to change, somehow, and soon. Before that happened, though, Lehigh & Hudson River, Ann Arbor, and Erie Lackawanna, among others, would join a long list of eastern bankrupts.[3]

Bankruptcies, of course, were hardly a new phenomenon. Bankruptcy for a railroad historically meant that a court oversaw controlled reduction of debt, operations continued, and—with creditors at bay—the property was improved. Minneapolis & St. Louis and the Denver & Rio Grand Western are twentieth-century examples of this process; both emerged from lengthy reorganization proceedings with strong managements, with well-groomed physical plants, and with improved competitive capacity. Penn Central was different. Track conditions deteriorated, service levels plummeted, and labor unrest in 1973 led to a strike. Investors talked of liquidation and politicians discussed nationalization. Penn Central would not survive. But Penn Central's service area was characterized by densely populated districts and heavy industry requiring reliable railroad service. A reluctant Congress finally moved, ordering the Department of Transportation in 1973 to study problems in the Northeast and to recommend plans for restructuring the rail industry there. Out of it came the Regional Rail Restructuring Act of 1973 (3Rs Act) which created the United States Railway Association (USRA) for the pur-

John Burdakin was comfortable with traditional duties as a railroad businessman in the political world—such as presenting this plaque to President and Mrs. Ford during the 1976 campaign. He would become more involved in the political scene as GTC addressed the new world of mega-mergers. Photograph courtesy of Grand Trunk Western Railroad.

pose of planning a Consolidated Rail Corporation (Conrail). USRA would do more than decide the fate of Penn Central and railroad properties. In the end, all eastern bankrupts save Ann Arbor and Boston & Maine would be plunged into Conrail—a monumental federally-sponsored experiment that combined public and private considerations, to be born on 1 April 1976. Before that, however, preliminary plans were formulated which boldly proclaimed that Conrail would not be a receptacle into which all lines of all predecessors would be thrown. Rather, Conrail would be a much slimmer model—shorn of many branches and even many main lines. This would result in dislocation for some rail customers and restructuring for all railroads in a broad area from Chicago, St. Louis, and Detroit to Washington, New York, and Boston. How would GTC's railroads—especially Grand Trunk Western—respond? That was John Burdakin's responsibility.[4]

To properly discharge that duty, Burdakin concluded, GTC required eyes and ears in Washington—senses of a person who knew the industry as well as the workings of the federal

government, a person who could monitor developments and make informed recommendations. In this, Burdakin had marvelously good fortune. Basil Cole, whose father had been an operating officer on the Union Pacific, and who had also become a railroader—heading the law department at Pennsylvania Railroad and then Penn Central—would be GTC's Washington emissary and would eventually be involved in important legal proceedings on GTC's behalf.[5]

Burdakin and Cole recognized that Conrail's ultimate configuration would be the outcome of often conflicting and always powerful forces—local, regional, and national transportation needs, public and private requirements, and political considerations of all stripes. USRA planners—"itinerant philosophers," Cole labeled them—might be relied on to carve out Conrail's core lines but there was sure to be much pulling and hauling. The East's large, healthy roads—Norfolk & Western, and Chessie System—would be principal players. Where did GTW fit in? Burdakin initially did not see the road expanding its service area by way of large strategic acquisition. Rather, he thought GTW could solidify its position in certain Michigan markets by selective acquisitions of Penn Central operations. Burdakin focused on Muskegon, Grand Rapids, Saginaw, Bay City, and Lansing which, he said, did "not generate enough rail traffic to sustain three railroads" (GTW, Chessie, and Conrail). GTW's plan, then, was to campaign against Conrail presence above Detroit and Battle Creek and to convince USRA to divide Penn Central lines lying north of those cities between GTW and Chessie. The effort was directed at Michigan politicians and business leaders ("Grand Trunk is basically a Michigan railroad") and took on a David and Goliath tone

Investment in and about Saginaw proved a good one. Property was improved, service strengthened, and traffic grew. Officers and contract employees congratulated one another in 1976. Photograph courtesy of Grand Trunk Western Railroad.

("Give Michigan's smaller railroads a chance to compete").[6]

That was not the whole cloth. Burdakin, Cole, Robert Adams, and others in Detroit whose earlier careers had been with Pennsylvania, New York Central, or Penn Central, fully understood the competitive implications of a slimmed down, modernized, and well-managed plant that might ultimately emerge from Penn Central ashes. Moreover, the debacle of Penn Central notwithstanding, the merger movement had continued. A huge Burlington Northern appeared in 1970 as the result of merging four western roads; Louisville & Nashville acquired Monon in 1971; Gulf, Mobile & Ohio and Illinois Central merged in 1972 to become Illinois Central Gulf; in 1973, Chesapeake & Ohio, Baltimore & Ohio, and Western Maryland became subsidiaries of Chessie System; and, of course, Conrail itself would appear in 1976. The shakeout in the East merely presaged another massive adjustment in

the Middle West where Chicago, Rock Island & Pacific declared bankruptcy in 1976 and would be followed into receivers court by Chicago, Milwaukee, St. Paul & Pacific in 1977.[7]

The arena in which GTC had evolved was rapidly disappearing. Burdakin was nervous. "I don't have misgivings about competing with an equal," Burdakin said at public hearings on USRA's final plan, "but I do have reservations about playing football in my undershorts against a fully equipped team supported by the federal government." Here was a double entendre. The reference, of course, was to Conrail and reflected Burdakin's concern as to GTW's ability to compete with that federally created and federally financed giant. It also reflected a larger concern: GTW's ability to compete with Conrail *and other increasingly powerful roads*—Norfolk & Western and Chessie. In the case of the Michigan lines, the most immediate issue, USRA eventually made available to Grand Trunk Western 118.5

Penn Central track miles in and about Bay City, Midland, and Saginaw plus 32.5 track miles from Ann Arbor between Durand and Ashley through Owosso (over which GTW previously had trackage rights). GTW bought well ($1.485 million) and quickly authorized a three-year improvement program ($5 million). It was money well spent. By 1979, a 23 percent return on investment would be realized.[8]

The fall of the eastern regionals, Penn Central, Rock Island, and Milwaukee, the creation of Conrail, and the rising power of Norfolk & Western and Chessie all served notice on GTC managers that they must move quickly to design strategy adequate to survival in an environment that was becoming more difficult with each passing day. A period of intense soul-searching at Grand Trunk Corporation had begun.

Burdakin, Cole, and team found themselves in a circumstance faced by countless railroad managers of the past: GTC roads, especially GTW, had to expand or expire. GTW had to expand its service area, as well as gain and hold friendly connections through additional gateways. This would not be accomplished by new construction, as had been the case a century earlier, but by line acquisitions—such as the purchase of the former Penn Central segments in Michigan—or on a grander scale by purchase or merger of entire companies. That prospect, though, would be awkward for GTC given its youth—not even ten years of age—and its delicate financial condition. Moreover, as always, there were considerations unique to GTC such as its ownership by foreigners—the need to have permission from "headquarters," from Parliament, and ultimately from the Canadian people. Such constraints weighed heavily on GTC's ability to respond nimbly. On the other hand, Burdakin had assembled a talented team; and Bandeen, as usual, would dare to do. There was no reason to count out Canadian National's American roads as the merger movement evolved into the era of megamerger.

Events conspired to focus on an opportunity close at hand—the Detroit, Toledo & Ironton Railroad (DT&I). Begun in 1849 as a local Ohio venture, the earliest predecessor experienced several transformations and emerged in 1905 as DT&I with a north-south route configuration from Detroit through Flat Rock in Michigan to Lima and Springfield and finally Ironton on the Ohio River. During the 1920s, DT&I was controlled by the hard-charging Henry Ford whose huge River Rouge Plant was served by the road. In 1929, however, Ford became disenchanted with railroading and sold DT&I to Pennroad Corporation, an offshoot of Pennsylvania Railroad, which heretofore had only a modest presence in traffic-rich Detroit. Eventually Pennroad sold DT&I to subsidiaries of Pennsylvania, which along with the parent, became parts of ill-starred Penn Central.[9]

DT&I's contribution to its owner's well being thinned during the first half of the 1970s just as Penn Central's creditors sought recompense. DT&I's earlier record had been quite different. Indeed, DT&I enjoyed impressive prosperity after the Great Depression. It had very little passenger expense, could count on monumental blocks of high-rated traffic from Ford Motor Company, connected with all of the region's east-west trunk roads, and boasted strong profit margins. It dieselized early and enjoyed prestige of ownership by "the standard railroad of the world." Eventually, however, modal competition, counterproductive work rules, Ford's difficult demands for equipment and service, and Penn Central's collapse sent dark clouds across DT&I's horizon. Moreover, hapless Ann Arbor, another of Pennco's holdings, had been thrust upon DT&I in the early 1960s only to fail a decade later and land in independent receivership. Because of DT&I's ownership by Pennco, USRA planners initially sought to abandon most of DT&I and parcel out the rest. This was averted, but the road's future was clouded at best.

Rumors circulated within the industry that Pennco would be willing to part with DT&I. Several carriers poked about and expressed interest in one way or another. Meanwhile, Pennco asked Salomon Brothers for a candid evaluation. The report was not encouraging. Salomon noted that DT&I's market share had slipped; that net profits per carload, coverage of interest and other fixed charges, and cash flow all had declined; and that the operating ratio had risen. Salomon attributed these problems to several factors: "a few large accounts" comprised DT&I's customer base, Penn Central's collapse and the collateral rise of other "neighboring and affiliated roads" had taken its toll, DT&I's costs had accelerated more rapidly than revenues, and DT&I had a restricted route structure. Worst of

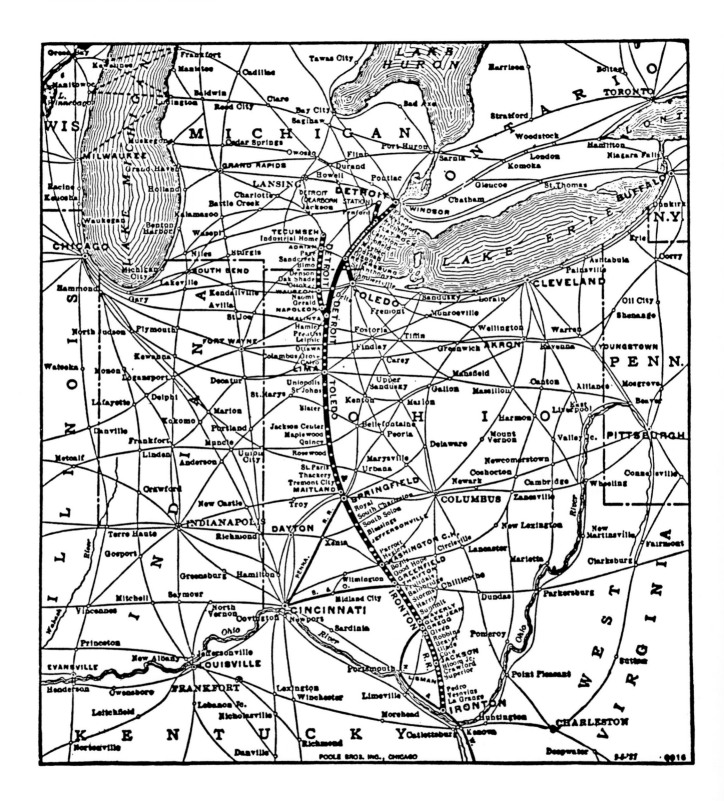

DT&I began as a local venture but ultimately reached from Detroit to the Ohio River. Courtesy of Grand Trunk Western Railroad.

84

Henry Ford built for the future as his electrification program for DT&I suggests. Photograph courtesy of Grand Trunk Western Railroad.

all, warned Salomon, DT&I could not "expect to refund bonds maturing in March 1976 using traditional external sources of capital."[10]

At the same time, Norfolk & Western Railway (N&W) analysts quietly scrutinized DT&I. They liked its potential and earnestly urged N&W's senior management to acquire the road. After all, the N&W team pointed out, DT&I had 30 junction points—10 of them with N&W, and N&W was DT&I's second largest interchange partner. The primary connection however, was Penn Central (soon to become Conrail) and, with DT&I in its pocket, N&W could divert most of this tonnage to its own gateways. There were other advantages. DT&I's long-term debt was reasonable, the company had not failed to pay interest on funded debt, the property and equipment fleet was in at least fair condition, and on "conveyance day" (1 April 1976, the advent of Conrail) DT&I would be relieved "of the devastating burden of Ann Arbor operations" and at the same time would gain full trackage rights to the important Cincinnati gateway (Louisville & Nashville's DeCoursey Yard and Southern Railway's Gest Yard). Additionally, DT&I's impressive Flat Rock Hump Yard had capacity to classify cars and make up run-through trains to and from Toronto

on behalf of Norfolk & Western and Canadian Pacific (DT&I held valuable operating rights through Penn Central's Detroit-Windsor tunnel). And there was defensive rationale. "The loss of DT&I to an unfriendly carrier could be damaging to gross revenues" because N&W would lose St. Louis and Kansas City business; Chicago traffic, too, "might be in jeopardy if a new owner wished to route via" Conrail, Grand Trunk Western, or Chesapeake & Ohio. Finally, N&W analysts reminded, an earlier team in 1959 had recommend acquisition of the Detroit road.[11]

N&W's senior managers did not react as quickly as the company's analysts had urged. Meanwhile, USRA plans were implemented on 1 April 1976; Conrail was born and DT&I was relieved of Ann Arbor. At the same time, DT&I established regular through service to Cincinnati and implemented direct connections with Grand Trunk Western in Detroit (bypassing the Detroit Terminal Railroad). In addition, DT&I's urgent need to satisfy bond requirements was met through the sale of impressive land holdings and leaseback of equipment. But problems remained. Maintenance was trimmed and derailments were costly and damaged the road's credibility. Ford suffered a strike costing huge chunks of traffic,

Robert A. Sharp was brought in to make DT&I attractive for suitors. Sharp predictably urged attention to the road's many connections. Photograph courtesy of Grand Trunk Western Railroad.

and Mother Nature played nasty and expensive tricks. Harsh cost controls were imposed during the fall of 1976.[12]

Pennco was increasingly restless. Did DT&I fit into Pennco—an organization that essentially oversaw Penn Central's non-rail assets? The answer, in short, was no; a railroad, Pennco concluded was, at best, a headache. The issue for Pennco then became how to maximize the value of the property. To address that issue and to make DT&I attractive for suitors, Pennco brought in Robert A. Sharp as president. Sharp made personal contact with major shippers and labor organizations, delegated managerial decisions, and promoted an aggressive marketing campaign. With Cincinnati service firmly in place, Sharp urged solicitation for the maximum haul. This included vigorous attempts to lure traffic from central Michigan, GTW country, toward which Walter Cramer showed little affection. Sharp thought that pressure from shippers might bring GTW around. Then, too, Canadian

Pacific was talking to Southern Railway about a Toronto-Atlanta run-through using DT&I's Cincinnati linkage. "This effort may also have favorable influence on the CN/GTW attitudes toward the DT&I," Sharp concluded.[13]

That may or may not have been the case. In any event, early in 1977, Burdakin asked Bandeen for permission to investigate acquisition of DT&I. Bandeen predictably responded in the affirmative but pointedly told Burdakin that it "would have to be achieved without CN cash support" because "the parent company cannot be seen to be investing in additional U.S. rail plant at a time when our capital demands in Canada exceed our ability to finance internally." Bandeen recognized the potential for moving heavy traffic onto DT&I through Cincinnati, but he also saw another advantage in acquiring DT&I. This might be, he pointed out, "the means by which we obtain external equity participation in GTC, or GTW, through a private sale rather than a public sale of stock." Burdakin had a mandate.

Robert A. Walker was borrowed from Cramer's marketing staff for work on the DT&I case. Photograph courtesy of Grand Trunk Western Railroad.

With Basil Cole, he met with Frank Loy, president of Pennco, and Jervis Langdon, former president of Penn Central and Pennco adviser. Burdakin knew that others—Southern, L&N, Chessie, and N&W—had expressed interest, but was surprised to learn that Langdon believed DT&I should be sold to a "group of railroads rather than one individual railroad." Failing that, however, Pennco would "issue a prospectus and solicit bids." Pennco promised to make traffic and financial data available but then stonewalled Burdakin's persistent requests. The reason became abundantly apparent on 31 May 1977, when Norfolk & Western and Chessie announced an agreement to jointly purchase DT&I for $15 million. Southern countered with an offer of more than $22 million, but on 13 June, Pennco signed a binding agreement with N&W/Chessie (technically N&W and Baltimore & Ohio, a unit of Chessie) for $23.6 million. GTW had been frozen out.[14]

How to respond? Burdakin felt he had two options: negotiate a deal with the new owners to protect GTW interests or oppose the transfer of ownership before the Interstate Commerce Commission (ICC). Burdakin chose the latter. But he felt GTW's chances with the ICC would be materially improved if he could provide a realistic alternative to the N&W/Chessie proposal. A project team was assembled, headed by Basil Cole and Robert A. Walker who was borrowed from Cramer's marketing staff.

When N&W/Chessie made formal application to the ICC in the fall, GTW denounced the plan because of the "serious impact this sale could have on the competitive position and solvency of smaller railroads—especially the GTW." Indeed, said Burdakin, Grand Trunk Western was "completely dependent upon the economy of Michigan" and this sale would "adversely affect the quality of service we render to the automobile industry and others . . . ." Moreover, there was the important matter of fairness. Selling DT&I to two of the nation's largest revenue producing railroads "was not equitable." The campaign mirrored earlier efforts to gain USRA concessions—a David and Goliath contest certain to harm David and his worthy constituents if hardhearted Goliath had his way. Burdakin turned up the heat. Sale of DT&I to N&W/Chessie would have "monopolistic impact" that would clearly have negative implications for "smaller railroads, shippers, communities, and taxpayers." GTW, he affirmed, would offer an alternative proposal. After all, "Detroit, Toledo & Ironton and Grand Trunk Western, Michigan-based railroads, have traditionally performed complimentary services especially in the highly industrialized southeastern section of the state."[15]

On 16 February, GTW and GTC boldly asked the ICC to disapprove the N&W/Chessie application and indicate, on an interim basis, conditions by which it would approve control by Grand Trunk Western of DT&I *and* the Detroit and Toledo Shore Line Railroad (D&TSL or Shore Line, presently owned in halves by GTW and N&W). The purpose of this, said Cole, would be to integrate GTW, DT&I, and Shore Line into an efficient unit that would provide competitive balance and produce greater return than any or all of the three roads operated independently. Financing had been arranged by which GTW would issue senior unsecured notes guaranteed by GTC adequate to pay for DT&I stock and debt, land held by a subsidiary, N&W's half of the Shore Line, labor protection, and start-up costs. All of it was consistent with the Interstate Commerce Commission Act (to improve adequacy of transportation service), the Regional Rail Reorganization Act of 1973 (continuation and improvement of essential rail service), and the Railroad Revitalization and Regulatory Reform Act of 1976 (4Rs Act, restructuring of the system on a more economically justified basis and foster competition among all carriers). Cole asserted that DT&I and GTW were "natural candidates" because their combination would result in an end-to-end merger. GTW pledged that these efforts were not, as N&W/Chessie charged, designed simply to derail the N&W/Chessie application. GTW would pay $15 million for DT&I stock, but was flexible in that regard if Pennco could demonstrate greater value.[16]

This campaign, Basil Cole readily admitted, would be "an uphill battle." Innovation and persistence would be required. It was incumbent on Grand Trunk Western to present itself as "the little guy" battling the "giants" on the basis of "everlasting right." Privately, Cole told Burdakin that Norfolk & Western and Chessie had the best argument. Burdakin bluntly responded that if N&W/Chessie succeeded it "would kill GTW as well as DT&I." GTW purposes were at once, Robert Walker urged, strategically offensive (get to Cincinnati and connections there) and strategically defensive (prevent any encroachment of Detroit's traffic base). GTW designs might be aided by altered public opinion; the broad issue of railroad mergers certainly was not as explosive as it once was. In fact the Railroad Revitalization and Regulatory Reform Act of 1976 passed ostensibly to address a growing crisis in the Midwest, actually enhanced opportunity for merger and rationalization of plant.

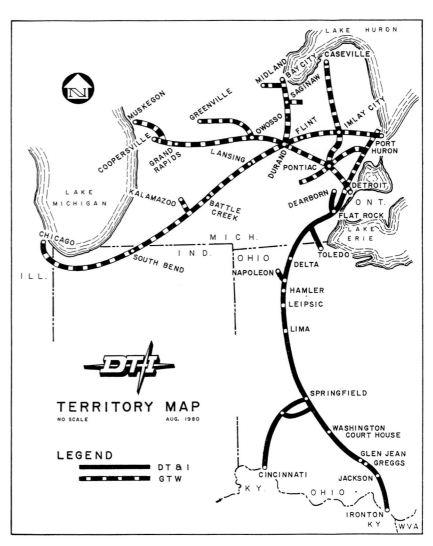

If approved, GTW and DT&I would be an end-to-end merger. Photograph courtesy of Grand Trunk Western Railroad.

Cole's burden as counsel would be to convince ICC staffers, the administrative law judge hearing the case, and ultimately the commissioners themselves that the GTW plan was better than that of N&W/Chessie in terms of "public interest."[17]

Big Guns were arrayed against Grand Trunk Western. Pennco, owner of DT&I, was put off by the fact that GTW had interrupted what seemed to be a fait acompli, that GTW—unlike N&W/Chessie—had not negotiated a sales contract and had not even made a solid dollar-value offer, and it clearly doubted GTW's ability to finance the deal. After all said Pennco, GTW has "a history of serious financial difficulty." And, sniffed Pennco attorneys, GTW's "bifurcated proceeding" was altogether "inappropriate."[18]

Others were less restrained. Since GTW had not tendered nor had it been awarded a contract to purchase, "its application offers a 'proposal' which is distinctly inconsistent with the public interest," asserted counsel for N&W/Chessie. Indeed, they hooted, GTW's application was "nothing but a speculative, disruptive and very possibly ruinous 'plan' for control of (and ultimately merger with) DT&I . . . . " Under GTW's proposal, DT&I would lose its identity, jobs would perish, and personnel would be dislocated. "GTW is, by any criterion, a marginal road . . . " and "to permit merger [of DT&I] with GTW (which is also heavily dependent upon the automobile industry) would be to accentuate and exacerbate its problems." Opposing attorneys took great issue with GTW's vaunted claims to recent financial success under the flag of Grand Trunk Corporation. There were, in fact, said N&W/Chessie, "sharp limits to the degree of [GTC's] 'independence and Americanization.'"[19]

Canadian National was not initially a party to these proceedings, but Robert Bandeen presented testimony in support of GTW's case. Bandeen seized the opportunity to explain CN's history and circumstance. CN was, he pointed out, "a crown corporation . . . and accordingly is accountable to the Parliament of Canada through the Minister of Transport. All capital stock is owned by the federal government with control and direction provided by a board of directors and with implementation of policy by a management selected by that board." CN, he reminded, "has always been required by law to be operated on a commercial basis . . . ."[20]

What were CN's intentions in the DT&I case? "CN is not seeking to expand its operations within the United States and is not even committed to maintaining full ownership of its American rail subsidiaries," said counsel. In other words, CN's interest in the DT&I case was a matter of enhancing the attractiveness of its U.S. investments rather than simply expanding the CN system. Success in this case by N&W/Chessie would damage GTW whereas a combined GTW-DT&I-D&TSL would "make outside investment in GTW more attractive." This was, of course, Bandeen's long-term desire and he had told Burdakin as much early in 1977: "My main reaction . . . is in seeing this proposal as a possible means by

which we obtain external equity participation in GTC, or the GTW . . . . " Was there more to the story? "The underlying motivation," speculated N&W/Chessie, might be "a combined GTW-DT&I that would give CN a more marketable product to sell." Would CN part with a combined GTW-DT&I? Perhaps. One possible effect of this consolidation, observed GTW counsel, would be "to make the GTW a more economically viable carrier and then to make it available for consolidation with other carriers."[21]

The whole matter of Canadian National—a "foreign corporation"—and its relationship to GTC and GTW was admittedly confusing and thus presented opportunities for opposing attorneys and others to fan xenophobic flames. Was there not something untoward about a "Crown Corporation," all of whose stock is owned by the Canadian government, doing business in the United States? Yes, implied N&W/Chessie and yes, said Canadian Pacific, CN's nemesis at home. This irked John Burdakin, who scorned those who contended that "Grand Trunk's acquisition of Ironton [DT&I] poses some sort of sinister threat to the United States by increasing Canadian investment in our [U.S.] railroad system." For his part, Bandeen found such assertions contradictory and bemusing. He noted that CN and CP were head-to-head competitors in Canada where they fell under the same regulatory framework and he pointed out that both had substantial investment in U.S. rail operations (CN through GTC and CP in Soo Line). Unlike CN, however, CP also had non-rail assets in the U.S.—lead and zinc refineries and oil and gas investments in the Gulf Coast area.

Consequently, "I am," Bandeen chuckled, "at a loss to understand why Canadian Pacific . . . has endeavored to paint a sinister picture in describing the modest investment of CN in United States enterprises." What of Norfolk & Western and Chessie? Each had lines in Ontario, Bandeen reminded, "where they themselves compete with Canadian roads in Canadian territory." For GTW, the Canadian-ownership issue remained nettlesome but not controlling.[22]

Stronger and more directly applicable arguments centered on reasons why DT&I should pass to ownership by N&W and Chessie which together pledged to "stabilize" DT&I as one of their "principal feeders." Indeed, more than 40 percent of DT&I's traffic moved to and from

Chessie alone. Furthermore, N&W/Chessie would maintain DT&I's identity "responsible to its own shippers" with "no changes in its management nor in the duties of its employees," and would discharge DT&I's debt "leaving it substantially debt-free except for equipment obligations." Pennco, of course, supported N&W/Chessie and had every right to be heard. Said Pennco: N&W/Chessie would "assure continued high quality DT&I service" and, in fact, improve it with sophisticated data processing, communication, and other staff services. In Pennco's view, assurance for this came implicitly from the fact that N&W and Chessie were "natural competitors." Consequently, "neither would allow the other to use DT&I to the other's advantage."[23]

Powerful arguments, Basil Cole agreed. But Cole was not without his own sharp swords. Despite assertions to the contrary, said Cole, N&W/Chessie would dry up DT&I by diverting its traffic: "The financial incentives of N&W/Chessie to favor their lines (to the detriment of DT&I) would be irresistible." N&W/Chessie, Cole sarcastically reminded, had pledged no changes in DT&I if they acquired the road. Nonsense! Why, then, would they want it? Changes were bound to follow, Cole thundered, should N&W/Chessie prevail and those changes would result in the disappearance of essential service rendered by DT&I. The public interest would suffer accordingly. After all, N&W and Chessie had historically viewed DT&I only in terms of what it could do for them. As a recent example, both had lobbied vigorously against giving DT&I access to Cincinnati under the USRA's final system plan. In truth, said Cole, the N&W/Chessie application—if granted—would be anticompetitive.[24]

On the other hand, GTW's application favored competition. Acquisition of DT&I by GTW would give it the following: access to lucrative traffic emanating from Ford's River Rouge industrial complex; lengthened line hauls; the ability to avoid congenitally congested terminals in Toledo; enhanced intermodal opportunities; and direct connections with Southern and Louisville & Nashville at Cincinnati. GTW promised to upgrade DT&I's plant, rolling stock, and motive power and pledged vital competition by a Detroit-based, service-oriented regional carrier in the important Detroit-Cincinnati corridor.[25]

Neither side relied solely on logic and merit. Both engaged in hyperbole. For example, friendly relationships between GTW and DT&I were, bellowed a GTW publicist, "historic." This assertion left Robert Sharp and DT&I's marketing force in a state of catatonic bemusement since a mere 2 percent of DT&I's business was interchanged with GTW and attempts to work together—on other than cooperative movements in Detroit—had left DT&I forces bewildered and discouraged.[26]

GTW's justification in stiff-arming DT&I was based on an understandable desire to route for its longest haul—in this case over Detroit & Toledo Shore Line—jointly owned with N&W. The earliest predecessor for the Shore Line had aspirations as a high capacity electric railroad, fell into financial difficulty, and emerged as D&TSL to be acquired jointly during 1902 in ownership halves by Grand Trunk and Toledo, St. Louis & Western (predecessor of New York, Chicago & St. Louis, "Nickel Plate," which merged into N&W during 1964). The Shore Line reached from Toledo to West Detroit and was a profitable and strategically important route. Before the advent of GTC, CN made numerous studies demonstrating advantages to GTW if GTW acquired N&W's half-ownership, but nothing came as a result of these recommendations—probably because N&W had no incentive to sell.[27]

Burdakin openly contended that D&TSL was "doomed as an independently operated railroad if either N&W/Chessie or the GTW application is approved." If GTW acquired DT&I, former Shore Line traffic would surely move to DT&I; if N&W/Chessie acquired DT&I, they would certainly move traffic away from the Shore Line. In either case, said Burdakin, D&TSL was "dead." N&W/Chessie contended that Burdakin's was an "extravagant claim."[28]

The case dragged on. Cole tried to stake a prior claim to DT&I for GTW. He reminded that Penn Central's Alfred E. Perlman had sought in 1968 to extend DT&I, which Penn Central then owned through Pennco, by acquisition of Grand Trunk Western. That effort failed, of course, as Penn Central succumbed. Cole also noted that GTW had lobbied unsuccessfully to have DT&I designated to GTW during developmental stages of USRA's final system plan. Others noted that N&W and Chessie had lobbied just as intensely and unsuccessfully toward the same end.[29]

In all cases, Cole drew focus to GTW's primary argument: GTW's plan favored competition while that of N&W/Chessie was anticompetitive. A decision for N&W/Chessie would kill the Shore Line and moreover, said Cole, "GTW's future is dim if DT&I is acquired by N&W and Chessie." On the other hand, consolidation of GTW with DT&I and the Shore Line would allow the surviving entity to live on as a competitive force in the Michigan-Ohio region and, significantly, would make outside investment in Grand Trunk Corporation more attractive.[30]

The Detroit, Toledo & Ironton case seemed a microcosm of the industry at the time. Tremendous flux reflected a growing recognition that change had come and that the industry needed to make appropriate adaptations. Merger was a continuing nostrum, but by most standards of the day the DT&I case was small potatoes. In the Midwest and West, Milwaukee Road ended service west of Miles City, Montana, early in 1980 and on 31 March of that year Rock Island died. Line abandonments and redefinition of service area would continue in those regions as a consequence. Unrelated to the problems of Milwaukee and Rock Island but of great consequence

otherwise was the merger of St. Louis-San Francisco into the already huge Burlington Northern—also in 1980. Big news also came from the East. Late in 1978, Chessie System announced renegotiations with Seaboard Coast Lines Industries that would result two years later in creation of CSX, a holding company for Chessie (Chesapeake & Ohio, Baltimore & Ohio, Western Maryland, etc.) and Seaboard (Seaboard Coast Line, Louisville & Nashville, etc.). Not surprisingly, Norfolk and Western and Southern then announced study plans that on 1 June 1982 would result in formation of Norfolk Southern.[31]

All of this was bound to have an impact on the GTC roads in one way or another. There were direct and indirect reflections in the DT&I case. For instance, the Burlington Northern-Frisco merger mirrored the ICC's then-current affection for end-to-end combinations. In addition, the demise of Rock Island and bankruptcy and massive line abandonment by Milwaukee—following as they did the crisis of eastern lines leading to painful loss of rail service and the creation of Conrail—made the public, politicians, and the ICC unwilling participants in further railroad misery. Thus GTW's contention that the Shore Line and maybe even itself were headed for the poorhouse hit a responsive cord. The David and Goliath routine worked. So did Cole's legal strategy. On 30 July 1979, the ICC administrative law judge who heard the case ruled that both applications (GTW's and that of N&W/Chessie) met public interest requirements, but he expressed preference for GTW. A formal decision would follow.[32]

A flurry of activity unfolded—appeals, negotiations, pulling and hauling of all types. Most interesting, perhaps, was the campaign of Robert Sharp and others of DT&I management who, with investors and Cincinnati businessmen, attempted to form a group to acquire DT&I. Sharp's proposal had appeal since the arrangement would not be subject to ICC authority and thus the consortium could undertake a direct sales arrangement with Pennco. As it turned out, Pennco was negotiating with "several other parties." Meanwhile, Norfolk & Western, Canadian Pacific, and others petitioned the ICC for review. Events moved quickly to resolution. GTW's board on 19 March 1980 authorized Burdakin to bid (not more than $33 million) for the outstanding stock of DT&I. On 1 April, Pennco agreed to an aggregate price of

On 18 June 1980, the ICC gave its blessing for merger of GTW and DT&I. Operating integration followed quickly. Photograph courtesy of Grand Trunk Western Railroad.

$25.2 million, and on 18 June the Interstate Commerce Commission gave its blessing. The Detroit, Toledo & Ironton Railway had a new shareholder, Grand Trunk Western railroad, and a new president—John H. Burdakin.[33]

The ICC appended a most important sidebar. Grand Trunk Western was required to either purchase the remaining one-half interest in the Detroit & Toledo Shore Line from Norfolk & Western or to divest its own interest. Stung by its defeat in the DT&I case, N&W resolutely refused to sell its stake. This placed GTW in difficult straits, made more so by ICC's further requirement that full responsibility for the matter rested with GTW. Matters remained awkward but when N&W sought merger with Southern, GTW finally found the chink in N&W's defense. GTW complained that a combination of these two companies would harm its welfare and, to smooth things, N&W grudgingly agreed to grant protective traffic concessions via Cincinnati and to sell its interest in the Shore Line. The agreed price was $1.9 million; GTW took full control on 13 April 1981. The Detroit & Toledo Shore Line Railroad was dissolved on 30 September 1981.[34]

It fell to the Shore Line's general manager, William C. Blades, to button up the affairs of the road. Photograph courtesy of Grand Trunk Western Railroad.

NOTES

1. Albro Martin, *Enterprise Denied: Origins of the Decline of American Railroads, 1897-1917* (New York: Columbia University Press, 1971); John W. Barringer, *Super Railroads for a Dynamic American Economy* (New York: Simmons-Boardman, 1955).

2. *Trains* 50 (November 1990): 22-47.

3. Ibid.

4. Richard Saunders, *The Railroad Mergers and the Coming of Conrail* (Westport: Greenwood Press, 1978), 301, 305, 309, 315, 319, 324, 325.

5. Basil Cole, interview by author, 21 March 1989.

6. Robert A. Walker, interview by author, 7 March 1990; GTW, Minute Book No. 5, 193; GTW, "USRA/Conrail: Give Michigan's Smaller Railroads a Chance to Compete" (1975).

7. *Trains* 50 (November 1990): 22-47.

8. *GT Reporter* (April 1975): 1; USRA, *Final System Plan*, 2 vols. (Washington: Government Printing Office, 1975), 1: 26-27, 234, 296-99, 359, 365 and 2: 171-79, 188-99; GTW, Minute Book No. 6, 219, 227; GTC, Annual Report (1976): 24; GTW, Minute Book No. 7, 310.

9. On the DT&I, see 141 ICC, 115; *Railway Age* (26 July 1920): 143-45 and (28 February 1925): 501-6; "Henry Ford's Railroad Experiment," *Railroad Magazine* (July 1938): 9-28; William D. Middleton, "Henry Ford and his Electric Locomotives," *Trains* 36 (September 1976): 22-26; Scott D. Trostel, *The Detroit, Toledo & Ironton Railroad: Henry Ford's Railroad* (Fletcher, Ohio: Cam-Tech Publishing, 1988); Scott D. Trostel, *Henry Ford: When I Ran the Railroads: A Chronicle of Henry Ford's Operation of the Detroit, Toledo & Ironton, 1920-1929* (Fletcher, Ohio: Cam-Tech Publishing, 1989).

10. DT&I, Financial Planning Study by Salomon Brothers, (n.d. [1975]), 1-3, PF.

11. Detroit, Toledo & Ironton Railroad Company-Norfolk & Western Railway Company System Analysis (Operations Planning Department, Roanoke, 13 January 1976) and Appendices A-D, PF 451.

12. DT&I, Corporate Records 16 (22 April, 30 June, 17 September, 27 October 1976).

13. Ibid., 15 December 1976; Robert A. Sharp, interview by author, 3 May 1989.

14. Robert A. Bandeen to John H. Burdakin, 28 February 1977; John H. Burdakin to R. A. Bandeen, 2 March 1977, (PF 105); *Wall Street Journal*, 31 May, 13 June 1977.

15. GTW, Press Release, 24 October 1977 and 5 January 1978.

16. GTC, Annual Report (1977): 3; GTW, Minute Book No. 7, 277-78; GTW/GTC, Application, Finance Docket 28499 (16 February 1978).

17. Basil Cole, interview by author, 21 March 1989; Saunders, *Railroad Mergers,* 325; John H. Burdakin, interview by author, 5 March 1991.

18. Post Hearing Brief for Pennsylvania Company and Detroit, Toledo & Ironton Railroad (21 May 1979): 12, 45, 47.

19. N&W/Chessie, Brief of Joint Applicants to Administrative Law Judge Richard H. Beddow, Jr. (21 May 1979): 2, 20, 23, 81, 83.

20. Statement for Robert A. Bandeen on Behalf of Canadian National Railway Company (8 April 1978): 9-10.

21. Brief of Canadian National Railway Company to Administrative Law Judge Beddow (21 May 1979): 30-31; Robert A. Bandeen to John H. Burdakin, 28 February 1977; Bandeen statement, 31; N&W/Chessie brief, 64; PC/DT&I, Post Hearing Brief for Pennsylvania Company and Detroit, Toledo & Ironton Railroad Company (21 May 1979), 46.

22. N&W/Chessie brief, 70; Verified Statement of John H. Burdakin, 27 June 1978, 17; Bandeen statement, 28.

23. N&W/Chessie brief, 7, 9; Pennco and DT&I, post hearing brief, 2, 13.

24. GTW/GTC, Post Hearing Brief of Grand Trunk Railroad Company and Grand Trunk Corporation (21 May 1979), 181-90.

25. Ibid.

26. *GT Reporter* (May/June 1979), 6.

27. CN, *Synoptical History*, 292-93; CN, Overview—Grand Trunk Western (July 1969), 75; GTW, Executive Committee Minute Book No. 6, 2 September 1970.

28. Burdakin statement, 15-16; N&W/Chessie brief, 42.

29. GTW/GTC post hearing brief, 13.

30. Burdakin statement, 15; GTW/GTC post hearing brief, 4.

31. *Railway Age* (27 November 1978): 13-14; Ibid. (30 April 1979): 9; Ibid. (27 July 1981): 24-27; Ibid. (12 September 1982): 12-13.

32. Basil Cole, interview, 21 March 1989; Robert P. vom Eigen, interview, 21 March 1989.

33. DT&I, Corporate Records 27 (6 December 1979 and 28 February 1980) and 28 (10 March 1980); GTW, Minute Book No. 7, 327; DT&I, Corporate Records 25 (1 April 1980); 363 ICC, 122-31; DT&I, Corporate Records 30: 1-5.

34. GTW, Executive Committee Book No. 8, Executive Minute No. 639; GTW, Minute Book No. 8, 357-58; D&TSL, Minute Book No. 5, 786-805.

6      "Truly a Marriage Made in Heaven"

Since the beginning of this decade GTC planning has been geared toward effectively dealing with major external forces such as recession, deregulation, mergers, and competitive structural changes.

GTC, Annual Report (1982): 5.

Grand Trunk Corporation's successful campaign to acquire Detroit, Toledo & Ironton and Detroit & Toledo Shore Line during the late 1970s played out at a time when the railroad industry in the Midwest was undergoing wrenching change. For example, Chicago, Rock Island & Pacific (Rock Island)—the "mighty fine line" of musical verse—had declared bankruptcy in 1975 and tottered toward oblivion. The end came on 31 March 1980; it was the largest abandonment ever—7,500 miles. Almost simultaneously Chicago, Milwaukee, St. Paul & Pacific Railroad (CMStP&P or Milwaukee Road), bankrupt since 19 December 1977, abandoned its Pacific Extension west of Miles City, Montana, as well as other trunk routes and various branches—paring down, its trustee said, to carry on as "Milwaukee II," a mere shadow of its former self and utterly without assurance of survival as a regional carrier or in any other form. In addition, neither Chicago & North Western Transportation Company (C&NW or North Western) nor Illinois Central Gulf could claim robust balance sheets at the time. Many observers gloomily concluded that the horrific "eastern bankrupts" malady was now abroad in the midlands. That raised the specter of government involvement with vast expense, a la Conrail, a specter not at all attractive to politicians or rail managers. Yet significant restructuring in the region was at hand, with or without government planning or financial involvement.[1]

Managers at Grand Trunk Western and Canadian National watched it all with captivated interest. They recognized the need to adjust to changed circumstance and they recognized that the flux created strategic threats but also strategic opportunities. On the other hand, the DT&I and Shore Line cases had been long and taxing and now John Burdakin and his colleagues were hard at the business of consolidation and integration. Burdakin and team pored over maps, exploring opportunities, but they acknowledged the immediate imperative—digesting the new acquisitions. Robert Bandeen cautioned Burdakin: The main objective for Grand Trunk Corporation was to protect Canadian National's interests. That *might* be accomplished by extending GTW's line haul through acquisition but, said Bandeen, ultimate benefits had to be clearly demonstrable. Moreover, Bandeen pointedly

95

Milwaukee would give GTC, among other advantages, a direct link between GTW and DW&P. Eastbound manifest near Dakota, Minnesota on CMStP&P's Chicago-Minneapolis thoroughfare. Photograph by Don L. Hofsommer.

reminded, CN *might* best be served by selling off parts or even all of GTW. Yes, replied Burdakin, but making GTW more attractive to potential suitors *might* require extension into additional gateways offering new and attractive marketing opportunities. Such opportunities were more likely for smaller roads and regional carriers, noted Burdakin, than for huge railroads born of the mega-merger movement. The "small vs. big" or "David and Goliath" approach had succeeded nicely for Grand Trunk Western in recent forays. There was no reason to expect less in future endeavors. Bandeen agreed.

Burdakin's eye increasingly fell on Kansas City as a potential outpost. Connections could be made there to the Gulf Coast through independent regionals Kansas City Southern (KCS) and Missouri-Kansas-Texas; to Texas points via Burlington Northern; to Texas, the Southwest, and Southern California by way of Santa Fe and after early 1980 by Southern Pacific; and to the central West via Missouri Pacific, Union Pacific,

and shortly Denver & Rio Grande Western. In this regard, Rock Island offered GTW twin alternatives from Chicago (Blue Island): via Des Moines to 1) Kansas City and 2) Omaha. GTW's strategic team, still led by Robert Walker, was dismayed, however, by the wretched physical condition of Rock Island property. "It became evident in looking at the Rock Island," said Burdakin, " . . . that the capital funds that were required to bring . . . [it] . . . back were far greater than our capability to finance."[2]

At the same time, however, CMStP&P continued to flounder in a sea of red ink. Initial plans for a "core" operation had not included Milwaukee's Chicago-to-Kansas City route, although eventually it was retained. Given Milwaukee's severe cash shortage and the nervousness of politicians and government bureaucrats over the growing Midwestern rail crisis, Burdakin reasoned that GTW might gain access to Kansas City by purchasing its line. But there was more in Milwaukee than just its Kansas City line which attracted GTW managers who increasingly studied acquisition of much of that company's then condensed route structure: Milwaukee would give GTW its coveted longer haul with a line to Kansas City; it would provide additional opportunities in and around Chicago; it would allow GTW to tap traffic-rich Milwaukee; it would extend line haul advantages to and from the Northwest via St. Paul/Minneapolis; and, more important, it would give GTW trackage rights between St. Paul and Duluth, a direct connection with the Duluth, Winnipeg & Pacific, and in that way satisfy historic urgings to link GTW solidly with CN's western traffic base.

There were liabilities along with additional advantages. Milwaukee's track, motive power, rolling stock, and reputation were suspect. On the other hand, its trustee was working to eliminate or restructure certain debts, and Milwaukee's heavy Chicago commuter responsibility would soon pass to the Regional Transit Authority. Moreover, federal loans of up to $250 million would be forgiven if substantially all of Milwaukee Road was merged with another carrier. Burdakin, Walker, and GTW staffers quietly pondered the matter.[3]

Milwaukee's struggle continued. The trustee, former Illinois Governor Richard B. Ogilvie, announced in May 1980 that wholesale abandonment except for a core of less than 4,000 miles had "staunched the overwhelming cash losses the Milwaukee Road had been experiencing and has for the first time allowed the Trustee to operate a railroad with an equipment fleet which is adequate to serve customer needs." Ogilvie considered that CMStP&P had three options: 1) reorganization into Milwaukee II, a pared down plant of perhaps 3,200 miles which might anticipate profitability by 1984, 2) sale of Milwaukee II, the core road, as a "going concern;" and 3) complete liquidation. The court and the Interstate Commerce Commission (ICC) had rejected the latter option with the effect that Ogilvie had but two choices: reorganization or sale. There was no time to dawdle. "The future of Milwaukee must depend on its performance during the remainder of 1980," Ogilvie warned.[4]

There followed a gallant struggle for life. Huge segments of embargoed line were sold—764 miles in South Dakota alone—to bring in cash. Scrap from abandoned lines and excess equipment pro-

duced further infusions. Track supplies rendered surplus were quickly installed to bolster surviving lines, and rolling stock was patched and painted. Employees, at least most of them, agreed to "wage deferrals." Observers detected an aggressive new spirit. Perhaps Milwaukee would not follow Rock Island to the boneyard. Ogilvie and Worthington L. Smith, Milwaukee's president, focused on the road's primary routes: Duluth-Twin Cities-Milwaukee-Chicago; Chicago-Louisville; and, Chicago-Kansas City. For example, transit time on the Kansas City line was improved by nearly 50 percent and in December, Milwaukee joined with Southern Pacific to establish time-sensitive perishable service—*The Golden State Express*—with fourth-day delivery in Chicago from California. Shortly thereafter Milwaukee signed an agreement with Kansas City Southern for the movement of chemicals from the Gulf Coast to points in Ohio and Michigan.[5]

Ogilvie's first objective was to establish Milwaukee as a freestanding core railroad on a cash basis. On the other hand, few railroad experts thought that Milwaukee, even as a slimmed-down system, could make it alone. But the core, Worthington Smith believed, would one day be part of another system. What system? "Anybody that connects with us," said Smith—stressing, however, that his prediction would come true only "if we prove ourselves in the market place . . . ."[6]

On 15 September 1981, Ogilvie filed a revised plan of reorganization—one that predicted a financially viable, 2,900-mile "north-south regional railroad." Pared from current operations would be about another 1,000 miles including 519 miles between Ortonville, Minnesota, and Miles City, Montana, plus branches and extensions elsewhere. Additional cash would come from sale of timber properties, scrap, and excess equipment. Further savings would derive from labor concessions including smaller train crews and pay cuts. The plan, said Ogilvie, anticipated profitability in 1983 and a 12.2 percent return on investment in 1986. The plan would also make the Milwaukee more attractive to other railroads, although Ogilvie said there were no acquisition discussions at that moment.[7]

No formal discussions, at least. On 23 June 1980, John S. Guest of Lehman Brothers Kuhn Loeb, Incorporated, told John Burdakin that

GTC was still digesting DT&I, but Burdakin and crew determined to take a close look at Milwaukee. Manifest train with integrated GTW/DT&I power at Flat Rock Yard. Photograph courtesy of Grand Trunk Western Railroad.

Milwaukee "would be available for acquisition at some point in the future" and wondered if there was interest at Grand Trunk Corporation. "We are on the verge of digesting a rather full plate with the DT&I," Burdakin had told Guest in reply, but, he added, "the subject has considerable interest to us." Considerable interest, indeed. On the same day Burdakin told Walter Cramer and Paul E. Tatro (who had succeeded Donald Wooden in the area of finance) that "sometime in the near future we should discuss the merits of becoming involved."[8]

Sixteen months later, on 27 October 1981, Grand Trunk Corporation and Ogilvie announced that "discussions concerning the possible integration of the Milwaukee Road into the GTC system of railroads" had begun. Rumors of GTC's interest had circulated since summer when GTW personnel toured Milwaukee properties and when Canadian National began routing increased volumes of lumber to Milwaukee at Duluth via DW&P.[9]

The strategic logic was obvious. The double-track Milwaukee main line between Chicago and St. Paul coupled with Milwaukee's trackage

rights over Burlington Northern to Duluth would provide a direct, high-speed, high-capacity means to link two disconnected properties—Grand Trunk Western and Duluth, Winnipeg & Pacific. The combination "would create a 5,000-mile system that practically would encircle the American side of the Great Lakes." More important, line hauls would be extended with commensurate increase in revenues. Milwaukee's Duluth-St. Paul-Chicago-Louisville leg would be of particular advantage to CN and DW&P for movements from western Canada, and the Chicago-Kansas City line would more than double GTW's haul on automobiles and parts. And the combined properties would boast an impressive traffic mix protecting revenues otherwise sensitive to the business cycle.[10]

GTC's move brought mixed comment. Speculators, who hoped Milwaukee would be liquidated in the fashion of Rock Island, were dismayed at the prospect of a reorganized Milwaukee and sale of it to GTC. Others worried that Canadian National would use an expanded GTC to benefit Canadian ports over American ports, especially those on the Great Lakes.

Rumors predictably erupted when GTW and Milwaukee officers made an inspection trip over certain CMStP&P lines. The train stopped briefly at Portage, Wisconsin, on 10 November 1981. Photograph by John Gruber.

Industry leaders, most of whom thought that even Milwaukee's core would be dismembered, were cautious in their early appraisal. Most, it seemed, were surprised by GTC's aggressive new personality. Managers of Milwaukee's neighbors—Burlington Northern, Soo Line, and Chicago & North Western—had profoundly hoped for Milwaukee's liquidation and thus pondered this unexpected turn of events and wondered what impact an expanded GTC would have on their fortunes.[11]

John Burdakin's face lit up at the prospect of acquiring Milwaukee, but in predictable form he demanded only a dry-eyed assessment of Milwaukee's capacity. Robert A. Walker, Paul Tatro, and Basil Cole, the nucleus of the GTC team, found that a difficult assignment. Milwaukee, after all, had just reduced itself from a transcontinental road to a regional carrier with the result that there was no history of traffic flows or earnings to inform their judgement. Milwaukee's recent "inordinately high rehabilitation and maintenance expenditures" and its curious bankruptcy proceedings also muddied the picture. Moreover, the nasty recession of 1981-82 reduced available traffic and increased competition for what remained. In the end, the team con-

cluded that "on a stand-alone basis, Milwaukee II can neither secure enough traffic, nor safely lower expense sufficiently, to be able to operate consistently with a positive cash flow." Neither did the team believe Milwaukee could attain a break-even position. Nevertheless, "the geographic relationship of Milwaukee II to DW&P and GTW coupled with the system marketing strength of CN Rail" did, they concluded, "create an opportunity for an integration of services." There were risks and caveats: potential retaliation by other railroads, the need for further reductions in Milwaukee's labor force with the potential for rebellion by the unions, and the categoric need to get out from under the backbreaking commuter responsibility in Chicago. There was much about Milwaukee that was troubling; there was much that was tantalizing.[12]

By mid-February 1982, Walker's staffers prepared internal documents that proposed reallocation of traffic from Canadian National, DW&P, and GTW adequate to "bring Milwaukee II sufficient revenue to lift it from bankruptcy, make it profitable, and enable it to return cash to its owner." These were bold words from staffers who frankly remained unconvinced but who understood Burdakin's increasingly positive position on the question. The arrangement they proposed would amount to perhaps 80,000 cars per year and would, they hoped, move Milwaukee from the category of pretax loss to net income. Still they were nervous and hedged their recommendations. Perhaps some "innovative quasi-affiliation would be best—an arrangement from which GTC could back out if Milwaukee faltered." Or perhaps "an option to purchase" would be appropriate. Burdakin headed for Montreal for a meeting with Bandeen. Both men agreed: the Milwaukee was worth pursuing, for it had potential to benefit parent and children as well.[13]

On 24 May 1982, John Burdakin and Richard Ogilvie jointly announced that they had signed a

Bandeen saw the potential in Milwaukee not only for the GTC roads but for the parent as well. Photograph courtesy of Canadian National.

letter of intent providing for transfer of stock ownership in Milwaukee to Grand Trunk Corporation—but only after Milwaukee was reorganized. GTC agreed to shoulder $250 million of Milwaukee debt and obligations but the estate, principally Chicago Milwaukee Corporation, would retain Milwaukee Land Company, a valuable subsidiary of the railroad. At the same time, GTC and Milwaukee agreed to immediate "operating initiatives" designed to increase traffic volumes and revenues to the Milwaukee.[14]

Burdakin invoked his best "David and Goliath" routine. Consolidation of Grand Trunk and Milwaukee was essential to survival "in an environment dominated by larger railroads that are growing even larger by the merger process." Government policy, Burdakin insisted, should encourage smaller railroads by giving them a chance to compete with industry giants. Failure to do so might result in further "emergency transfusions from the taxpayers to support tottering finances of bankrupt railroads." The proposal to consolidate GTC and Milwaukee would preserve most Milwaukee jobs and would be "an opportunity for two relatively small end-to-end rail systems to gain strength through cooperative efforts while improving their service to the pub-

lic." Indeed, GTC/Milwaukee would create strong competition in the Midwest with the Kansas City gateway as the focal point. Did GTC have aspirations beyond Kansas City—to the Gulf Coast, for example? "Opportunities exist," said Burdakin, but he denied any interest in Missouri-Kansas-Texas (long shopped to prospective buyers) or Kansas City Southern (occasionally rumored as a merger candidate).[15]

A "marketing blitz" is what *Railway Age* called a six-week GTC/Milwaukee campaign ramrodded by Walter Cramer with full cooperation of Peter C. White, head of Milwaukee's marketing group, to acquaint shippers with "unprecedented joint

On 24 May 1982, John Burdakin, right, and Richard Ogilvie, center, signed a letter of intent providing for transfer of stock ownership in Milwaukee to GTC. CMStP&P President Worthington Smith, a descendent of Smith's association with the early CV, stands at left. Photograph courtesy of Chicago, Milwaukee, St. Paul & Pacific Railroad.

train operations" and other advantages offered as a part of what the roads jointly labeled their voluntary coordination agreement (VCA). These advantages often extended beyond the service territory of GTC/Milwaukee. For instance, Southern Pacific—which had recently acquired

THE Saga of THE MILWAUKEE ROAD

THE·CANADIENS·ARE·COMING, THE·CANADIENS·ARE·COMING...

This homespun cartoon suggests that employees of the Milwaukee Road were well pleased with news that GTC was interested in their company. Source unknown.

and upgraded Rock Island's portion of the Golden State Route west of Kansas City—joined with Grand Trunk Western, Canadian National, and Milwaukee to improve transit time on lading moving to and from Montreal and Toronto and Southern California via Port Huron, Chicago, and Kansas City. GTC and Milwaukee also engaged in an innovative and attractive advertising campaign pointing to "one great service from two great rail systems."[16]

Attention was diverted elsewhere to matters that, at first blush, seemed unrelated to GTC's efforts to acquire Milwaukee. In fact, there was a direct relationship to the realignment resulting from Milwaukee's departure from many markets coupled with the total collapse of the Rock Island, on the one hand, and GTC's campaign to acquire Milwaukee's core, on the other. Particularly at issue was Rock Island's route between St. Paul and Kansas City—the "Spine Line" as many dubbed it—and Rock Island's impressive grain-gathering branches in Iowa. As early as 1979, Chicago & North Western had promoted a bold plan to take over Rock Island and Milwaukee lines in Iowa and southern Minnesota. Iowa authorities bridled at the notion, citing potential antitrust problems, and openly backed counterproposals by Kansas City Southern whose new presence would encourage competition and prevent monopoly by C&NW. Milwaukee itself coveted the Spine Line as did Burlington Northern, which even offhandedly proposed joint ownership of it with KCS to form a new operator, Kansas City Northern. Bidders haggled with the Rock Island's stern trustee to no avail and, when the Rock Island went down for the count on 31 March 1980, the trustee gave C&NW only a short-term lease before the ICC designated North Western as operator of the Spine Line under directed service order.[17]

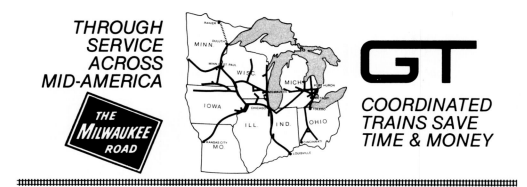

A marketing blitz advertised the innovative voluntary coordination agreement which proved to be wildly successful. Courtesy of Grand Trunk Western Railroad.

Matters became increasingly muddled when Soo Line entered the fray. Fresh from its recent acquisition of tiny Minneapolis, Northfield & Southern (MN&S), Soo Line—nearly 56 percent owned by CN's historic rival, Canadian Pacific—entered a bid on 14 September. Acquisition of MN&S, incidentally, provided Soo a direct short-mile connection from the west side of Minneapolis to the Spine Line south of St. Paul at Northfield. Moreover, the Spine Line had clear strategic importance for Soo, traditionally a grain handling road. But was that the whole cloth? Several observers considered Soo's activity simple retaliation, orchestrated by Canadian Pacific, in reaction to GTC's plan (read, in this case, Canadian National's plan) to acquire Milwaukee. Indeed, Senator Charles H. Percy along with Representative Dan Rostenkowski and others from the Illinois congressional delegation charged that "this Soo Line bid is seen by many as a defensive move by one Canadian railroad competing against another, and not primarily as an effort to improve the U.S. rail system."[18]

Soo managers found such speculation bemusing since Canadian Pacific took little notice of the entire matter. In fact, said Byron D. Olsen, vice president-law at Soo, "our problem . . . was getting CP interested in what we wanted to do." Olsen and others at Soo were frightened, however, by C&NW's aggressive posture and urged a policy to build Soo "into a size that could better balance the main competition in its service region [C&NW]." But the process was halting. CP had little strategic interest in Soo, and Soo itself had no culture of acquisition to speak of, although

some senior managers held lingering regrets that Soo had not gathered in Chicago Great Western when it was available during the late 1960s. And, noted Dennis M. Cavanaugh, the road's president, Soo suffered like much of the industry as deregulation dissolved traditions where "all rules were defined" and labored under its own traditional burden of "protecting the dividend." Consequently Soo groped to define itself anew with little direction from its principal shareholder.[19]

The spotlight shifted to Chicago & North Western, whose president vociferously complained of what he called "the Canadian invasion," an obvious reference to Grand Trunk Corporation in pursuing Milwaukee and Soo's attempt to acquire the Spine Line and attendant branches. It was a shrewd and calculated public relations ploy, especially in the long term, but C&NW's immediate problem was to find money adequate to challenge Soo. A bidding war ensued and the Interstate Commerce Commission, at sixes and sevens, approved both bids; it would fall to Rock Island's trustee to make the decision.[20]

GTC and CN kept deliberately low profiles in the Spine Line case. Internally, however, the position was clear: C&NW was favored over Soo, since a decision favoring Soo would strengthen CP/Soo over CN/GTC/Milwaukee. CN's view was especially pointed because, of the many advantages Milwaukee offered, the greatest—insofar as CN was concerned—was the Duluth-St. Paul-Chicago route to which CN planned to route heavy traffic from western Canada if GTC acquired Milwaukee. In that same Duluth-Chicago rail corridor were, of course, C&NW and Soo Line but, more important in CN's strategic calculations, were historic CP/Soo linkages from western Canada to Chicago (CP to Portal, North Dakota and/or Noyes, Minnesota, Soo beyond).[21]

The Rock Island trustee finally came down on C&NW's side. Trackage in the amount of 720 miles passed to C&NW on 29 June 1983, and North Western quickly made good on its promise of major reha-bilitation. There was relief at GTC and especially at CN. Without good reason.[22]

The Spine Line case, as it developed, merely anticipated a much greater struggle with far greater stakes, i.e., resolution of Grand Trunk Corporation's proposal to acquire Milwaukee. Menacing rumblings were heard from two camps. Soo's chair-man, Thomas M. Beckley, told his shareholders following the Spine Line deci-sion that Soo was "reviewing alternative arrangements which might be made to secure better access to the Kansas City gate-way." Another Soo offi-cer was more direct:

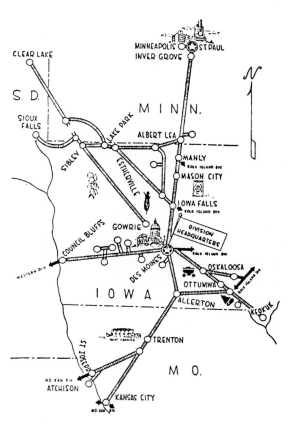

A portion of the Rock Island system, including the Twin City to Kansas City spine line.

"We may ask for operating rights . . . [into Kansas City] . . . over the bankrupt Milwaukee Road." More ominous mutterings came from C&NW's James R. Wolfe who energetically pro-pounded on the "Canadian invasion" theme. "I'm not too anxious to compete in a capital formation contest with the Canadian government," said Wolfe in direct reference to the "government-owned Canadian National Railway." Wolfe's provocative assessment was shared by others. "We're not worried about competing with Grand Trunk Western," said an officer of another road, "but we are concerned about competing with the Canadian government." Particularly galling to some was a provision of law forgiving certain debts owed the federal government in the event of Milwaukee's successful reorganization and subsequent acquisition by another carrier—at least if that carrier was owned by Canadian National. That possibility seemed to some as an indirect subsidy to the government of Canada by American taxpayers.[23]

Earlier, in 1981, when Milwaukee was paring to its core, John Burdakin had canvassed numerous railroads with the idea that they severally acquire the Milwaukee core, put traffic on it, and operate the road as a joint facility. Burdakin was dis-gusted to learn that there was no support for the idea. Most saw Milwaukee as redun-dant, except perhaps for its Chicago-Milwaukee-St. Paul thoroughfare. The implication was clear: few would weep at the death of Milwaukee and abandonment of most of its route miles. That likely explained the lack of response and subsequent lack of complaint when GTC announced its inten-tion of buying Milwaukee. There was, in fact, surprise that any carrier would be interested in it. "Ours was the only life preserver floating on the ocean," said Burdakin, and Ogilvie now exclaimed gleefully that a combined GTC/Milwaukee would be "a marriage made in heaven." Chicago Milwaukee Corporation protested, however, saying that "we believe it is a giveaway," and tiny Green Bay & Western early on suggested that it be given "various operating and market trade-offs to improve its position" in the event of a combined GTC and Milwaukee. On the other hand, there was widespread support among shippers and politicians for the project.[24]

Yet, as it developed, the voluntary coordination agreement curiously proved all too successful. By putting traffic on Milwaukee two powerful points were made: 1) traffic diverted to Milwaukee from

While the Spine Line case wound its way to resolution, GTW and CN labored to pour traffic into the VCA with Milwaukee Road. The success of that venture is suggested by this view showing a heavily-laden train on the DW&P heading for Duluth. Photograph courtesy of Duluth, Winnipeg & Pacific Railway.

other carriers (from C&NW and Soo at Duluth, for example) had hurt those carriers and, more important, 2) Milwaukee Road was increasingly vibrant. Only then, after GTC's boldly innovative voluntary coordination agreement—rerouting business before the fact of combination—had most clearly demonstrated the great potential in a consolidated GTC/Milwaukee, was there criticism or protest. "Who would buy that streak of rust?" was the often-heard rhetorical question of 1981 and 1982, but former naysayers then gathered to take a covetous look at the formerly cadaverous Milwaukee.

On 31 March 1983, Ogilvie presented an amended plan of reorganization to the federal court overseeing the case. The reorganized Milwaukee would "emerge from bankruptcy as an efficient organization, relieved of unprofitable lines, deficient equipment and facilities," and would become a subsidiary of Grand Trunk Corporation. Milwaukee's performance in 1982, said Ogilvie, "had proved its financial viability and the current plan," he continued, "satisfied various public interest criteria." Through consolidation with GTC and affiliation with CN, Ogilvie

concluded, "we will preserve service on the Milwaukee and assure financial stability to benefit shippers and employees."[25]

The Interstate Commerce Commission, like the federal district court, had to rule on Milwaukee's reorganization plan and potential acquisition by others. It set 27 July 1983 as the deadline for bids. With only a few hours to spare, Chicago & North Western breathlessly delivered on its threat to file a contrary bid for Milwaukee. The ICC announced that it would consider C&NW's last-minute proposal, but Ogilvie denounced it. C&NW's offer, he contended, was inferior to his plan under which Milwaukee would be acquired by GTC. Ogilvie also opposed a rival plan offered by Chicago Milwaukee Corporation which claimed CMStP&P's improved financial condition and operating results should enable recovery as an independent road. Turning again to C&NW's proposal, however, Ogilvie hedged; his opposition was not unalterable. Ogilvie's waffling sent a profound shudder through the Detroit offices. Would all the work on this project be in vain? Had GTC enabled Milwaukee to prosper only to lose it?[26]

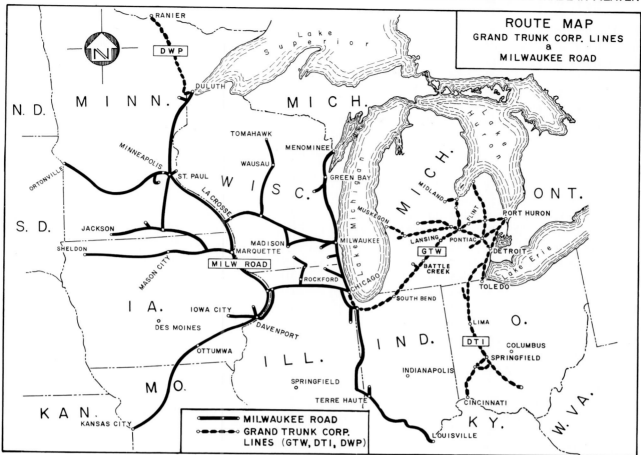

The strategic advantages for GTC in a merger with Milwaukee were all too apparent. Courtesy of Grand Trunk Western Railroad.

There was but a single common thread in the GTC and C&NW proposals: each wanted to acquire the Milwaukee. GTC's plan, if approved, would link properties end-to-end: DW&P with Milwaukee at Duluth and GTW with Milwaukee at Chicago (by way of Indiana Harbor Belt, 49 percent owned by CMStP&P). Projected benefits would come from additional traffic tendered by each new partner to the other, not from consolidation; neither the GTC roads nor Milwaukee would experience substantial changes in modus operandi; no abandonments or downgrading of service was planned; no employees would lose their jobs as a result of the operating plan. And GTC roads combined with Milwaukee would encourage competition. C&NW's proposal, however, boldly proclaimed that too much competition remained in the service area of C&NW and Milwaukee and that combination of these two would have the very useful impact of reducing redundant service and trackage. Yes, admitted C&NW, that would have a negative impact on some communities and, yes, several hundred jobs would be lost. Approval of C&NW's plan, it noted, would improve the position of a medium-sized American carrier while approval of the GTC proposal would aid a foreign railroad and its owners (Canadian National and Canadian taxpayers). Both plans included assumption of Milwaukee's debt, but C&NW's differed in that it contained operating loss and investment tax credit carry-forward tax benefits for the Milwaukee estate (principally Chicago Milwaukee Corporation).[27]

An intense public relations campaign followed. Factions quickly took sides. Labor understandably favored GTC's end-to-end plan for it would yield employment stability whereas C&NW openly admitted plans for line abandonments and job reduction. That stance, according to the

Des Moines Register, was C&NW's Achilles' heel. "Remember the Chicago Great Western and the Minneapolis & St. Louis?," the *Register* asked. Both roads had been acquired by North Western during the 1960s only to have their traffic diverted and most of their lines torn up. The *Register* envisioned the same fate for Milwaukee in C&NW's plans. So did the governors of Minnesota, Wisconsin, and Iowa—the states that made up Milwaukee's principal service area—who sided with GTC. "By its end-to-end merger, the proposal maintains competitive service in the major markets of the states and maintains essential service in the smaller communities," these governors concluded.[28]

Some parties saw it otherwise. The Green Bay Economic Development Authority gave conditional support to North Western and the Duluth Seaway Port Authority sided with C&NW, complaining that GTC, if successful, would siphon business from the Great Lakes. And C&NW spokesmen picked at GTC's own Achilles' heel—Grand Trunk Western's historically poor financial performance and the relationship of GTC properties to the Canadian National and thus to the Canadian government. The issue was ticklish. GTC's Paul E. Tatro said the "GTC's future financial performance might be at levels not viewed as acceptable by management . . . if GTC were to remain as it is without acquiring Milwaukee or without otherwise joining into partnership with any other carrier in order to extend its hauls and obtain further gateways." True enough. But that implied a frightening financial anemia. What about the vaunted power of GTC's parent, Canadian National? CN's Ronald E. Lawless, in defining the relationship of the parent to GTC had been emphatic: The U.S. subsidiaries "would have to make it on their own . . . [and] . . . further develop traffic and pay dividends." They could not, he emphasized, "depend on CN to finance deficit operations." That being the case, asserted C&NW, GTC was nothing but a "floundering" enterprise that would "perpetuate instability in the Midwestern rail system" if it gained Milwaukee. "The Midwest does not need a mini-Penn Central," C&NW concluded in a shrewd reference to the Penn Central debacle and the resulting expensive governmental involvement to stabilize the industry in the Northeast.[29]

The matter was about to become even more complicated. In the fall of 1983, Soo Line's chairman, Thomas M. Beckley, told his shareholders that Soo was "opposed to both proposals [GTC and C&NW] and continues to study possible alternatives with regard to restructuring the Milwaukee Road." Before year's end the *Chicago Tribune* reported that Soo would make a bid for Milwaukee. It was correct. Soo announced on 19 January 1984 that it would file a motion with the bankruptcy court to buy Milwaukee with a cash payment of $40 million and assumption of debt. The powerful smell of cash had an immediate impact on Judge Thomas R. McMillen, who was overseeing the proceedings and reopened the bidding. There was predictable distress at C&NW and dismay at GTC.[30]

Judge McMillen did indeed accept Soo's application and a bidding war erupted—reminiscent of that for Rock Island's Spine Line. GTC amended its position to permit the estate to retain tax benefits. Soo increased its cash offer to $148 million, and C&NW dropped its plan to abandon Milwaukee trackage. GTC's was clearly an inferior bid on a comparative basis, a disappointment to Ogilvie, who admitted that the voluntary coordination agreement with GTC roads had much to do with Milwaukee's improved fortunes and who seemed a bit embarrassed at this turn of events. GTC portrayed the contest as a public-interest issue—with GTC wearing a "white hat," but with Soo Line, C&NW, and Chicago Milwaukee Corporation all wearing "black hats" as they played a game of high-stakes poker with the public welfare at stake. It was clever, but not effective. Neither were legal or public relations attempts to show both C&NW and Soo as "Johnny-come-latelys." Cash bidding continued, but only with Soo and C&NW as contestants. GTC was reduced to complaining "we had a deal" and to preaching the wisdom of forming joint operating agreements by which all applicants could be served. The ICC promised a decision by late summer.[31]

The regulatory agency had a very hot potato on its hands, and so a public conference was scheduled for 26 July. The ICC was obliged to address several major areas: 1) The long-term operating viability of the resulting entity and the effect on adequacy of transportation to the public; 2) financial viability and fairness of terms; 3) effect on competition; 4) effect on employees; and 5) effect on energy and environment. First, however, it fell to the commission to deal with GTC's

The VCA with Milwaukee proved marvelously successful but would perish when Milwaukee passed to Soo. Here a VCA train moves to Milwaukee's trackage rights over Burlington Northern in Duluth. Photograph courtesy of Duluth, Winnipeg & Pacific Railway.

request for dismissal of C&NW and Soo applications. The motion was summarily denied without comment; it was an ominous sign. Yet commissioners and staffers alike were captivated by the voluntary coordination agreement creatively devised by GTC and implemented in 1982. Chairman Reese Taylor recalled the earlier testimony of Robert P. vom Eigen, a GTC attorney who worked closely on the case.

> We went out and looked at our options, took a chance on the Milwaukee, negotiated with the trustee for seven months, and came up with a transaction. For two years we have been working to implement the voluntary coordination. This is an investment. We invested our marketing skills, we invested our corporate efforts in promoting the Milwaukee Road.

The ICC's staff admitted the result: "It has brought the Milwaukee to the position that it is in today. As our analysis points out, it has made the Milwaukee profitable and a salable item."

Specifically, "it [the VCA] is probably the most important reason for the Commission having a number of suitors for the Milwaukee before it today . . . ." Taylor put it cryptically: " . . . the voluntary coordination agreement prettied up the girl when she went to the dance." But, wondered John Burdakin, would GTC's admittedly successful efforts to rescue Milwaukee bear any fruit?[32]

The commissioners turned to merits of the various proposals. GTC's bid received high marks for public benefit since it was an end-to-end proposition, C&NW's received low marks because it included or implied line abandonment, and Soo's was viewed as a mixture of rationalization and lengthened line haul. No plan would have a negative impact on energy and environment, but in terms of employment GTC ranked high, C&NW low, and Soo between. All were judged as financially acceptable although commissioners concluded that C&NW's offer was best for shareholders and claimants. In the end, however, they could only agree to dismiss Chicago Milwaukee Corporation and Grand Trunk Corporation as contenders. They could not agree between the remaining candidates, C&NW and Soo, but approved Soo's proposal and took no action on C&NW's request. A divided commission sent its report to the applicants and to the bankruptcy court on 10 September.[33]

Disappointed GTC managers had already decided to drop out of the contest which continued along its bizarre path. Bidding continued to escalate, as did a nasty verbal war between C&NW and Soo. Richard Ogilvie, who as trustee

had long supported GTC's bid, now favored a $781 million offer of cash and debt assumption by C&NW over Soo's $571 million offer. Citing public-interest factors, however, Federal Judge McMillen surprised all hands—especially Soo which had consigned its records to storage—by accepting the lower bid. C&NW promptly withdrew its bid, provoking general comment from observers that senior management at the North Western finally realized how inflated its offer was. C&NW counsel took exception, defending North Western's high offer and feeling the road would prevail on appeal. But appeal would be lengthy and expensive. C&NW backed off. In any event, the Chicago, Milwaukee, St. Paul & Pacific Railroad became a subsidiary of Soo Line Corporation at 11:58 P.M. on 19 February 1985 when final papers were signed.[34]

Why had John Burdakin's dream foundered? Why had the "marriage made in heaven" dissolved at the altar? Basil Cole, GTC's seasoned attorney, maintained that "GTC had the best public interest argument," but a close associate, Robert P. vom Eigen, declared that "we were in town with the wrong argument"—meaning that GTC had trumpeted the virtues of public interest, an approach that had served it well in the earlier DT&I case, while the prevailing mood in Washington had shifted. The Reagan administration placed full value on deregulation and marketplace solutions of the type put forward by C&NW and Soo, putting much less emphasis on public-interest arguments. Cole further observed

that GTC's position had been to "buy the debt and pay nothing for the property." That was fine as long as Milwaukee was financially anemic and perceived generally as without competitive ability; it was not fine when Milwaukee displayed vigor and threatened to live on as a competitive thorn abroad the Midwest landscape. That prospect, of course, aroused other contenders—those who had hoped to pick at the Milwaukee's carcass. Then there was the matter of timing. C&NW and Soo both were wrangling over the Spine Line and might have remained sufficiently off balance if the GTC/Milwaukee case had gone forward even a few weeks earlier. GTC legal maneuverings also had delayed proceedings so that C&NW and then Soo time to gather their wits. C&NW attorneys sensed that GTC would lose if the contest became a bidding war for they perceived that GTW was hard-pressed for requisite cash. They also perceived that Canadian National, standing always in the wings, was either unable or unwilling to take a monetary position in Milwaukee. Soo attorneys agreed: "We felt . . . that if GTC had the courage of its convictions early on and moved faster, it could have easily concluded acquisition of Milwaukee before North Western got off the mark . . . I appreciate that the foot dragging may not have been GTC's; CN obviously had much to say," concluded Byron D. Olsen. Yes, said Basil Cole, "We knew if the auction began, GTC would lose." That is exactly what happened.[35]

There were other problems. GTC's proposal clearly favored competition, but it was solely earnings-based in concept—an end-to-end combination with virtually no chance to derive savings from consolidation. By contrast, C&NW and Soo brought cash to the table, and they could afford to since each saw greater potential synergetic benefits through cost savings and, in either case, could see further and continuing advantages through the disappearance of a primary competitor. GTC, on the other hand, saw no such benefits and, moreover, did not have deep pockets.

Fate had been unkind to GTC in the Milwaukee case. Indeed, GTC missed the brass ring. Photograph courtesy of Grand Trunk Western Railroad.

And GTC's recent foray into the merger field had not yielded predicted returns; DT&I, proved a depressing cash drain during the soft economy of the early 1980s.

Circumstances north of the border surely influenced GTC's course of action. As always, Canadian traditions and political realities were key variables. In this case, at least some Canadians thought it untoward for Canadian National to consider acquisition of substantial rail operations in the United States (albeit through an American subsidiary) when at the same time CN was trying to unburden itself of certain lines and functions in Canada.

Finally, when Bandeen left Canadian National in 1982, GTC lost an ardent friend as well as a powerful advocate for strategic growth. Thereafter support was lukewarm at best in Montreal where many at CN and on CN's board

viewed the Milwaukee deal as a cash transaction and not as an assumption of debt for rolling stock, mortgages, etc. J. Maurice LeClair, Bandeen's successor, bluntly inquired of John Burdakin: "Why do you want to buy a bankrupt railroad?" The very question was significant. Indeed, Detroit had been obliged to prosecute the Milwaukee opportunity against long internal odds.

The David and Goliath strategy, used so successfully earlier, was ineffective in the Milwaukee instance. In the end, John Burdakin, Robert Walker, Paul Tatro, Basil Cole, Robert vom Eigen, Walter Cramer, and all who had worked so diligently on the case were left to shake their heads and mutter of things that might have been. "Yes," said an emphatic Burdakin, "Ogilvie was right: It was 'truly a marriage made in heaven.'" Or so it might have been.

NOTES

1. There is no reliable, comprehensive history of the Milwaukee Road. See, however, August Derleth, *The Milwaukee Road: Its First Hundred Years* (New York: Creative Age Press, 1948); *Trains* 51 (November 1990): 39-41.
2. Jim Scribbins, "Interview with John H. Burdakin," *The Milwaukee Railroader* 18 (September 1988): 4-7.
3. *Railway Age* 180 (28 May 1979): 20 and 181 (10 March 1980): 14; Scribbins, "Interview," 4-7; Thomas H. Ploss, *The Nation Pays Again* (Self published, 1983), 153; See the Milwaukee Restructuring Act, 45 USC ¢900, signed into law on 4 November 1979.
4. "Report and Recommendations for the Future of the Milwaukee Road." Filed with the Court by Richard B. Ogilvie, 15 May 1980, 1-8, 91-96.
5. *Railway Age* 182 (12 January 1981): 8; First Monday/Third Monday (15 December 1980); F. Stewart Mitchell, "Milwaukee II: A Transformation of Assets," *Modern Railroads* 36 (August 1981): 47-48.
6. Ibid.; *Business Week* (10 August 1981): 20-21.
7. Trustee's Revised Plan of Reorganization, Finance Docket No. 28640 (15 September 1981), 1-28; *Railway Age* 182 (28 September 1981): 12.
8. John H. Burdakin to John S. Guest, 23 June 1980; John H. Burdakin to E. R. Adams et al., 23 June 1980, (PF 150).
9. Milwaukee Road press release, 27 October 1981; *Wall Street Journal*, 28 October 1981; Scribbins, "Interview," 4.
10. *Wall Street Journal*, 28 October 1981.
11. *Chicago Tribune*, 1 November 1981; *New York Journal of Commerce*, 3 November 1981.
12. GTC, "Acquisition Evaluation Chicago, Milwaukee, St. Paul & Pacific Railroad Company" (2 February 1982); GTC, "GTC and Milwaukee II Objectives Can Be Achieved Through Cooperative Action," 2 February 1982, (PF 107).
13. GTC, "Results of GTC/CN Study of Chicago, Milwaukee, St. Paul & Pacific Railroad Company," 15 February 1982, (PF) 107.
14. *Trains* 42 (August 1982): 8-10.
15. GTC, Press release, 24 May 1982; *Railway Age* 183 (14 June 1982), 26; *Modern Railroads* 37 (June 1982): 10.
16. *Railway Age* 183 (5 October 1982): 4; First Monday/Third Monday, 1 November 1982; *Wall Street Journal*, 3 February 1983.
17. *Railway Age* 180 (31 December 1979): 28-29; Ibid. 181 (29 December 1980): 14; *Modern Railroads* 35 (January 1980): 17.
18. *Des Moines Register*, 15 September 1982; *Kansas City Business Journal* 22/28 November 1982; *Modern Railroads* 37 (October 1982): 10; Senator Charles H. Percy et al. to The Honorable Reese Taylor, 12 May 1983, (PF 950).
19. Byron D. Olsen to the author, 11 October 1991; Dennis M. Cavanaugh, interview, 17 September 1991.
20. *Chicago Tribune*, 26 January 1983; *Modern Railroads* 38 (April 1983): 7 and (June 1983): 11; *Des Moines Register*, 9 June 1983.
21. E. Maroti to J. Burdakin, 28 June 1983, (PF 950).
22. *Kansas City Business Journal*, 4/10 July 1983; *Railway Age* 185 (April 1984): 62-63.
23. Soo Line, Second Quarter Report 1983; *Chicago Tribune*, 9, 26 January 1983.
24. Basil Cole, interview, 21 March 1989; Scribbins, "Interview," 5; *Railway Age* 183 (13 September 1982): 4; John H. Burdakin to Richard B. Ogilvie, 11 October 1982, (PF 950).
25. Trustee's Amended Plan of Reorganization, 31 March 1983.
26. *Wall Street Journal*, 29 July, 9 November 1983.
27. Scribbins, "Interview," 7; Amended Plan of Reorganization, Appendix 4: 4, 6, 8 *Chicago Tribune*, 29 July 1983; *Crane's Chicago Business*, 1 August 1983.
28. *Des Moines Register*, 14 September 1983; *Milwaukee Sentinel*, 1 November 1983.
29. *Green Bay News Chronicle*, 25 October 1983; *Minneapolis Star Tribune*, 1 November 1983; *Des Moines Register*, 6 November 1983; *Chicago Tribune*, 13 November 1983; Amended Plan of Reorganization, Appendix 1: 59, 68, 136.
30. Soo Line, Third Quarter Report 1983; *Chicago Tribune*, 14 December 1983; *Wall Street Journal*, 20 January, 8, 21 February 1984; *New York Journal of Commerce*, 8 February 1984.
31. *Chicago Tribune*, 1, 27 March, 16 April 1984; *Wall Street Journal*, 1 March, 7, 16 April 1984; *Railway Age* 185 (April 1984): 21; *New York Journal of Commerce*, 12 July 1984.
32. ICC, Official Transcript, F.D. 28640, Washington, 26 July 1984, 8, 14, 42, 50.

33. Ibid., 1-30; *Minneapolis Star Tribune,* 27 July 1984; *Wall Street Journal*, 11 September 1984.

34. *Minneapolis Tribune*, 11 October 1984; *Wall Street Journal*, 17, 19, 30 October 1984, and 11 February 1985; *Business Week* (25 February 1985): 34; *Railway Age* 186 (March 1985): 27; Soo Line, Special Report to Shareholders, 21 February 1985.

35. Ogilvie was fond of using the term "truly a marriage made in heaven," and is quoted thusly in the *Chicago Tribune*, 27 March 1984; Basil Cole, interview, 21 March 1989; Robert P. vom Eigen, interview, 22 March 1989.

7  A BUCKET FILLED WITH HOLES

The problem of productivity continues to concern the railroad industry despite the 26.5% gain in output per employee hour since 1967. At the same time, constant-dollar labor costs increased more than 50% . . . leaving . . . railroads . . . vulnerable to traffic erosion by the competition.

John H. Burdakin, GTC,
Annual Report (1984): 2.

Failure in the Milwaukee case was a monumental setback for Grand Trunk Corporation. For nearly a half-decade, managerial energies and focus had been directed toward tying Grand Trunk Western and Duluth, Winnipeg & Pacific together by way of Milwaukee Road; untold time and money had been expended in soliciting business for the "new system." All had gone for naught. And the business environment in 1985 was even more ferociously competitive than earlier. As always, GTC was expected to protect the best interests of Canadian National and, as always, managers of GTC properties confronted the need to be nimble and creative.

The competitive environment had changed—and was continuing to change—in dramatic and unalterable ways, as the American and Canadian economies moved from basic production or manufacturing to service. Industries long dependent on railroads—iron and steel, ferroalloy and copper mining, stone and clay quarrying, forgings, etc.—declined, when lighter materials were substituted for heavier ones, and both countries became increasingly dependent on imports from Europe and Asia. The problems of the railroads in the United States were further exacerbated when the already vigorous trucking industry was deregulated during the late 1970s.[1]

Further changes on the traditional competitive landscape resulted from passage of the Staggers Act, signed into law in October 1980 by President Jimmy Carter. Carter recognized that the modal monopoly of railroads had long since passed, that most transportation in the United States was subject to competition, that nearly two-thirds of the nation's intercity freight now moved by means other than rail, that the rail system was shunned by the financial community with resulting capital malnourishment, and that nationalization of the railroads would be inordinately expensive and otherwise undesirable. The Staggers Act, although it stopped short of wholesale deregulation, nevertheless substantially eased the regulatory burden on railroads, and it provided significant changes in rate-making procedures, legalized contract rates, established new cost-accounting principles, and streamlined

Modal competition would not disappear simply because Congress passed progressive legislation. For GTW, such competition was fierce in its primary corridors—Detroit-Chicago and Detroit-Cincinnati. Photograph courtesy of Grand Trunk Western Railroad.

abandonment and merger standards among other things.[2]

None of this occurred without difficulty. As the chief executive of one carrier said, "the industry was strong for the principle of deregulation, but weak on the practice." Competition, especially for contract business, proved unexpectedly keen. Traffic managers of major shippers were bemused as railroaders sorted through their new circumstance. One said: "If a railroad moves freight at a loss today, it is usually because it is deliberately implementing a short range strategy to capture traffic or because it is not yet used to competing in the market place." There were other problems. Single-line service, single-carrier control of transportation from origin to destination, always desirable from the carriers' point of view, became even more so as the result of Staggers. Previously, railroads had been protected from antitrust action in the making of joint rates, but under deregulation they had reason to worry about prosecution by the Justice Department when they sought to negotiate rates on point-to-point shipments. The easiest way to avoid such potential liability was, of course, to own the track from origin to destination—in other words, expand the system through line acquisition or merger. Short of this, and in an attempt to force shippers to accept, as much as possible, single-carrier service, the large railroads closed traditional gateways and raised rates via others.[3]

Competition was hardly restricted to that among railroad companies; most, in fact, was with other modes. The volume of intercity freight transported by rail carriers had dropped from 74.9 percent in 1929 to a disappointing 35.8 percent in 1982, although the number of tons handled nearly doubled over the same years. Trucks, waterway operators, and pipelines had exacted devastating tolls on railroads. The Staggers Act, of course, significantly reduced artificial restrictions on the inherent efficiency of steel-wheel-on-steel-rail transport, but modal competition was not going to disappear simply because of progressive legislation. The American railroads had dieselized, purchased thousands of high-capacity cars, dumped their money-losing passenger service, and trimmed branches. Yet they remained an asset-rich, cash-poor, high-labor-cost industry with clearly inadequate return on investment. Other than investment in property, the only immediate opportunity seemed to be further effort in the merger field.[4]

Rumors were rife; reality was not far behind. In the West in 1982, Union Pacific gathered in neighboring Missouri Pacific and Western Pacific to become what many observers called an "unstoppable monster," and Southern Pacific and Santa Fe talked confidently of marriage. Closer to home, and far more ominous as far as GTC roads were concerned, CSX Corporation was formed in 1980 to acquire the assets of Chessie System Incorporated (Chesapeake & Ohio, Baltimore & Ohio, etc.) and Seaboard Coast Line Industries (Seaboard Coast Line, Louisville & Nashville, etc.). Old rivals Southern Railway and Norfolk & Western then pledged their troth on 1 June 1982. Included in these two new giants were historic competitors of Grand Trunk Western—Chesapeake & Ohio and Norfolk & Western—

each of which had obtained intraline access to southern and southeastern markets via Cincinnati—Chesapeake & Ohio with Louisville & Nashville and Norfolk & Western with Southern. All of this, warned Walter Cramer, was sure to have a negative impact on the fortunes of Detroit, Toledo & Ironton—recently acquired, in large part for the purpose of gaining traffic advantages for GTW and CN through Cincinnati. Elsewhere, Timothy Mellon, a wealthy nabob who had briefly chased DT&I before it came under GTC's flag, acquired Maine Central in 1981, Boston & Maine in 1983, and Delaware & Hudson in 1984. Mellon combined these as parts of Guilford Transportation Industries, clearly a power to be reckoned with in New England. The impact of these acquisitions on Central Vermont was not immediately apparent.[5]

Then there was Conrail, birthed with the federal government as midwife and suckled with federal funds and beneficial legislation, but also a political conundrum. Conrail served the densely populated Northeast, historically a prime manufacturing region, but one that suffered wrenching dislocation as the American economy changed course. Conrail shuddered under these continuing changes, under onerous labor requirements, under vicissitudes of extremely harsh winters, and under the simple pain of birth and early life. Many leaders in manufacturing, transportation, and government doubted its success and, in fact, freely predicted its demise. Policy planners in the Reagan administration found Conrail an acute embarrassment, an awful contradiction to their firm devotion to marketplace solutions. Not surprisingly, the Northeast Rail Services Act of 1981 permitted Conrail to stop functioning as an instrument of social policy and—like all other carriers under the Staggers Act—to respond to traditional business needs and challenges. This unshackling gave heart to an invigorated management team; shippers soon reported improved performance. Politicians remained impatient. Secretary of Transportation Elizabeth Dole announced that bids would be received for the property but she was disappointed for the only early interest was from Conrail employees. Then, in the summer of 1984, came several offers with varying caveats and conditions. CSX, for example, proposed a split-up of Conrail; Norfolk Southern (NS), on the other hand, proposed outright acquisition.[6]

Grand Trunk Corporation was busy with the Milwaukee case as the Conrail story unfolded, but ramifications were clear enough to John Burdakin, Walter Cramer, and Robert Walker who viewed an energized Conrail as a great threat to GTC's Grand Trunk Western and predicted dire consequences if either CSX or Norfolk Southern gained parts or all of Conrail. Burdakin was especially concerned with Norfolk Southern which, he told GTW directors, if successful in its attempt to purchase Conrail, "would be positioned to inflict serious adverse financial" pain. A merger of Conrail and Norfolk Southern, said Burdakin in testimony before a congressional committee, would alter traffic patterns, threaten the existence of small railroads, and destroy rail competition in the upper Midwest. Specifically, the merger would cost GTW 68,000 revenue carloads per year, force GTW to reduce its employment by 15 percent, and threaten the company's ability to remain competitive. "The public interest and the National Transportation Policy as most recently defined by the Staggers Act" and "the competitive impact" were issues of profound consequence in the Conrail case, Burdakin told Senator Donald W. Riegel (D-Michigan).[7]

Burdakin dug in his heels when the Department of Transportation supported Norfolk Southern's application—"a transaction," he said, promoted by the "U.S. government . . . that threatened GTW with insolvency." John H. Riley, head of the Federal Railroad Administration (FRA), asserted that Norfolk Southern would surely make concessions to salve GTW's wounds but Burdakin responded testily: ". . . to date NS has offered nothing that would permit GTW to survive and remain a competitive force within the market it serves." Burdakin accused Riley's agency of misrepresentation as did Harry J. Bruce, chairman of Illinois Central Gulf who, like Burdakin, argued that "the merger of Conrail with a major southeastern railroad such as Norfolk Southern would have serious anticompetitive consequences" and thus "would divert substantial amounts of traffic from smaller, regional railroads . . . ."[8]

GTC managers recognized that a defensive posture alone was inadequate. They must do more than complain; a positive alternative was required. To that end, Robert Walker unveiled "Prorail," a system that would include GTW, Pittsburgh & Lake Erie (P&LE), and lines

Prorail would enhance GTC's investment in the former DT&I and would give it important new gateways. Photograph courtesy of Grand Trunk Western Railroad.

redundant to Conrail or made redundant by a Conrail/NS merger. Prorail would reach from Buffalo and Pittsburgh on the east to St. Louis and Chicago on the west. Among advantages to GTW and P&LE were added gateways and extended line hauls; the shipping public would benefit by preservation of at least a degree of competition in the heartland. Furthermore, Prorail would obviate most antitrust problems in a Conrail/NS combination.[9]

The dogged and dogmatic determination of Secretary Dole and FRA's Riley in support of Norfolk Southern eventually aroused the ire of Representative John Dingell (D-Michigan), chairman of the House Energy and Commerce Committee which had jurisdiction over legislation necessary to consummate sale. Dingell became increasingly suspicious that a combined Conrail/NS would substantially reduce competition and harm regional roads. Dingell had reason. By Conrail's own admission, it was "the largest railroad freight system in the Northeast-Midwest quadrant of the United States" . . .

[serving] . . . "a heavily industrial and consumer region that includes six of the nation's ten largest population centers." Moreover, it boasted: "Conrail is one of the largest rail transporters of automobile parts and finished vehicles. . . ." Momentum finally shifted. In 1985, Burdakin told a congressional panel that a premier alternative to acquisition and merger was a public offering plan. Jervis Langdon, Jr., who had been president and then trustee of ill-fated Penn Central, saw the matter similarly. So did many others. In the end, the federal government on 26 March 1987 sold its ownership interest in Conrail—the largest initial public stock offering in the nation's history. The immediate challenge—merger of Conrail and Norfolk Southern—had been thwarted and GTC's Prorail plan perished accordingly. In the long term, though, GTW was still confronted with CSX, Norfolk Southern, and Conrail—powerful rail competition throughout its service area. Such powerful rail competition simply added to the greatest competition of all—trucks.[10]

Collaterally with the Conrail case Burdakin ordered a vigorous campaign to reopen routings and gateways closed by Conrail in 1981. The problem actually dated from the spring of 1979, when Conrail began imposing surcharges to improve its revenues. This was, of course, in advance of the Staggers Act and had led Walter Cramer to complain that "Conrail is starting to act like we already have deregulation." The matter clearly anticipated Conrail's growing independence and aggressiveness. Conrail managers discussed gateway and route closings early in 1981 and made them effective on 25 July. A howl of protest went up from shippers and connecting carriers. GTW managers saw the action as "a midnight raid to steal traffic." Midnight or not, Conrail was making policy designed to win for itself maximum haulage. With gateways closed and optional routings voided, Conrail instituted single-line rates over its own routes that did little, if anything, to reduce shipper costs but required shippers, in many cases, to deal with it in a captive way. Other major carriers retaliated in kind, and smaller carriers suffered. Toledo, Peoria and Western, for example, vainly fought to retain its bridge business between Conrail and Santa Fe, and in Texas, Roscoe, Snyder & Pacific terminated line haul operation when deprived of overhead traffic.[11]

Burdakin was not amused; and he was hardly a patsy. In addition to the very important economic issue, a profound principle was at stake: integrity. After all, Burdakin himself had affixed his signature to an agreement of 18 December 1975 that obligated GTW and Conrail "to each other in respect to rates, divisions, and through routes via existing junctions and gateways." A deal was a deal. Conrail had abrogated the deal, but no retaliation in kind was permissible. Burdakin reminded senior managers that the agreement was binding on both parties: "Our belief that they have violated the agreement does not permit GTW/DTI to violate the agreement in fact, principle, or intent." The matter had broad implications. Giant railroads already controlled the bulk of traffic, and Burdakin felt compelled to ask: "Is it sensible to reduce rail competition further by wholesale elimination of competitive joint rates and routes?" Had it been the intent of Congress in passing the Staggers Act to assure the absence of competition among railroads? "If allowed to go unchecked," Burdakin told a Senate

subcommittee, "current trends will foster a non-competitive system of giant railroads, each dominant in a section of the country and facing no meaningful rail competition." It was "David and Goliath" reborn.[12]

The issue headed for the courts. Early results were mixed. A preliminary injunction went against Conrail, Conrail sued Grand Trunk, and Grand Trunk sued Conrail. Burdakin was adamant that the company see the issue through to resolution. GTW charged violation of the 1975 contract and that Conrail had, on a premeditated basis, closed gateways and routings for the purpose of monopolizing traffic. Finally, on 18 April 1986, a settlement was reached; Grand Trunk won injunctive relief and compensatory damages, but exact terms were sealed by the court. In an important related development, Conrail lost a crucial gateway routings case before the Interstate Commerce Commission (ICC) with the result that shippers and carriers could seek restoration of routes closed earlier by Conrail. GTW's John C. Danielson, who orchestrated the case, gleefully concluded: "Goliath 0, David 2."[13]

These were no small victories. The war continued, however, and Grand Trunk Western remained a small regional carrier confronted on the east and south and throughout its service area by powerful rail competitors—Conrail, CSX, and NS—and thwarted beyond Chicago by failure in the Milwaukee case. Yet Walter Cramer's force had arrows in their quiver that, if cleverly employed, could give GTW much needed leverage. There was no disputing the fact that GTW originated and terminated large chunks of traffic and that it acted as an important conduit for business moving to and from Canada. And the voluntary coordination experiment with Milwaukee had proved how impressive that innovative marketing device could be once thoroughly and enthusiastically embraced. In 1981, prior to implementation of the VCA, 25,260 units were interchanged between GTC roads and Milwaukee. In 1983, when fully operational, 78,375 units were interchanged, and forecasters predicted nearly 100,000 units for 1984. This was not simply an exercise in moving tonnage; the VCA was profitable for the GTC roads and Milwaukee alike. Eyebrows had been raised at other carriers and at the ICC when the arrangement went into effect, but in the mid-1980s the ICC and most railroads viewed the VCA concept as an appropriate pro-competitive, inter-corporation approach. A VCA, in fact, could be consummated without ICC approval and the interminable delay and expense of such proceedings.[14]

GTC managers had predictably looked for options should the Milwaukee case be lost. The development of post-Milwaukee strategy was vigorously pursued by Robert A. Walker who had previously held traffic-related discussions with Soo, C&NW, and Burlington Northern (BN). Soo and C&NW were regional roads larger than GTW but small compared to BN which had lines through the Midwest to the Texas Gulf Coast and to Puget Sound. BN had exploited its monopoly in the Powder River Basin only to excite recent intrusion by C&NW (with profound backing by Union Pacific), resulting in a notable contest for lucrative low sulfur coal traffic. There was little love, then, between BN and C&NW and, while C&NW had fought GTC in the Milwaukee case, BN had given GTC at least passive support in those proceedings. For its part, Soo had the liability of having fought GTC for Milwaukee and, let there be no mistake, was more than 50 percent owned by Canadian Pacific. Any of the three—BN, Soo, or C&NW—could link GTW with DW&P via Chicago and Duluth and—after Soo got Milwaukee—could provide access to Kansas City. But the dependence of C&NW and, to a lesser extent Soo, on the health and cyclical nature of Midwestern agriculture made them less desirable than BN which had a more stable traffic mix and the ability to directly tap the markets of Dallas/Fort Worth, Denver, Memphis, and Birmingham. A VCA with BN would provide a link between

GTW and DW&P, would expand the traffic base and market mix of GTC roads, and would be compatible with GTC's goal of long-term profitability as Canadian National's arm in the United States. On 21 August 1984, directors of GTC approved cancellation of the Milwaukee VCA and institution of a more expansive VCA with Burlington Northern effective 2 January 1985.[15]

The new agreement provided for coordinated marketing and operations among GTC roads, Burlington Northern, and Canadian National over a 63,000-mile network in Canada and the United States. One part of the arrangement pertained to carload business routed via Duluth and Chicago, and the second related to intermodal traffic through the same gateways. All parties professed confidence in the deal, but Burdakin predicted that it "would draw a great deal of attention and fire." He was sure "we will step on many toes when one considers that the little Grand Trunk Western is the link between the two largest systems in North America." CN's J. Maurice LeClair, who had replaced Robert

This publicity view, made before the new VCA with Burlington Northern went into effect, shows the power of each participating carrier. The location is on the rough escarpment leading to DW&P's old yard facility in West Duluth—trackage soon made redundant by DW&P's move to Pokegema. Photograph courtesy of Canadian National.

Bandeen as president, assured Burdakin and BN's chairman of his personal enthusiasm: "The prospects for significant benefits to all parties seem to be bright, both because the concept is sound, and because the spirit of cooperation between officials of our companies is high." Additionally, said LeClair, "I think the affiliation among Canadian National, Grand Trunk and Burlington Northern is an important development, and it will help strengthen the North American rail network, which is a goal I am sure we share."[16]

GTC's experience with the Milwaukee VCA had been most positive—in part because GTC, with giant Canadian National in the wings, was the dominant force. With the Burlington Northern VCA, however, GTC found itself between two headstrong giants, each of which took defensive or egotistical positions occasionally which contradicted the concept of "voluntary coordination." Indeed, the gestation period and early months following birth were typified by pulling and hauling, much of it at upper middle management levels at both BN and CN. In other cases, rates and routes on certain commodities became a problem as more traffic moved under contract. One GTW staffer put it bluntly: "It's going to require a lot of teamwork and hard work to achieve the full potential of our BN-GT-CN VCA." Early results were disappointing. Figures for 1985 were well short of prediction, but service improvements and a more aggressive posture by BN in 1986 achieved results. Volume in 1987 was 30 percent more than the previous year. Robert Walker and others who had fashioned the pioneer venture with Milwaukee in 1982 had reason to smile. The new agreement with BN was successful, and the concept had caught on and was embraced by many other carriers as they sought access to new markets, sought to increase equipment utilization, and sought to streamline inter-carrier pricing. BN, for example, had six VCAs in place in 1989. Shippers applauded. This kind of cooperation "would have been out of the question" only a few years earlier, said a representative of the Ford Motor Company, "because railroads were totally territorial."[17]

Although GTC managers longed to control events that affected their company, they found this an elusive goal; especially in the transportation industry did managers find themselves subject to buffeting by gyrations in the national and international economies. So it was during the hard years of the early 1980s which proved particularly vexing for those of GTC persuasion. Anticipating low billings in 1981, Burdakin ordered reductions in capital accounts, which turned out a prudent decision. Recovery would not come until mid-decade, and the recession pasted the Midwest, "home to most of our rail lines," with a vengeance. Unemployment in Michigan hit a frightening 17.9 percent, and on GTC properties manpower was reduced by 9.3 percent in 1982 alone. Train operations were trimmed modestly, but this was a delicate matter considering the firm demands of shippers, particularly on GTW. The crunch came in 1983 when GTC was forced to borrow $20 million from Canadian National, a fact that thoroughly alarmed the parent.[18]

Part of the problem, ironically, was purchase of Detroit, Toledo & Ironton, which came into the GTW family almost simultaneously with the onset of the recession. After acquisition of DT&I, one CN executive remarked, "the blood was running." DT&I, of course, like GTW, was tied in large measure to the fortunes of the automobile industry, which was down by the heels during the early 1980s. At the same time, DT&I's route structure and historic traffic patterns were subject to attack as Conrail closed gateways and otherwise flexed its muscles, and as the prized Cincinnati gateway lost allure when friendly Louisville & Nashville combined with unfriendly Chessie and when friendly Southern joined unfriendly Norfolk & Western. All of it, warned Burdakin late in 1980, "bore ominous warnings for the GTW-DT&I future." Despite innovations such as *Thunderbolt*, new through train service between Port Huron and Atlanta (via Southern at Cincinnati), DT&I operating statistics reflected slack revenues and high expenses, the cumulative result of the recession and unanticipated competitive forces. DT&I's operating ratio leapt to 121.3 in 1982. Burdakin, perhaps recalling the horrific problems in merging Pennsylvania and New York Central, had promised a slow process in joining DT&I with GTC properties, but during the summer of 1983 plans were accelerated to "simplify the corporate structure" and to "implement economies in operation" by merging DT&I into GTW. Much had been done already to combine operations and marketing, so there was little notice on 31

The *Thunderbolt* offered premium service to Cincinnati but the loss of friendly connections through merger took the bloom off of expectations for that gateway. Photograph courtesy of Grand Trunk Western Railroad.

December 1983, when the proud Detroit, Toledo & Ironton Railroad Company passed from the scene to be fully integrated by GTW.[19]

Slack business on Grand Trunk put great pressure on Walter Cramer to locate, sell, and retain traffic and on Gerald Maas to run a more efficient operation. It sounded like a pat prescription from a graduate school of management, but in the real world of GTW this simple strategy amounted to a monumental challenge. Historically, of course, the North American automobile industry

provided a strong business base for the company. That foundation was eroded by the oil embargo of the mid-1970s, by growing foreign competition in the late 1970s, and by the serious recession of the early 1980s. The North American auto industry responded haltingly to all of this with the result that railroad prognosticators predicted only modest growth for the foreseeable future. In addition, smaller and lighter vehicles ratcheted down important market segments such as steel, scrap iron, glass, and

As it goes for General Motors, so it goes for Grand Trunk Western. Photograph courtesy of Grand Trunk Western Railroad.

chemicals. Of challenges there were plenty; nothing new in that.

Yet there were new opportunities—the result of deregulation. Prior to passage of the Staggers Act, GTW was very much like other American carriers. The operating department ran the railroad and the sales department sold the business. Rates were determined through the Traffic Executive Association where powerful personalities prevailed and where there was little if any cost analysis. All carriers were bound by common pricing and company salesmen were left to sell service—reliability, settlement of claims, car tracing, etc. On GTW, for example, salesmen peddled: Good track, Good equipment, and Good tickets to ball games. Deregulation changed much of that by exposing railroaders to traditional business practice where pricing was a primary factor. Shippers changed, too; traffic managers became more like purchasing managers, procuring transportation on the best terms for their companies. In the new era, GTW had to sell: Good track, Good equipment, Good service, and Good price.

Fortunately for GTW, the transition was easier than it was for some other carriers because Cramer, long devoted to marketing as opposed to traditional "traffic solicitation," had laid good and proper groundwork.[20]

Following successful tests of commodity-based development in the intermodal and automobile groups, the marketing department was reorganized in 1982. The merchandise group was restructured on a commodity basis, with market development and pricing assigned within each major commodity classification. At the same time, CN and the GTC roads began common solicitation and, following acquisition of DT&I and introduction of the Burlington Northern voluntary coordination agreement, advertised "CN/GT" as a "bigger railroad" offering "better performance." CN/GT promoted "growth potential in the industrial heartland of the United States" and pointed to Canada as "land of business opportunities."[21]

Cramer's forces looked constantly for means to wean the road from an unhealthy dependence on

121

the automobile industry with its roller-coaster tradition of boom or bust. Great energy was expended to provide distribution centers based on economy-of-scale logic. One of the earliest of these was FoodTerm, opened in Detroit in 1975 for the purpose of handling bulk shipment and transfer of edible liquids such as syrups, fructose, starches, and vegetable oils for beverage companies, bakeries, food processors, and ice cream manufacturers. PolyTerm, a warehouse-transfer facility for bulk plastic pellets, granules,

One area of market development—intermodal—was exhilarating. Was it profitable? Photograph courtesy of Grand Trunk Western Railroad.

and powders, opened at Warren, Michigan, in 1978. Additional facilities included a one-million-square-foot newsprint warehouse at Ada, Michigan; a distributing center for newsprint and woodpulp at Springfield, Ohio; a coil steel warehouse at Trenton, Michigan; a lumber and plywood distribution center at Taylor, Michigan; and a reload facility for scrap paper and woodpulp at Kalamazoo, Michigan. GTW also provided distribution or "unload/reload" opportunities at Chicago and Grand Rapids. Much of this business moved under contract; indeed, by the end of 1984, 40 percent of all GTW tonnage was billed that way.[22]

There was one area of market development—intermodal—that was at once exhilarating and depressing. Volume increased consistently and in 1981 revenues in this category were 40 percent above 1980. The question at GTW, and within the industry generally, was twofold: Was this business coming out of boxcars or from highway competitors, and was it compensatory? There was no question at GTW that its traditional boxcar business, especially that related to the cereal and auto industries, was deteriorating—not because of "rail pricing," said Robert Walker, but as "a result of structural and philosophical changes in distribution concepts." Shippers

placed emphasis on price, service, and flexibility. Railroads might meet demands of price but were notoriously inflexible and thus only marginally attuned to service demands. Walker insisted that, in partial response to growing modal competition, the realities of deregulation, and pressures from giant rail carriers, GTW "must significantly reduce" its "labor costs to remain competitive" and "look at new business arrangements not restricted to the movement of merchandise freight in boxcars." Cutting costs would be painful and might invite labor unrest; soliciting intermodal business was possible, but would it be remunerative? GTW's route structure—short legs from Port Huron and Detroit to Chicago, and Port Huron and Detroit to Cincinnati—required high costs in train operations and yarding at RailPort (Chicago) and MoTerm (Detroit) without offsetting income from long hauls. Red ink from intermodal operations, a trickle in 1983, was a torrent in 1985. Many managers argued for total discontinuance.[23]

John Burdakin felt himself in a tight spot, especially when intermodal issues involved General Motors. That was the case when GM became interested in RoadRailer, trailers with dual highway and railway capacity, as a means

Gerald Maas directed activity regarding the impressive Lansing facility. Photograph courtesy of Grand Trunk Western Railroad.

GTW earned *Modern Railroads'* Golden Freight Car Award in 1985 for its efforts on the Lansing loading facility. *MRs'* Tom Shedd, left, presented the award to GTW's Walter Cramer. Photograph courtesy of *Modern Railroads.*

and Chicago. *Lasers* would feature new motive power and specially designed equipment allowing for heavy loads and would be low enough to allow passage through the Sarnia-Port Huron tunnel. The new trains would operate six days per week on twenty-three-hour schedules, would be handled in the United States by GTW crews, and would yard at RailPort in Chicago. Would *Laser* make money for GTW or even cover costs? That remained to be seen. Not at issue, however, was demand, which started strong and got stronger.[25]

to forward auto parts to and from Michigan plants. Burlington Northern also took an interest in RoadRailer and, in fact, GTW cooperated with BN and General Motors to run a test train between Flint and Kansas City in the fall of 1985. GTW's interest, said Burdakin rather defensively, "was motivated by GM's interest." After all, he reiterated, "if our number one customer is interested, we should be also." That did not imply that Burdakin was hostile to new technology. Indeed, Burdakin saw in RoadRailer "the best innovation on the horizon that has the potential to make truck-rail operations profitable for railroads." He was simply concerned about GTW's very sizable investment in standard equipment—an investment threatened if parts were diverted to RoadRailer. General Motors remained interested, although the matter went "on hold."[24]

GTC managers could not ignore the needs of their largest customer nor could they ignore the needs of GTC's parent. CN's views regarding intermodal business were undergoing change that would certainly have an impact on GTW. In 1985, CN announced massive spending in support of *Laser* service, dedicated new intermodal trains for the 845-mile run between Montreal

GTW occasionally was party to distinctive or unusual lading. In 1986, GTW handled hay to drought-plagued areas in the Southeast and to the Upper Peninsula of Michigan. Earlier, in 1983, GTW joined with Fruit Growers Express in an innovative campaign to move bulk beer in mechanical refrigerator cars (fitted with stainless steel containers) from Stroh Brewing Company's plant in Detroit. Three years later, GTW handled eighty-two fermentation tanks from the Detroit plant to Allentown, Pennsylvania, and St. Paul, Minnesota, when Detroit-based Stroh shut down the home brewery.[26]

In all seasons, however, the apple of GTW's eye, clearly king of the traffic mix, was auto business. There was great pleasure at GTW in 1980 when GM announced a huge assembly plant to be built near Pontiac, in 1983 when Chrysler signed an agreement to ship vehicles from a new loading facility in Highland Park, Michigan, and in 1985 when production began at GM's Detroit-Hamtramck assembly plant. There was no pleasure, however, when GM announced reconstruction of its Lansing plant in a way that threatened loss of traffic there to a competitor. That ominous news thoroughly galvanized

Gerald Maas, who responded nimbly and worked with GM to design a sophisticated multilevel "direct from the production line" loading facility that served well the needs of the giant automaker and saved the lucrative business for GTW. It was no small accomplishment. GTW's main line had to be relocated and a retaining wall installed along the Grand River, and twelve new loading tracks had to be built. The effort received positive comment and earned for GTW *Modern Railroads'* 1985 Golden Freight Car Award in the shipper commitment category. Assembled autos and parts remained the premier revenue producer at GTW and General Motors continued as GTC's best customer, providing 24 percent of consolidated operating revenue from 1980 through 1985.[27]

Walter Cramer wryly observed that his job was much like pouring water into a bucket filled with holes; the more water you poured in the more it leaked out. He was referring, of course, to the constant need to solicit business in a world filled with eager and aggressive competitors. It was frustrating to spend great time and effort building up some aspect of the business only to see it undercut by a cunning rival. Gerald Maas faced similar frustration as he looked for means to make GTW's operations more efficient. Maas confronted GTW's historic problem of high expenses without offsetting compensatory line hauls as well as stubborn traditions inherent in this mature industry. Some of these customs and institutions were exaggerated on the GTW because of its long association with Canadian National, which was bound by conventions that not even progressive managers such as Donald Gordon and Robert Bandeen could overcome. For Maas and others in the area of operations, it was a constant campaign to position GTC in such a way that the company could continue to serve the needs of shippers, employees, and the parent.

Maas also found himself in the ironic position of spending appreciable amounts of money to maintain service standards, in some cases, and to improve efficiency, in other cases. Expenditures might be as mundane as replacing a timber trestle on Saginaw Subdivision or as expansive as increasing the size and scope of function at RailPort. New ties and adequate surfacing of track were constants. Burdakin had promoted GTW as the "Good Track Road"; to make good on that assertion required such effort. Maas sup-

ported the idea. Under his leadership GTW replaced nearly six million ties and installed 58.2 miles of continuous welded rail (CWR) in 1980-82. Track improvements turned downward in 1983-84, but in 1985 alone GTW installed 52.3 miles of CWR.[28]

Monies were also expended to improve and expand communication by replacing trackside pole lines and wire with a microwave system providing high-frequency radio for direct dial long-distance and train dispatching telephone needs as well as teleprinter and facsimile circuits. The first installation was made in 1968 and by the end of 1974 the entire GTW system was operational. Capacity was added as needed and the equipment, including towers and associated components, was purchased in 1983 after an initial leasing period.[29]

Efficiencies were also gained by upgrading GTW's computer system. An IBM 3033S was acquired in 1981 to replace an IBM 370/148. The new package added capacity necessary, in part, to absorb responsibilities formerly handled by DT&I's computers, shut down subsequent to merger. Capacity was further increased in 1985.[30]

GTW also worked with others to reduce plant by implementing trackage rights agreements. Louisville & Nashville, for instance, used GTW for a few miles near the Illinois-Indiana border, Detroit & Mackinac gained rights over GTW at Bay City Michigan, and CSX used the former DT&I between Carleton, Michigan, and Frankfort, Ohio. For its part, GTW succeeded in gaining agreements with Conrail and CSX, especially in Ohio.[31]

Such trackage rights agreements usually reflected a willingness on the part of two carriers to put aside parochial interest and corporate pride in favor of efficiencies gained from putting trains of both roads on a common track. When such agreements occurred, unused trackage could be retired. In other cases there was no parallel competing railroad and when business slumped abandonment was the only viable option. The GTW board in 1974 had authorized management "to take whatever action it deemed necessary and prudent to relieve the company of the economic burden of continuing to operate certain branch lines . . . ." Shortly thereafter the branch from Pontiac to Jackson was pared back to Lakeland and was further trimmed to South

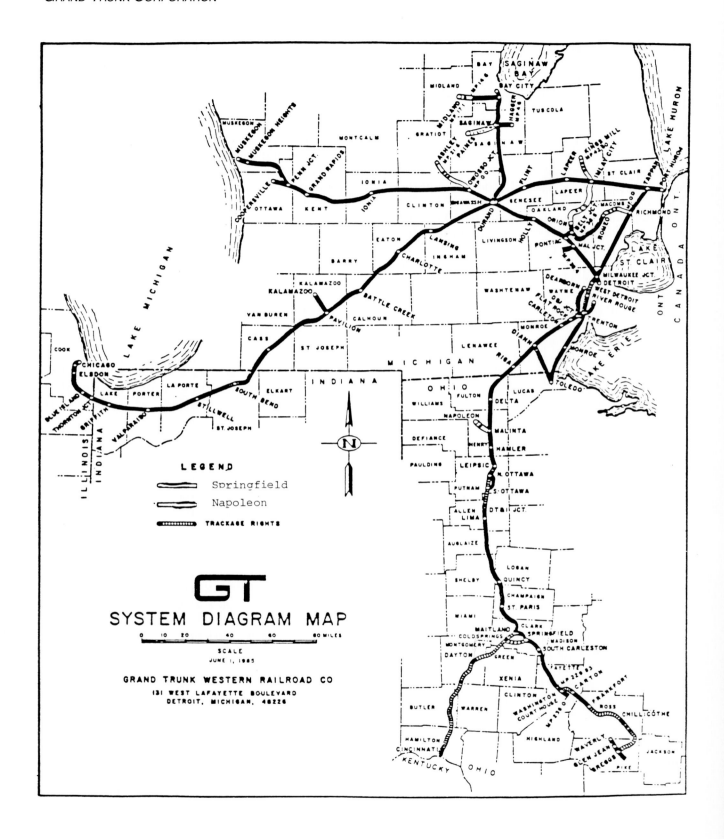

L E G E N D

Springfield

Napoleon

TRACKAGE RIGHTS

N

GT
SYSTEM DIAGRAM MAP

0   10   20   40   60   80 MILES

SCALE
JUNE 1, 1985

GRAND TRUNK WESTERN RAILROAD CO
131 WEST LAFAYETTE BOULEVARD
DETROIT, MICHIGAN, 48226

Lyon in 1985. The economic downturn in the early 1980s predictably accelerated the process of evaluating marginal lines. The top end of the Pontiac-Imlay City-Caseville line, seven miles from Pigeon to Caseville, came out in 1983. Other pieces of lightly used trackage were abandoned in place; dismantling would follow after regulatory review.[32]

On the DT&I the story had a different twist. As a condition of the Chessie/Seaboard merger creating CSX, DT&I gained trackage rights in Ohio between Washington Court House and Greggs, 50 miles. Then, when CSX later asked to abandon the line, DT&I (GTW) purchased 14.2 miles to assure service to Greggs and especially to Waverly, a source of important tonnage, and to Jackson, site of DT&I's shops. Consequently DT&I could abandon its poorer line. Jackson to Greggs disappeared in 1984-85; Ironton to Jackson had come out in 1983. Much of the remaining former DT&I remained subject to outright abandonment or to abandonment after a switch to the superior route of a competitor.[33]

The DT&I shop at Jackson provided a backdrop to the broad issue of labor productivity. After acquisition by GTW that repair facility was redundant but subject to a 1964 agreement providing severance pay if closed before the passage of twenty years; premature closing would cost GTW $2 million or more. As a consequence, GTW was forced to keep the place open until early 1984, whether there was need or not. It reflected a broader pattern of labor agreements that had evolved during times when the railroad industry held a virtual modal monopoly or when the industry was fully regulated and thus felt competitive impulses only as they reflected the culture of a particular company—and then almost solely between one railroad and another. Labor and management alike found the 1980s a brave new world, but one that was profoundly frightening. There was little from the past to serve as a rudder in defining a proper course for a deregulated environment characterized by fierce contests for business among the various railroads and, more important, among the multiple modes of transportation now available to shippers. Moreover, labor and management equally bore the heavy burden of tradition: Relationships derived from the military—officers and enlisted men modified in the railroad industry to managers and laborers, those who give orders and those who take them. In the army an officer threatened an enlisted man with court martial and the brig; on the railroad a manager (almost universally called an officer) threatened an employee with an investigation and his job. Few on either side took the time to consider whether this was a good and proper arrangement; the solitary frame of reference was: "This is the way we have always done it." Gerald Maas was one who thought there might be better ways; he looked for means to improve employee relations and for those who saw the world as he did.

Of course GTW had made an effort to improve employee relations before. But usual procedure there and in the industry generally was to negotiate from strength and, from at least the era of World War I, unions had wielded great power through the political process and the court system. That power eroded only as railroads lost relative position compared to other forms of transport. Not until 1972, for example, was the Indiana Full Crew Law amended to allow railroads in the Hoosier State to operate trains without a fireman and a third brakeman "under certain conditions." Success in dealing with unions was measured by management in traditional form. "The company experienced no strikes in 1972," GTC boasted in 1972. Peace had been achieved, in part, through a national agreement giving members of one union representing 18 percent of GTC employees wage increases of approximately 45 percent over a three-and-one-half-year period. Could the industry, faced by modal competition on all sides, stand that? Could the GTC properties, increasingly smaller railroads on a comparative basis, stand that? Was it possible to do business as usual?[34]

Business as usual was not good enough—certainly not at GTW. In 1973, Walter Cramer had dolefully reported that "the rise in wage rates and material costs was more than twice the amount received from freight rate increases." That was during the era of regulation when the ICC pegged rates. How would it be after deregulation? Different pressures would emerge, but the problem of gaining and holding business at compensatory rates would be more intense than ever. The cost of providing service had to be carefully considered in such an environment.. In 1979, a full 61 percent of GTW's expenses came from wages, salaries, and benefits (50 percent was the industry average). That very unattractive figure reflected a sad reality—GTW was out of step.[35]

Another statistic was even more depressing. GTW's operating ratio for the six-year period 1980-85 was a wretched 101 percent.

Change was necessary and change came; its impact depended on one's point of view. Improvements in communication and computer technology reduced the need for telegraph operators and station agents; blending of GTW and DT&I operations meant fewer staff jobs; the closing of Chicago's historic Elsdon Yard and moving terminal operations to the Belt Railway of Chicago's Clearing Yard claimed many engine, clerk, and switchman jobs; elimination of classification switching at Toledo's Lang Yard and the shutting down of the shops at Jackson cost jobs in several crafts; and reduced crew size and the removal of cabooses on some trains further trimmed GTW employee numbers. All of this fell under the rubric of "cost control." GTC promised

"further mechanization of clerical and operations control functions to improve efficiency and . . . [allow] . . . reduced employment." Quite so. And quite necessary. But terribly costly. The whole process was expensive for the company (in machines, technology, and training; in separation payments or relocation costs for personnel) and for employees (in loss of income and benefits). It also exacted a toll in a psychological sense, for change was traumatic for all hands. To his credit, Maas understood the issue. In the main, leaders of unions represented on the GTW came to respect him for his vision and convictions. Changes in work rules and in other areas became the legacy of this respect. Managers and contract employees alike came to believe as Maas did that "the business environment . . . will be progressively less forgiving to industry segments and companies which do not continue to improve productivity."[36]

The need to recognize and meaningfully address new realities, so apparent on Grand Trunk Western, was no less acute on Central Vermont. CV's problems, to an extent, reflected the trials of New England, a region where traffic-producing business was increasingly scarce. The railroad industry suffered accordingly. The efforts of Timothy Mellon to put order into New England's railroad web through consolidation as Guilford Transportation Industries ultimately drew frowns as service levels fell and as labor unrest mounted. Other nostrums were no more successful. Deregulation, for example, eventually gave Conrail enough leverage to choke off traditional New

Maas had the ticklish job of driving down costs while maintaining high services levels as well as morale among employees. It would prove a difficult balancing act. Photograph courtesy of Grand Trunk Western Railroad.

This pleasant nocturnal scene at White River Junction belied reality. What was CV's future? Photograph courtesy of Central Vermont.

England gateways and traffic flows. Deteriorated service levels on Guilford (Boston & Maine), together with the disappearance of outlets to the south (Conrail), cost CV dearly. Its overhead business, upon which it was so dependent, dried up. CV, it was quite clear, would have to innovate in every way simply to stay alive.

In the summer of 1982, a thoroughly alarmed John Burdakin sought opinions regarding Central Vermont from CN's senior management and was modestly surprised at initial forthrightness from Montreal. The current circumstance, he was told, demanded "an urgent re-appraisal of our thinking about CV." In fact, if CV was "no longer an attractive investment, then this is the time to recognize that fact and plan for its disposition and/or dismantlement under the most favorable possible terms." CV's "future, or lack of one," Burdakin was told, "will be determined by its interchange with CN." Put differently, Montreal asked bluntly: "Does CN need CV as a competitive alternative?" But what about the "family relationship"? CN would protect its "own

best interests" and would be "influenced by service and contract rebates offered by the competing routes (Delaware & Hudson, then a part of the Guilford empire, via Rouses Point, New York, and Conrail via Huntingdon, Quebec)." In 1982 CV received 55 percent of CN's southbound movement into New England, but there was no doubt that CN would shop the entire package to its greatest reward. GTC could not complain. After all, Bandeen's promise had been that every one of CN's properties should be allowed to compete on a standalone basis. It was this very argument that GTC made quite often to CN; CN was now reciprocating in kind.[37]

After studying the matter, Burdakin and Paul Tatro concluded that Central Vermont "under the present corporate structure and political climate" would have "a negative value from both an earnings and cash flow standpoint." A harsh judgment; CV went on the market in December 1982. Consequently it was written down to $5 million, "a reasonable sales price," and recorded a $28.9 million loss. The salvage value of CV,

CV had lost most of its overhead business; now it was a destination carrier, with most of its billings moving to locations on the south end of the road. The company's historic office building is at the right. Photograph courtesy of Central Vermont.

Burdakin admitted, exceeded $5 million but, he concluded, abandonment was not "a viable option available to GTC or CN."[38]

CN waffled. Only three bids were received—one from CV employees, one from a smaller American railroad, and one from unidentified investors. None of the bids was appealing from a monetary point of view and all prospects demanded traffic guarantees from CN. Staffers in Montreal brooded and eventually concluded that CN's "strategic interest" vis-à-vis Guilford and Conrail, "might best be served by keeping CV." CN's board concurred, adding that "consideration should be given to the eventual integration of CV's operations with those of CN." As GTC's 1983 annual report dryly noted, CV remained a corporate member—"strategically located, in spite of the Guilford competitive threat."[39]

Blithe comments notwithstanding, CV's future looked bleak. Heads-up management, innovative marketing, and dry-eyed bargaining to lower costs was essential. General Manager Phillip Larson turned to Robert L. Rixon, a longtime officer with

a broad background who knew the region and its potential. Rixon was a good choice but, like Walter Cramer at GTW, he found the job of locating and retaining business taxing in the extreme. Rixon watched in dismay as CV's overhead business—its meat, potatoes, and gravy—slipped away, as traditional boxcar business was lost to truckers, and as connecting roads failed in service requirements or closed gateways. In 1981, approximately 67 percent of CV's business was overhead, but in 1985 the figure was a mere 37 percent. That was reflected when *Washingtonian/Montrealer* freight service, dependent on Boston & Maine and Conrail, perished.[40]

Rixon looked valiantly for means to replace lost business. He believed trailer-on-flat-car (TOFC or piggyback) might hold or regain accounts and so, to that end, CV instituted dedicated overnight *Rocket* service between Montreal and Palmer, west of Boston, in 1978. A small terminal was provided at Palmer and the trains attracted positive comment as well as volume. New manufacturing plants capable of producing significant carload business were hard to come by, but Phelps Dodge

130

located a large copper wire plant at Yantic, Connecticut. Rixon was much more successful in attracting several break-bulk distribution centers, which included several impressive terminals: cement at Belchertown and Palmer, Massachusetts, and Montpelier Junction, Vermont; gypsum products, plastics, and carbon dioxide at Palmer Massachusetts; newsprint at Norwich, Connecticut, and Monson and Palmer, Massachusetts; and lumber at Sharon, Vermont, Belchertown and Palmer, Massachusetts, and South Windham, Connecticut. Indeed, by the mid-1980s, most of CV's business derived in Canada and moved to distribution centers.[41]

In other areas Rixon had mixed results. CV's *Rocket* intermodal train service was eventually modified to start from St. Albans, Vermont, instead of Montreal, and extended to New Haven (over Boston & Maine); trailers were trucked to and from St. Albans and New Haven (as well as Palmer). *Rocket* trains were operated with smaller crews and without cabooses, but these reductions in operating costs were inadequate. Competition from truckers, especially from "gypsies," was too much; CV could not raise rates and retain business. *Rocket* service ended in 1984, although intermodal service returned briefly with an outside firm supplying all equipment with CV crews operating the trains. Rixon enjoyed much greater success, however, moving woodchips under contract in specially designed hopper cars from Swanton, above St. Albans, to Burlington Electric's generating plant located just east of Burlington, Vermont, 36 miles. The deal proved a good one for shipper and carrier alike. Chips were a low-cost, readily available fuel for Burlington Electric, and the efficient use of labor and equipment provided profit for CV. The woodchip unit train venture earned *Modern Railroads*' 1985 Golden Freight Car Award in the shipper commitment category.[42]

Robert Rixon put great faith in distribution centers such as this one at Palmer, Massachusetts. Photograph courtesy of Central Vermont.

While Rixon wrestled with challenges of sales and marketing, Phillip Larson sought ways to make CV a more productive plant. In 1983, agreements were signed with operating crafts that permitted, under conditions of seniority and availability of personnel, train operations with three-person crews—down by one brakeman—and the right to remove cabooses from one-quarter of train movements. It was inadequate. Larson concluded, at Burdakin's firm urging, that CV could not be party to national labor processes and agreements and in 1984 notified all unions representing CV employees of this decision. Larson would negotiate locally thereafter. At the same time he introduced the "quality circle" concept and practice at St. Albans and New London. All of this represented disruption, change from the usual ways of doing business, and was resisted to some degree by lower management and contract workers alike. Despite misgivings on many levels, however, all parties pulled in harness when it came to the crucial

Rocket intermodal service typified CV's aggressive stance. The train is shown here at the Palmer, Massachusetts ramp. Photograph courtesy of Central Vermont.

CV's woodchip train proved profitable and earned a Golden Freight Car award. Photograph courtesy of Central Vermont.

132

CV's future remained problematic. Photograph courtesy of Central Vermont.

matter of safety in the workplace. CV won prestigious Harriman awards in every year from 1976 through 1981.[43]

As Larson looked back on the first half of the 1980s and ahead to the remaining years of that decade he had mixed feelings. Larson took pride in CV's physical condition—"the best main line track in northern New England"—and the road was popular with rail enthusiasts who flocked to see the fifteen Alco RS-11 locomotives transferred in 1984 from DW&P to burble and gurgle and smoke their way across CV's undulating profile. More important, gross ton miles and revenue ton miles increased nicely. But costs outran receipts in some seasons. The operating ratio, 92 in 1980, dropped to 85.5 in 1981 and then raced to a depressing 111.2 in 1984. Larson was compelled to trim employee numbers; 412 persons were on the payroll in 1980, but only 308 were employed in 1984. The road had total income of $7.6 million for the years 1980-85, inclusive, but only $5.7 million in operating income. Nonoperating income, Larson knew, tended to come from sources that

could not be renewed. CV's fate, as a consequence, would be decided in part by Rixon's ability to attract and retain traffic, by Larson's ability to bring down operating costs, and by Canadian National—which had to weigh the merits of putting more traffic on Central Vermont against other strategic options.[44]

Canadian National managers had no similar constraints when it came to Duluth, Winnipeg & Pacific. As CN's Yvon H. Masse tartly observed, DW&P was a "good revenue maker" with "fine connections" at the Lakehead. CN would "guard it jealously." With ample reason. DW&P produced an average of 2.42 million gross ton miles annually for the first half of the 1980s; trains averaged a very respectable 6,147 tons. Lumber predominated among traffic commodities with 35.8 percent of the total, followed by potash (24.9 percent), and paper and woodpulp (16.5 percent). With the vast majority of its business moving from western Canada into the United States, DW&P had little reason for an inhouse marketing staff such as that found on CV. Canadian

Work was well along on the Pokegama facility in July 1984. Photograph by Don L. Hofsommer.

National, instead, handled these duties under Walter Cramer's scrutiny. The favored connection in 1980 was Chicago & North Western, but during the lengthy Milwaukee acquisition case DW&P predictably moved more business to CMStP&P; in 1985, with consummation of a new VCA, Burlington Northern got the nod.[45]

There was temptation to compare DW&P with CV. Both connected with Canadian National and, in fact, were appendages into the United States. That is where the analogy ended. CV had a long historic traffic association with CN; DW&P's was relatively new. CV's business had been stronger earlier and became weaker; DW&P's traffic had been weak earlier but became stronger. CV had been primarily a bridge road but became dependent on billings to and from on-line locations; DW&P had once lived on local loadings but then found fame as an overhead carrier. CV had expensive classification expense; DW&P had little.

DW&P's principal yard expense was at the Lakehead where its vestpocket West Duluth facility hugged a rugged escarpment overlooking the St. Louis River Valley and Lake Superior. Yard tracks were not level and tilted dangerously toward the lake, and to get from West Duluth to connections required impressive but extremely expensive trestlework plus trackage rights. Traditionally, road crews handled trains only into and out of West Duluth with a yard crew required to move cuts to and from connections. DW&P's terminal operation was, in sum, operationally difficult and expensive; it also caused irksome delay to lading and added car hire cost.

Throughout the 1970s, those responsible for DW&P's welfare brooded about problems at Duluth. On the other hand, they were loath to move quickly since they knew that Minnesota transportation authorities were contemplating an extension of the interstate highway system that was likely to have an impact on all rail operations downtown and in the industrialized area along the lake. Meanwhile, managers looked for property across the way in Wisconsin for a new yard and talked with other railroaders about opportunities to rationalize plant and means by which to expedite traffic moving among the several carriers. Finally, in 1979, a verbal agreement was made with highway authorities but progress was slow; negotiations were required with three cities, two states, and six railroads.

134

The anguish was worth it. In 1981, DW&P management was authorized to make all arrangements necessary to move from West Duluth to Pokegama, near Superior, Wisconsin, and to join in trackage/yardage/interchange agreements with cooperating roads. DW&P managers, in public and in private, referred to the move as "forced" by the "I-35 highway relocation project," but in reality they were overjoyed by the new arrangement—especially since the federal government through the state of Minnesota would reimburse most of the cost ($15,490,000 of $18,511,000). Work began in 1983 on the 18-track yard and on connections with Duluth, Missabe & Iron Range Railway

The sign outside DW&P's new office building at Pokegama was simple, bold, and muscular—typical of the company. Photograph by Don L. Hofsommer.

(DM&IR) to reach tracks and yards of Burlington Northern (which CMStP&P also used), Soo Line in Superior, and Chicago & North Western at Itasca, as well as with the DM&IR to Nopeming Junction, milepost 10.5, and a junction there with DW&P's route to Virginia and Ranier. Forces from the accounting department in downtown Duluth and all departments from West Duluth moved to the handsome new Pokegema facility on 1 December 1984; revenue trains began use of Pokegama six days later. The entire property was Spartan yet attractive and functional—typical of DW&P.[46]

The company's motto, "Delivered With Pride," proved to be more than boastful rhetoric. DW&P's small workforce (389 persons in 1980, 291 in 1984) produced extremely efficient transportation; the operating ratio for the first half of the 1980s averaged a very respectable 80.3. Sophisticated computers and communication systems including a system-wide microwave network aided DW&P personnel and shippers alike. More hotbox/dragging detectors, persistent tie renewal programs, additional welded rail, and a fleet of General Motors SD-40 locomotives carefully maintained by DW&P mechanical forces spelled reliability that was noticed by customers and connecting carriers alike. Productivity was enhanced by the introduction of unit trains of potash in 1980, and in 1985 by granting trackage rights to Burlington Northern over 153 miles to Ranier (giving DW&P added revenue and allowing BN to abandon its own line to International Falls). Employee morale was heightened by knowledge that the company had a policy of constantly spending money to improve the property and this was well and properly reflected in DW&P's safety record: Harriman awards in 1978, 1980, 1983, and 1984.[47]

DW&P's excellent record was best reflected by its income statements. The road had total net income of $21 million for the five-year period 1980-84. Ironically, that very satisfactory performance caused a bit of indigestion in Montreal where for years CN staffers felt that rate divisions unjustifiably favored DW&P over CN. Their argument was that the vast majority of DW&P's traffic was lading from Canada, that CN was the originating carrier, and that CN had the bulk of expense in handling (line haul and switching). DW&P, they noted, was a "hook and haul" operation with minimal comparative expenses. When the DW&P achieved profitable status in the mid-1960s, divisions for DW&P were reduced to about 9 percent—this to advantage CN but also to reduce DW&P's tax exposure. The debate flared again in 1972 when Bandeen wondered if DW&P was being "short changed" and frequently thereafter as forces in Montreal and Detroit debated the merits of increased revenue to CN or support for CN through Grand Trunk Corporation.[48]

DW&P was, in fact, the heart of the GTC concept. Losses at GTW, and more recently at CV, served to shelter DW&P's income; DW&P had also been used to provide cross guarantees for

GTW and CN had worked to move prodigious amounts of traffic on the Milwaukee Road. Here one of the final Milwaukee VCA trains moves across the DM&IR's Oliver Bridge; moments later it will enter DW&P's new facility at Pokegama before proceeding on to St. Paul and Chicago. Photograph courtesy of Grand Trunk Western Railroad.

DW&P's general manager, Marc Higginbotham, smiles broadly in accepting the 1980 Harriman safety award. Photograph courtesy of Duluth, Winnepeg & Pacific Railway.

debts incurred by GTW. All of this was necessary since CN had determined that GTW was an essential component but one that could no longer receive cash infusions from the parent. DW&P, through GTC, in effect replaced CN as GTW's financial backbone. It was a practical arrangement by which CN's investment and marketing requirements in the American properties could be protected. And in the 1970s, GTC had been profitable—by $53,754,000. The deep recession of the early 1980s proved disastrous, however; GTC lost $53.8 million (of which $27.5 million was for the writedown of CV).[49]

Had Bandeen's experiment run out of steam? The picture was unclear. GTC celebrated its fourteenth birthday in 1984 and had been profitable in all but four of those years. But the very author of GTC, Robert A. Bandeen, was no longer around to champion the cause. Bandeen resigned his multiple positions as head of CN and subsidiaries including GTC effective 31 March 1982. "I have always believed that five to eight years was the most that anyone should spend in this job," said Bandeen; "I am in the eighth year as head of CN, have achieved what I set out to accomplish and feel in need of a new challenge." He was soon named to head Crown Insurance.[50]

What would this mean for GTC? Bandeen had been predictably popular among managers and directors of GTC roads. Bandeen was "one of the greatest things ever to come down the pike," said an unabashed William K. Smith, vice president of General Mills and a GTW director. CN's Ron Lawless credited Bandeen with "letting managers do their own thing," and stressed that he had been "impressive in the strategic development of the company." Bandeen was also popular with the business community and with most CN managers; he was less popular with members of Parliament and civil servants. Bandeen had tried to run CN and its subsidiaries in a businesslike way and enjoyed much success in doing so, but as one senior CN officer observed, he was "not politically sensitive." Bandeen, in truth, suffered fools badly; politicians were put off by his arrogance. "You can operate in a political environment," said CN's Yvon H. Masse, "but it takes more patience." Bandeen, however, was a man in a hurry, a man with a purpose; he had little patience with those who inhibited his course of flight. Bandeen was succeeded by Dr. J. Maurice LeClair, a trained physician and well-known federal bureaucrat who most recently had been CN's senior corporate vice president. GTC managers were apprehensive. Bandeen, after all, had stood in the breach between GTC's independent management and the forces of tradition in Montreal—"Bandeen was the insulation," as GTW's Earl C. Opperthauser observed. Even then there had been tension, especially between the sales and marketing forces at CN and the GTC roads.[51]

Changes also came to GTC's leadership in Detroit. Gerald Maas, executive vice president of GTW since 1984, became president of the GTC roads on 1 January 1986. Burdakin was named to the new position of vice chairman. The two men were quite different and casual observers might have predicted a disastrous relationship. Maas was tall and broad; Burdakin was shorter and of slighter build. Maas held a degree from a modest midwestern public university; Burdakin graduated from MIT. Maas was Congregationalist; Burdakin was Presbyterian. Maas came up the ranks at New York Central; Burdakin was Pennsylvania Railroad to the core. Maas favored a casual style; Burdakin was formal. Of differ-

ences there were many. But Burdakin and Maas proved a good team; their respective assets and liabilities were offsetting.[52]

NOTES

1. James F. Willis and Martin L. Primack, *An Economic History of the United States,* 2d ed. (Englewood Cliffs: Prentice Hall, 1989), 417-37; Jonathan Hughes, *American Economic History,* 3d ed. (Glenview: Scott Foresman/Little Brown, 1990), 589-97.

2. Robert Roberts, "Deregulation: The Turning Point," *Modern Railroads* 35 (December 1980): 58-62. F. Stewart Mitchell, "Loosening the Grip," *Modern Railroads* 36 (April 1981): 34-35; Frank D. Shaffer, "We Now Have the Tools," *Modern Railroads* 36 (April 1981): 36-39; Frank Malone, "Contract Rates are Catching On," *Railway Age* 183 (22 February 1982): 42-44; Gus Welty, "Change!," *Railway Age* 185 (January 1984): 37-44.

3. G. B. Aydelott, interview, 22 September 1982; *New York Journal of Commerce,* 17 June 1982, 22 March 1983; *Wall Street Journal,* 22 February, 13 July 1983.

4. *Railroad Facts* (Washington: Association of American Railroads, 1984), 32.

5. Don L. Hofsommer, *The Southern Pacific, 1901-1985* (College Station: Texas A & M University Press, 1986), 302-3; Vance Richardson, "A Marriage of Equals," *CSX Quarterly* (Fall 1990), 9-25; *Railway Age* 183 (12 September 1982): 11-13; Gus Welty, "The Meaning of Merger," *Railway Age* 185 (July 1984): 73-76; GTW, Minute Book No. 8, 355-56; *Modern Railroads* 37 (June 1982): 10.

6. Gus Welty, "The Meaning of Merger," *Railway Age* 185 (July 1984): 73-76.

7. GTW, Minute Book No. 9, 472; *GT Reporter* (August 1985), 1; John H. Burdakin to Hon. Donald W. Riegel, Jr., 19 June 1985, (PF 108).

8. GTC, Annual Report (1985): 6-7; John H. Burdakin to Hon. John H. Riley, 10 January 1986; John H. Riley to John H. Burdakin, 19 November 1985; *Journal of Commerce,* 3 February 1986; Hon. John D. Dingell to Hon. Elizabeth Hanford Dole, 7 February 1986; John H. Burdakin to Hon. John C. Danforth, 19 June 1985; Harry J. Bruce to Hon. Richard J. Durbin, 8 April 1986, (PF 109).

9. *Railway Age* 186 (February 1985): 23.

10. *GT Reporter* (August 1985): 1; *New York Times,* 17 June 1985; Conrail, Annual Report (1986): 1-2; GTC, Annual Report (1986): 5.

11. Walter H. Cramer to John H. Burdakin, 23 May 1979, (PF 108); Don L. Hofsommer, *The Quanah Route: A History of the Quanah, Acme & Pacific Railway* (College Station: Texas A&M University Press, 1991), 183.

12. GTC, Annual Report (1985): 10; *GT Reporter* (May 1983): 1; Agreement between Consolidated Rail Corporation and Grand Trunk Western Railroad Company, 12-18-1975; John H. Burdakin to W. H. Cramer and G. L. Maas, 12 November 1982, (PF 108); *Modern Railroads* 38 (August 1983): 9; GTW, "Are Giant Rail Systems Foreclosing Rail Competition?: A Grand Trunk Point of View" (1983).

13. Earl Opperthauser, interview, 6 November 1989; ICC, Changes in Routing Provisions—Conrail—July 1981, Docket No. 38676 (5 September 1986); John C. Danielson to Carl V. Lyon, 17 October 1986, (PF 108).

14. Affidavit of Peter C. White, 5 October 1984, 2 (PF 108).

15. GTC, Executive Briefing Summary, 21 August 1984; GTC, Minute Book No. 3, 192-93.

16. *Detroit Free Press*, 6 September 1984; John H. Burdakin to R. E. Lawless, 22 August 1984; J. Maurice LeClair to W. A. Drexel, 9 November 1989; J. H. D. Sturgess to J. H. Burdakin, 7 January 1985; John H. Burdakin to W. H. Cramer, 3 June 1985; Richard M. Gleason to S. B. Hall, 19 June 1985 (PF 116).

17. E. J. Stasio to W. H. Cramer with VCA review and status report from D. A. Johnson, 11 March 1986 (PF 116); CNGTBN, Coordinated Train Service, March 1986; GTC, Annual Report (1987): 17; *Santa Fe Railway News* (March 1989): 4; *BN News* (Spring 1989): 16-17; *Wall Street Journal*, 20 December 1989.

18. GTC, Annual Report (1980): 3; Ibid. (1982): 2; Ibid. (1983): 21; GTW, Minute Book No. 9, 434-35.

19. Yvon Masse, interview, 24 May 1989; GTW, Minute Book No. 7, 339; GTC, Annual Report (1980): 2; GTC, Five Year Statistical Supplement 1980-1984; Frank Malone, "GTW-DT&I: A Slow Transition to Avoid Merger Shock," *Railway Age* 181 (30 June 1981): 38-42; DT&I, Corporate Records, 31: 98, 102-3; GTC, Annual Report (1983): 4.

20. Walter Cramer, interview, 11 August 1989, 6 March 1990; Tom Shedd, ". . . Cigars are Out," *Modern Railroads* 33 (October 1978): 43-45.

21. GTC, Annual Report (1982): 9; GTW, Minute Book No. 7, 315; Peter A. Clarke, interview, 7 August 1989; CNGT, "Bigger Railroad, Better Performance" (9/85); CNGT, "United States: Growth Potential in the Industrial Heartland" (2/85); CNGT, "Canada: A Land of Business Opportunities" (7/84).

22. GTC, Annual Report (1981): 6; *GTC Reporter* (August 1986): 2 and (September 1979): 2; *Railway Age* 183 (30 August 1982): 4; GTC, Annual Report (1984): 8.

23. GTC, Annual Report (1981): 6; Robert A. Walker to John H. Burdakin, 11 August 1983; Robert A. Walker to John H. Burdakin, 15 November 1985; M. H. Weisman to Productivity Committee, undated [December 1985] (PF 301); GTC, Annual Report (1985): 16.

24. R. E. Lawless to John H. Burdakin, 11 July 1985; John H. Burdakin to R. E. Lawless, 8 October 1985 (PF 504).

25. *Railway Age* 186 (June 1985): 59-60; Ibid. (October 1985): 26.

26. *GT Reporter* (November 1983): 5; Ibid. (October 1986): 26.

27. *GT Reporter* (March 1980): 1; GTC Annual Report (1983): 8; *Railway Age* 186 (January 1985): 36-37; GTC, Annual Report (1984): 8; *Modern Railroads* 40 (June 1985): 24-25; Ibid. (September 1985): 74-76.

28. GTW, Minute Book No. 7, 328, 345; GTC, Annual Report (1988): 14.

29. *GT Reporter* (September/October 1983): 5; GTC, Annual Report (1975): 7; GTW, Minute Book No. 9, 422-23.

30. GTW, Minute Book No. 8, 365-66, 396; GTW, Minute Book No. 9, 466, 474, 480.

31. GTW, Minute Book No. 6, 211, 243; GTW, Minute Book No. 9, 475-76.

32. GTW, Executive Minute No. 657 (23 July 1983); GTW, Minute Book No. 9, 416.

33. DT&I, Corporate Records, 31: 94, 103-6; GTW, Minute Book No. 9, 439-40; GTC, Annual Report (1984): 8.

34. GTC, Annual Report (1972), 27-28.

35. GTC, Annual Report (1973): 25; Ibid. (1979): 6.

36. *GT Reporter* (July-August 1973): 1, (March-April 1979): 1, (November 1983): 4, (May 1984): 5, and (August 1984): 2; GTC, Annual Report (1981): 6; Ibid. (1984): 8; Ibid. (1985), 4, 5, 14, 15; *Railway Age* 185 (September 1984): 11.

37. Charles F. Armstrong to J. H. Burdakin, 9 September 1982 (PF 102.11).

38. J. H. Burdakin and P. E. Tatro to Coopers & Lybrand, 17 February 1983 (PF 102.11); GTC, Annual Report (1982): 2, 14, 20.

39. CN, Analysis of Options for the Central Vermont Railway (undated, 1983); P. A. Quesnal to J. M. LeClair, 17 May 1983 (PF 102.11); GTC Annual Report (1983): 5.

40. *GT Reporter* (October 1978): 3; CV, "Piggyback Works for You" (undated, [1982]); *Railway Age* 180 (30 April 1979): 3; Ibid. 184 (February 1983): 44-45.

41. GTC, Annual Report (1980): 14; Ibid. (1983): 14; *GTC Reporter* (August 1986): 2.

42. GTC, Annual Report (1982): 14; Ibid. (1984): 14; *GT Reporter* (March 1984): 2; Ibid. (August 1985): 1; *Modern Railroads* 40 (June 1985): 20-21.

43. GTC, Annual Report (1983): 14; Ibid. (1984): 14; *GT Reporter* (March 1985): 2; GTC, Annual Report (1982): 14.

44. GTC, Annual Report (1983): 14; *GT Reporter* (May 1984): 3; GTC, Five Year Statistical Supplement 1980-84 and 1984-88.

45. Yvon H. Masse, interview, 24 May 1989; DW&P, Duluth Gateway: Loads Handled by Connections, 7 January 1983. DW&P, General Manager files, Pokegema.

46. DW&P, Corporate Records Book 4, 23 May 1973; GTC, Annual Report (1979): 12; DW&P, Executive Minute No. 51; DW&P, Corporate Record Book 4, 25 June 1982; DW&P, Pokegama Fact Sheet (undated, [1984]) (PF 103); "I-35 and the Great Yard Swap," *Railway Age* 186 (April 1985): 45-46.

47. GTC, Annual Report (1974): 11; Ibid. (1980): 12; Ibid. (1985): 18.

48. Memorandum, Recent History of CN-DWP Divisions Negotiations, 8 December 1982, (PF 103).

49. John H. Burdakin to J. M. LeClair, 19 October 1984, PF 103; Tabular data from GTC annual reports.

50. *Modern Railroads* 37 (March 1982): 11.

51. William K. Smith, interview, 24 September 1989; Ronald Lawless, interview, 7 August 1989; Peter L. Schwartz, interview, 7 August 1989; Peter A. Clarke, interview, 7 August 1989; Lorne C. Perry, interview, 23 May 1989; Yvon H. Masse, interview, 24 May 1989; David Thomas, "Tough Enough to Hurt," *Canadian Business* 55 (November 1982): 28-34; John H. Burdakin, interview, 4 November 1989 and 21 February 1991; Earl C. Opperthauser, interview, 6 March 1990.

52. GTW, Minute Book No. 9, 486.

8  CONTINUOUS CHANGE

If anything can be said to be certain in these uncertain times, it is that significant changes will continue to be needed in the activities and organization of Canadian National.

> J. M. LeClair, Canadian National Annual Report (1984): 9.

Just as the Grand Trunk Corporation roads sought to find and hold rightful places in the sun during times of stress and change, so, too, did its parent. Canada, after all, felt the same challenges resulting from globalization of trade and finance, accelerated technological change, regulatory alterations, and the consolidation of business enterprises as did the United States during the late 1970s and throughout the 1980s. But senior managers at Canadian National also had to deal with expectations of politicians and government bureaucrats to a degree that would have left their compatriots south of the border breathless and bewildered.

CN made impressive strides during the late 1970s. In 1976, it earned the first overall profit—$11.8 million—in two decades, and in 1978 CN experienced its best financial performance to that time. There were several reasons for this happy development: Parliament had made adjustments in CN's capital structure; stringent internal cost control; alert marketing; technologi-

cal advances; and improved organizational structure. In addition, a new Crown Corporation, VIA, relieved CN Rail of burdensome costs in the passenger carrying trade. But problems remained. CN Express was a loser, capital-hungry CN Hotels was marginal, statutory rates resulting from the infamous Crowsnest Pass Law harnessed CN Rail to impossible losses in the carriage of western grain and Montreal commuter operations were a drag on earnings as were rail operations in Newfoundland. Furthermore, CN needed staggering amounts of capital to finance expansion and to improve rail services abroad its huge landscape.[1]

When Robert Bandeen left CN early in 1982 he could properly claim that "working together we have given new shape and direction to Canadian National . . . ." During his tenure as head of CN the company had sustained losses only in 1974 and 1975 and had net earnings of $758,200,000. In addition, during the Bandeen years CN paid over to the shareholder, the Canadian government, a dividend of $145.9 million—certainly sound accomplishments.[2]

J. Maurice LeClair followed Bandeen in the corner suite. Although bright, talented, and well educated, LeClair was not as dynamic and charismatic as Bandeen, and he carried other heavy baggage. LeClair was a trained physician

J. Maurice LeClair had the unenviable task of following Robert A. Bandeen at CN. Photograph courtesy of Canadian National.

to spin off CN Marine as a separate Crown Corporation in 1984.[3]

LeClair increasingly enlisted in a campaign to educate opinion makers and government leaders that CN was "part of a changing national and world order." Consequently, he warned, "Canadian National must be concerned with factors that affect its customers and vigilant in its efforts to improve service to them." That would not be possible without fundamental change in CN's financial picture but under federal law, CN could not enter the equity market and for capital had to rely on internally generated profits (a part of which was obligated to the federal government) and on borrowing. Since recapitalization in 1978, the company's debt rose to $3.5 billion by the end of 1986—creating, said a worried LeClair, "a barely tolerable debt ratio and urgent need to reduce costs." Unable to issue stock as a means of generating capital and unable to draw on the government for capital, CN had only two

and former government bureaucrat, not a railroader and not even a businessman; his power derived from without, not within. Few at CN welcomed him. And he was unlucky. He was barely ensconced in 1982 when the full force of recession hit. LeClair boldly called for "restraint and retrenchment," layoffs, terminations, and early retirements. Such nostrums were appropriate but scarcely served to make him popular. CN, said LeClair, "can best serve Canada as a financially self-sufficient, commercially oriented Crown corporation." He was philosophically attuned to Bandeen's belief in a business-like policy if his style and approach were different. To his credit, LeClair worked diligently and successfully to resolve the Crowsnest issue in 1983 and

options: borrow money or trim. Much remained to trim, but trimming was politically risky. LeClair concluded that CN was obligated to impose a debt ceiling: unfortunately, that put CN's ability to deliver service and prepare for the future at risk.[4]

Conflicting public expectations contributed greatly to the problems facing CN. Many Canadians continued to perceive CN's role as essentially philanthropic—to provide jobs, to support communities, to exercise its considerable purchasing power in parochial ways. Other Canadians perceived CN's role as a self-sustaining and efficient business. A mixed view among the public was reflected in governmental position and, predictably, in schizophrenia at CN.

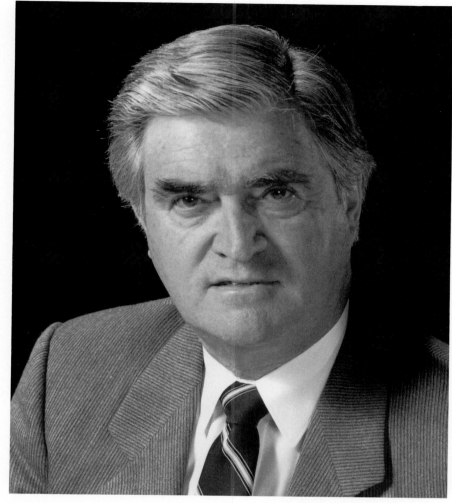

Ronald E. Lawless, a career railroader at CN, followed LeClair to become president and chief executive officer on 1 January 1987. Photograph courtesy of Canadian National.

Meanwhile, Gerald Maas labored to put his own personal imprint on the affairs of Grand Trunk Corporation. Like Bandeen and Burdakin before him, Maas found ample challenges. And, as always, Grand Trunk Western was the greatest test.

Maas recognized that one of GTW's greatest liabilities was a distressingly high percentage of operating expense attributable to wages, salaries, and benefits. Strides had been made within the industry and at GTW to improve productivity, but much work remained in that crucial area. Failing that, railroads in general, and GTW in particular, were bound to lose even more market share. American railroads during the 1980s still claimed slightly more than one-third of intercity ton miles, but the percentage of total revenues earned by railroads among all modes of transportation in the United States dropped from 26.7 in 1981 to 21.1 in 1986. Employee numbers were down, too, from 532,000 at the beginning of the 1980s to 346,000 at mid-decade. Ironically and distressingly, however, railroads ranked second in average total compensation among the modes in 1981 and copped first place in 1986.[6]

Any changes in the industry's conventions were sure to encounter resistance since most contract employees and managers, too, were wedded to the status quo. Changes in operating procedures at Durand, Michigan, provide a case in point. During the early summer of 1986, GTW managers determined to end yard service there after studies showed potential savings of approximately $1 million. A union representative complained, however, saying that cuts would result "in inconsistent service" leading "to the loss of business and the loss of jobs." The whole idea, he thought, was "foolish."

LeClair, who in a very real way was a political appointee, eventually surprised many with his firmness. "Regular bursts of single-minded philanthropy" by CN should not be expected and could not be tolerated: "Profitability must be CN's primary goal and there is not a moment to lose in its pursuit." Correct but impolitic; LeClair would leave office at the end of 1986. LeClair had, in his own words, "stimulated, challenged, stretched, and energized" CN. Indeed, under his direction the company had earned net of $262.6 million over five years and had paid $114.4 million in dividends to the federal government. Ronald E. Lawless, a career railroader at CN, followed LeClair to become president and chief executive on 1 January 1987.[5]

Indeed, the union man concluded, "this move is motivated by a deliberate desire to chase business away." The only other possibility, he said, was "stupidity." A hot response from management was not long in coming. "Whether or not you (and the other General Chairmen) care to believe it, Grand Trunk is in a fierce fight, not just for profits, but for basic survival," said a highly offended senior officer. "We do not have the luxury of 'business as usual', hoping and praying to muddle through to better times." He was correct: "business as usual" was categorically inadequate.[7]

The Durand episode—with harsh feelings on the part of labor and management alike—was sadly typical of the way railroads and unions usually dealt with each other. It was incredibly counterproductive. There had to be a better way; and Maas was determined to find it. One thing he could do, and do well, was communicate with "the men in the trenches." He would insist on a broad campaign to open communications at all levels,

Gerald L. Maas embraced a "tell it like it is" philosophy. Photograph courtesy of Grand Trunk Western Railroad.

which did not seem complex. GTW simply had to shrink its labor force; "just tell it like it is." Change came, if slowly and reluctantly, as Maas and David L. Wilson, whom Maas had brought in as vice president of operations, gained credibility among contract employees. Yard facilities at Blue Island (Illinois) were closed and terminal work at Toledo (Ohio) was reduced; dispatching was centralized at Pontiac (Michigan); a mechanized payroll system replaced earlier software; crew size was reduced from two brakemen to one; and GTW negotiated an employee severance program. But Maas admitted, "Changes at any and every level are hard to take."[8]

Maas was happy to announce in 1986 the establishment of a comprehensive effort to forge more productive agreements with unions. Maas calculated that GTW needed to trim annual expenses from $55 to $70 million by 1991. Yes, he and Wilson realized that would have an impact on loyal, hardworking employees. They urged union leaders to help in "finding the best solution to reduce costs with the least amount of hardship." GTW found itself in an awkward position, Maas told the company's board of directors. "Solid profitability" could "not be obtained until traffic growth is realized," but that would not happen until "a lower cost operating structure is in place." Maas noted that GTW employee costs in 1987 were approximately 60 percent while the industry average was 45.5 percent.[9]

David L. Wilson. Photograph courtesy of Grand Trunk Western Railroad.

New agreements would lower labor costs which, in turn, would give Walter Cramer's marketing group more flexibility in pricing. As an example, one of these agreements, with the United Transportation Union (UTU) and the Brotherhood of Locomotive Engineers (BLE), allowed GTW to use only two persons on Short Crew Automobile Trains (SCAT) if these hauled new business gained under competitive bidding. A more comprehensive package followed when GTW and UTU agreed to a general policy of operating freight trains of up to thirty-five cars with two crewman and trains of more than thirty-five cars with three. What did labor get in return? Security, or at least the prospect of security. "Grand Trunk Western is surrounded by railroad giants," noted one union negotiator, and could not "compete when those giants already have crew reduction and we do not." In addition, those who lost jobs secured a one-time severance payment; those who stayed could participate in a 401-K savings plan and a productivity pool in which they would share in the company's labor savings.[10]

Maas had reason to be pleased. GTW had chosen a difficult and potentially dangerous path by

negotiating independently instead of submitting to national agreements. "A labor contract negotiated by a 10,000-mile system does not address the operating characteristics of a high cost, short haul carrier . . . such as GTW," Maas explained. Success in this regard had come as the result of several factors converging during Maas's watch. There was, of course, the firm legacy of those who had gone before, but Maas also profited from new and invigorating breezes. After all, the recent demise of well-known rail carriers and public support for President Reagan's demolition of the air controllers union were realities at least grudgingly recognized by rail labor leaders and many in the ranks. And CN sent new signals: It would go along with a strike at GTW if it came to that. Maas was at the right spot at the right time to orchestrate change and he had a talented cadre of senior officers in support. Candor was essential in building good faith. Employee meetings were continued around the system and videotapes were made available; in all cases company officials bluntly explained what they wanted to do and why. "We have a surprise-free policy" because "not being forthright would only create problems farther down the line," said Maas. Candor also required GTW to admit that it had developed a mature business-interruption plan (i.e., strike plan) because, Maas noted dryly, "major portions of our rail market . . . would be permanently lost to motor carriers . . . under a work stoppage." Fortunately, however, the GTW-UTU agreement was hammered out without resorting to federal legislation, a strike, or bankruptcy. If Maas was happy, CN's Ronald Lawless was ecstatic. "I am viewing this as a real breakthrough in our labour contracts. . . . Please accept my congratulations for a job well done," Lawless enthused.[11]

Maas, with support from other senior managers, pressed the campaign for open communication. A pamphlet entitled *Straight Talk About Grand Trunk Western and Proposed Labor Agreement* was mailed to all contract employees, and Maas and others continued to produce videotapes and to hold employee meetings around the system. Questions were often hard-hitting; responses were equally direct. The overarching message was the same: GTW's survival was dependent on increasing business by "providing high quality service at reduced cost." GTW's strategy of openness was reflected in *GT Focus*, which received the Best Newsletter Award and the highest commendation as the "Best Contribution to Labor Management Understanding" from the Association of Railroad Communicators in 1988.[12]

Further gains in productivity followed. In 1989, GTW entered into an agreement with BLE which allowed the company to do away with the three-year apprenticeship requirement for locomotive firemen. Thereafter, GTW established a six-month training period for prospective enginemen. GTW then turned to the nonoperating side. For instance, in 1988 and 1989, data entry responsibility was removed from wayside stations and centralized at GTW's Detroit headquarters. The change reduced employee expenses by $4.5 million. Still, in 1989, wages, salaries, and benefits at GTW remained a stubbornly high percentage of total operating expense—57 percent as opposed to the national average of 45.3.[13]

Burdakin and then Maas instituted several programs and policies that subsequently received varying degrees of support from employees and mid-level managers alike. As early as 1972, Burdakin instituted an affirmative action plan to assure equal opportunity for minorities and women. In the same year, GTW introduced a program to combat alcoholism and drugs. Affirmative action was underscored by federal legislation and the drug plan enjoyed growing support at all levels. More problematic was Transportation Problem Solving, a program to improve the quality of work life through employee-management involvement groups. Middle managers were skeptical while at the same time admitting a dire need to involve contract employees more directly in the company's decision-making processes. They worried, in part, about a lack of support from top management, observing that they had seen other programs come and go with little to show for them. Contract employees were similarly skeptical, for the same reasons, but plans went forward and committees with representation from various crafts and management were established at Battle Creek, Detroit, Flint, Flat Rock, Pontiac, and Port Huron. They were characterized by varying enthusiasm and success but, with only halting support from senior management, essentially perished. This failure was uncharacteristic for Maas, who otherwise scored well in such matters.[14]

One area to which Burdakin and Maas gave unstinting support was safety. Burdakin had been appalled by the lax attitude he found at GTW and immediately moved to institute an aggressive policy. Results were dramatic; reportable injuries dropped by 44 percent in 1972 alone. Diligent efforts were rewarded when GTW won E. H. Harriman Memorial Safety Awards in 1981, 1982, 1983, 1988, and 1989.[15]

Meanwhile, Walter Cramer continued to refine GTW's marketing and sales group to meet the continuing challenges of deregulation, ferocious competition from giant railroads and other modes, a growing movement for free trade in North America, and a rapidly changing world economy. Customers, too, adjusted to these alterations and constantly demanded higher levels of service at lower rates. Railroads, including GTW, responded by more fully embracing the marketing concept, by becoming more market-driven and customer-oriented. They also turned increasingly to contracts which prescribed time limits, service levels, and rates. By the end of 1986, about 70 percent of all traffic on GTW moved under contract—good news and bad news, as it turned out. Contract agreements were designed to attract business, but GTW—with its high terminal costs and short line hauls—found itself in the unenviable position of having to grant "allowances" (discounts) in order to compete. Allowances paid under contracts in 1986 totaled $25.8 million, in 1988 $25.9 million.[16]

If GTW enjoyed few competitive advantages, it had the opportunity to excel in one area—customer relations. Two factors were crucial to GTW's benefit: the location of principal customers in near proximity to the Detroit headquarters and GTW's relatively small size. Consequently, GTW managers had opportunity to study most customer needs at close range, to detect trends readily, and to respond quickly. At least the opportunity was there. The advantage of smaller size would fade quickly, though, if it was not exercised continuously and aggressively. For the most part, Cramer's forces did well in this regard. Indeed, GTW in 1987 and 1988 was one of four North American railroads cited by *Distribution Magazine* for high ratings in service, convenience, pricing, and sales.[17]

There was no chance to rest on laurels. Flexibility and responsiveness were the twin watchwords. Sales offices were closed; hence-

146

During the last half of the 1980s, GM business represented 30 percent of GTW revenue. Photograph courtesy of Grand Trunk Western Railroad.

according to demand, with generally strong years beginning in 1984 and running through the rest of the decade. With assembly plants, parts plants, and loading and unloading facilities dotting GTW's landscape, the road was predictably a beneficiary of better times for the auto industry's "Big Three."[19]

During the last half of the 1980s, General Motors produced 30 percent of GTW's revenues. But GM's market share was slipping, from 46 percent of new car sales in the United States in 1980 to 36.1 percent in 1988. As the huge automaker took stock of its circumstance it focused, in part, on transportation service and cost. Frankly, GM was not satisfied with what railroads were supplying. GM called a meeting for 7 June 1989; the topic— "Integrated Rail Strategy"—was announced; and invitations went forward to every principal railroad in the United States and Canada. "Change and the necessity to manage it," GM gruffly pointed out, "is paramount to meeting competitive forces facing both our industries." In fact, GM had specific requirements in mind for its business moving from Canadian and Michigan points via Chicago: reduced rates, improved and guaranteed transit times; electronic data interchange; increased frequency of train movements and full coordination among connecting carriers for loads and empties as well; consistent high-quality service; and upgraded equipment. The threat was clear enough to railroaders; any carrier or any combination of carriers that could not or would not deliver on GM's demands was to be cut out. For GTW, there was utterly no choice: cars moved to the shops at Port Huron for modifications; dispatchers were alerted to the "new order"; and Dedicated Automobile Rapid Transit (DART) trains joined Short Crew Automobile Trains.[20]

forth, GTW would rely on CN's offices to handle whatever was required away from the road's immediate service area. Solicitation as such would be accomplished from Detroit by a small staff in telemarketing. At the same time, heavy emphasis would be placed on areas of direct contact between customer and carrier—loss and damage, claims, equipment management, billing, tracing, diversions, and expediting. Customers, Cramer noted, often felt they were victims of an uncaring bureaucracy, shunted from department to department in search of information or resolution. To overcome this problem, or at least to minimize it, in 1989 GTW established a customer-service wing under marketing as a single contact for handling questions in these categories.[18]

"GTW does well," recalled former director William K. Smith, "when the cyclical industries do well." Smith, of course, was thinking of the North American motor vehicle industry which recovered at least some of its poise and profitability during the 1980s. Chrysler had tottered toward oblivion, but regained strength; Ford was invigorated; and giant General Motors plodded toward a redefined but still very substantial place in the sun. Production ebbed and flowed

147

Ford was equally demanding. GTW had not been a major player in Ford's transportation spectrum until acquisition of DT&I in 1980, but Ford had taken GTW's side in that case and thus became GTW's second largest customer. Ford's respected Richard Haupt worried about GTW's sometimes weak financial performance, but noted with pleasure that the company was not mired in bureaucratic procedures. "It has great ability to respond," said Haupt, who had ample opportunity to compare GTW with other transportation companies. After all, he noted, Norfolk Southern, Conrail, and CSX—each one powerful and well managed—were readily at hand and constantly bid fair to be Ford's favorite railroad transportation provider. Haupt minced no words. He did not consider GTW "the *best* managed railroad around these days," adding quickly however that GTW was "pretty sophisticated in dealing with a huge shipper"—hardly "characteristic of a regional railroad."[21]

GTW/DT&I handled no fewer than 293,823 carloads for Ford during the years 1980 through 1984. These included parts, automobiles, and trucks—all remunerative but requiring constant attention. The logistics in moving parts from vendors to assembly plants was especially complex; failure to deliver on a timely basis resulted in expensive lost production and very unhappy managers at Ford. Such was the case when cars from Woodhaven and Dearborn were "completely mishandled" in Chicago with subsequent distress at Ford's St. Paul assembly plant. A low key manager there dryly observed that "this type of performance is detrimental to our premium freight objective," but another Ford manager was much less tolerant when GTW failed in delivery of specialized equipment for the Lima engine plant where a shift had to be shut down. "Reliable service by GTW is mandatory to sufficiently run this plant," he fumed. "If you cannot get empty cars returned each day, Lima Engine Plant will examine other methods of transportation." Ford's Dearborn headquarters sternly added: "GTW must have a system in place to move rail cars we ship without being monitored by Ford personnel."[22]

Just as General Motors tightened its transportation requirements, so, too, did Ford. "We will do business only with railroads that demonstrate the ability to deliver our products reliably, undamaged and at a competitive price," Walter Cramer was told in the fall of 1989. Ford was as categoric as it was emphatic. "We expect our railroads to demonstrate the reliability of all aspects of the service they provide." Neither was this warning for a limited period of time. "We expect our railroads to demonstrate a commitment to never ending productivity improvement." Ford invited response. At GTW it came from Walter Cramer who agreed with Ford's basic premise that railroads must assume "more responsibility for the total transportation function." Cramer also pledged GTW to provide Ford with an adequate supply of enclosed bi-level and tri-level auto racks; pre-loading inspection of equipment; state of the art ramps and facilities; competitive contracts; reduced claims and reduced delay in claim processing; and electronic data exchange to improve data communication between Ford and GTW. Cramer reminded that GTW and the rail industry at large had "come a long way," but admitted that "we still have a long way to becoming market driven." There was reason for optimism, Cramer told Ford, on the productivity issue where GTW was making strides with unions to become more flexible. Ultimately, though, GTW had no option. "We must be a vastly different company by the early 1990s if we are to survive," Cramer properly concluded.[23]

Aside from the "Big Three" automakers, other motor vehicle manufacturers—including foreign-owned Mazda Motor Corporation would have an impact on GTW. This Hiroshima-based firm had produced more than 15 million vehicles since its founding in 1920 and by 1983 was exporting to 120 countries. Ranked third among Japanese automakers, Mazda produced 1.3 million vehicles annually and early in the 1980s anticipated the establishment of its first assembly plant in the United States. Other Japanese firms—Nissan and Honda, for example—had or soon would announce similar plans, and Toyota unveiled its intention of working jointly with General Motors to reopen a GM plant in California. Ford owned a 24.4 percent stake in Mazda and few were surprised when the two companies announced that they were looking at sites in the Midwest and South for a new facility. At stake for the railroad serving this plant would be at least 1,800 inbound containers per month and 800 carloads of finished automobiles. There was predictable elation at GTW in 1984 when Mazda picked a location at Flat Rock, southwest of Detroit, near the GTW (former DT&I) hump yard.[24]

There was no axiomatic assurance, however, that GTW would gain the Mazda business. After all, I-75 and other railroads were immediately at hand; truckers and competing railroads would surely present Mazda with attractive alternative packages leaving GTW with only the burden of switching chores. Mazda candidly admitted "receiving proposals from a number of companies." Gerald Maas was the point man in GTW's campaign. GTW "has more than a keen interest in the Mazda

Gerald Maas shakes hands with Osamu Nobuto, president of Mazda, to complete negotiations establishing GTW as the provider of rail transportation at the new Flat Rock plant. John Burdakin and Edward J. Stasio, standing behind Maas, smile in approval. Photograph courtesy of Grand Trunk Western Railroad.

Motor Corporation," Maas affirmed. "We see our role as the continuation to and from Mazda's assembly lines . . . [and we promise] . . . to explore innovative and efficient operating . . . [procedures] . . . and to share those savings with new partners in Michigan." Mazda executives impassively added GTW's portfolio to an impressive pile of others; Maas was left to brood over the prospects. He was fully aware of Mazda's tradition that called for intense scrutiny of potential business partners and he was also aware that once Mazda committed it was "for the duration." Finally, during the summer of 1985, Mazda announced that it would establish "loading and unloading facilities on the plant site and would execute effective operations with GTW's full assistance," but asked for GTW's "continued concrete assistance and cooperation." Those assurances came quickly and eagerly from Maas. "Our joint efforts to date are only the beginning of what I know will be a long and fruitful partnership," he gleefully responded. GTW had caught the brass ring.[25]

Ground breaking ceremonies were held in May 1985, and the $550 million plant began production

in September 1987. One of the most advanced assembly facilities in the world, Flat Rock could produce 240,000 vehicles annually bearing either Mazda or Ford labels. GTW worked with western carriers to arrange delivery of containers via Chicago after Mazda rejected Canadian National's proposal to handle them through Vancouver. GTW also had exclusive access to Mazda's vehicle shipping yard for outbound set up automobiles, noted a smiling Gerald Maas.[26]

Containers handled for Mazda's account provided a regular and profitable flow of traffic. The rest of GTW's intermodal story was not as pleasant. Container and trailer volumes on GTW shrunk disappointingly at mid-decade while such business among other carriers grew. Yes, GTW could point to astonishing growth on CN's Toronto-Chicago *Laser* intermodal trains. But GTW suffered from unfortunately short corridors (Detroit to Chicago and Detroit to Cincinnati); hostile or ambivalent connections at Cincinnati; and the unfortunate need to "rubber tire interchange" (i.e., deramp, dray, and reramp trailers) in Chicago. Moreover, GTW's high labor costs

149

gave the company little flexibility in setting rates. And an overarching question remained unresolved: Was intermodal operation compensatory? There was sharp division of opinion among GTW managers. An outside study produced a thunderous "perhaps." Cramer referred to the whole issue as "the intemodal dilemma," and believed that "if we cannot achieve profitability we should withdraw from all or parts of these markets." On the other hand, if GTW should get out of intermodal business altogether the company might lose important customers who increasingly looked for alternatives to conventional—spelled boxcar—movement. It *was* a dilemma. GTW chose a conservative course, hedged its bets, and stayed with intermodal service.[27]

Canadian National was not uninterested in GTW's "intermodal dilemma." In the view of CN's W. H. Morin, intermodal opportunity was "not made of two markets (GTW and CN) but really only one." He went on to say, "The necessity to balance flows to competitively price domestic and international containers versus piggybacks, the need to address the competitiveness of various ports, both U.S. and Canadian, and to have a consistent marketing approach with the steamship lines, etc., all point to the requirement for one business approach in this marketplace." "It was," said Morin, "unrealistic and counterproductive to try to compete separately in this unusual market." Consequently, Morin proposed that CN "take over the responsibility and expense for marketing of intermodal on Grand Trunk Western, and take over the responsibility for operation of intermodal

terminals in Detroit and Chicago and integrate them into our Hub Network concept." Maas demurred, seeing Morin's idea as a "major departure from our present structure and mandate." GTW would continue to go it alone in this area and see where the chips fell.[28]

Fortunately, positive change was in the offing. During the summer of 1987, GTW and Burlington Northern implemented an innovative marketing agreement by which BN's Expediter Service reached Detroit—BN's cabooseless intermodal trains handled from Chicago to Detroit by two-person crews and yarded at GTW's MoTerm

Demand at MoTerm was so great that another $7.2 million was required for expansion. Photograph courtesy of Grand Trunk Western Railroad.

facility. MoTerm was further utilized when GTW landed contracts from European and Asian steamship lines for containers. That business received yet another shot in the arm when American President Company signed an agreement for the movement of double-stack containers to Woodhaven, near Detroit. Intermodal volume also increased with establishment of through trains to the Southeast from Detroit in cooperation with CSX, and when

GTW locomotive 5854 once had been Rock Island's 4372. Photograph courtesy of Grand Trunk Western Railroad.

arrangements were made in Chicago for direct rail-to-rail interchange with the Atchison, Topeka & Santa Fe and with Burlington Northern. Pressure was so great at MoTerm that $7.2 million was required to nearly triple its capacity. "This expansion and modernization program reflects the health of Grand Trunk Western's international and domestic container business," enthused Andrew J. Kalabus, director of intermodal marketing. Indeed, GTW's volume of intermodal units increased from 54,523 in 1986 to 119,140 in 1988, moving from loss to profit in the process.[29]

Revenue from other commodity groups showed a mixed pattern. Business from way stations, ordinarily of an agricultural nature, was subject to severe truck competition and volumes ebbed and flowed with demand and rates. In 1989, an important contract with National Steel resulted in unit train movements of coil steel between Ecorse, Michigan, and Portage, Indiana. Coke and coal, nearly 100,000 carloads annually, also added substantially to GTW'a traffic mix. Coke was bound for steel mills in the Detroit area and some coal moved to General Motors plants. Most of the coal, however, was low-sulfur from the West and from Appalachian fields billed in unit-train lots under long-term contracts to various power plants.[30]

Few changes occurred in GTW's traffic patterns during the last half of the decade. Motor vehicles and parts claimed first place with 49.2 percent of total revenues, followed distantly by fuel and chemicals with 19.94 percent.[31]

Burdakin had preached the "good track gospel" to which Maas and David Wilson similarly subscribed. Jointed rail on GTW, they knew, had a maximum lifespan of 30 years given the road's substantial gross ton miles. Engineering reports showed starkly that the functional life of much main line rail would mature in the mid-1980s. An accelerated relay program was called for but, with GTW's mixed financial fortunes, only 87.1 miles of continuously welded rail was installed from 1985 through 1989—much of it in 1985-1986 when significant funding was also allocated for ties and ballast. In addition, 20 miles on the South Bend Subdivision were single-tracked, but enhanced with centralized traffic control (CTC) to maximize fluidity.[32]

Another area that demanded attention was GTW's motive power fleet. By 1985, the company's 255 units had an average age of 19.9 years. David Wilson and his staff contemplated several options: acquisitions of new power, purchase of used power, a massive rebuilding program, and some combination of these. A

151

Shop forces at Port Huron could take special pride in GTW's track inspection car. Photograph courtesy of Grand Trunk Western Railroad.

auto racks, trailer-on-flat-cars (TOFC) flats, covered hoppers, air-slide covered hoppers, as well as common boxcars and humble gondolas. Part of GTW's "new" rolling stock arrived early in the decade when an impressive block of equipment was subleased after demise of the Rock Island. The entire 9,500-car fleet was maintained, modified, and upgraded by forces at the car shop in Port Huron. Shopmen there properly took special pride in track inspection car no. 15013 which they fashioned from a former Amtrak lounge car in 1982.[34]

necessary corollary was the need to finance such activity. Beginning in the mid-1980s, GTW entered into several agreements by which it leased equipment, bought equipment formerly leased, and sold and leased back equipment. Locomotives, all of General Motors derivation, included GP-38, SD-38, GP-40, and SD-40 models. The sale/leaseback program was attractive on several counts: GTW could use outside financing, could take advantage of the sale of tax benefits, and could provide power less expensively than buying new. For shop forces at Battle Creek there was a special benefit: jobs. Talented workers and thrifty managers there rebuilt an average of 21 units annually between 1982 and 1985, and with continuation of leaseback programs this pattern continued. Consequently, by 1990 actual ownership of locomotives by the company stood at about 60 percent, and with various banks and leasing companies about 40 percent.[33]

Similarly, GTW purchased or leased great numbers of new and used rolling stock during the 1980s. Included were high-cube 86-foot boxcars, damage free boxes, flat cars, bi-level and tri-level

Maas persisted in the earlier policy of pruning line segments. The reasons were many and varied, but the process was less painful than previously because of the Staggers Act and a more relaxed posture at the Interstate Commerce Commission. A particularly intriguing corollary was the dramatic rise of short line and even regional railroads. Late in 1985, for example, Illinois Central Gulf sold its 681-mile Iowa Division to Chicago, Central & Pacific; in 1986, Chicago & North Western sold 965 miles of line to Dakota, Minnesota & Eastern; and in 1987 Soo Line conveyed more than 2,000 miles to Wisconsin Central Ltd. In all cases large established carriers sold properties to newly created companies that promised greater responsiveness to shipper needs and, in many cases, featured more flexible agreements with workers. The short line movement did not miss Michigan where several organizations looked to life or expansion of operation through acquisition of GTW lines. Much activity centered on Durand, GTW's historic crossbands. The Bay City branch, to which trackage owned by the former Penn

Central recently had been added, was sold in 1987 to Central Michigan Railway, a new organization allied with Detroit & Mackinac Railway. The line to Grand Rapids and Muskegon, which also emanated from Durand, was sold to Central Michigan at the same time. A branch from this line, striking northwestward from near Owosso to Greenville, was parceled out in chunks. Owosso Junction to Ashley was sold to the state of Michigan and Ashley to Carson City was acquired by a group of shippers. Both segments were then leased to Tuscola & Saginaw Bay Railway. The remaining portion, Carson City to Greenville, met the scrapper's torch. Elsewhere, the former Jackson line was further pared from South Lyon to Lakeland in 1985 and Orchard Lake, near Pontiac, to South Lyon in 1987. The Caseville line was also peeled back in 1984 and 1987 from Pigeon to Imlay City and from Orion to South Dryden. Neither was the former DT&I spared. Temperance Yard in Toledo and the Napoleon branch (Malinta to Napoleon, Ohio) disappeared in 1988 and everything south of Springfield, Ohio, in 1987 and 1990. (Springfield to Fayne, 27 miles, was sold to a governmental authority which leased the line to Indiana & Ohio Rail System.) By the end of 1990, the only surviving branches were short pieces of the Caseville and Jackson lines, Pavilion to Kalamazoo, and Richmond to Pontiac, plus a few important lines in the Detroit terminal area.[35]

GTW, noted Robert A. Walker, was motivated to lop off these 482 miles of line for several reasons. Perhaps most important was the need for enough cash to properly maintain primary routes—Port Huron-Chicago and Port Huron-Detroit-Flat Rock-Springfield—so as to provide the high-speed requirements of principal customers. In some cases, important shippers on branches were lost and in other cases revenue predictions had proved too optimistic. Portions of these lines showed little or no potential for

Gerald Maas (center); chief mechanical officer, Robert G. Lipmyer (left); and shop superintendent, Raymond W. Kelly (right), admire the craftsmanship shown in the interior of the new inspection car. Photograph courtesy of Grand Trunk Western Railroad.

improved revenues and were salvaged while others were attractive to short line operators which, in their own way, also prospered as a consequence of the Staggers Act. Moreover, from GTW's point of view, these short lines would serve as valuable feeders. In any event, proceeds from sales or salvage yielded $7.01 million in nonoperating revenues for the years 1987-90, inclusive.[36]

Additional non-operating revenues derived severally. Fiber-optic contracts concluded with American Telephone & Telegraph, Michigan Bell, and several others were nonexclusive, renewable agreements that yielded $2.4 million in 1985 alone and gave GTW free use of more than 195 miles of cable for transmission of long-distance calls and computer data. In the case of Trailer Train, a corporation owned by American railroads and in the business of owning and leasing freight cars and making them available to railroads on a daily car-hire basis, GTW sold half of its interest in 1987 contributing substantially to the nonoperating revenue account.[37]

Another way to improve financial performance was to reduce claims of all types. GTW was especially vulnerable to thieves, vandals, and trespassers because of the high-value lading it

Substantial savings could be realized from abandonment of low-density lines such as the Caseville branch which was especially vulnerable to snowed-in cuts. Photograph courtesy of Grand Trunk Western Railroad.

handled and because of some of the distressed neighborhoods through which its trains passed. Amateur and journeyman thieves alike were particularly drawn to loaded auto racks for the purpose of stealing radios, tape decks, batteries, and the like. They also favored tires and wheel covers from fully loaded auto parts cars as well as liquor, tobacco, and electronic goods from trailers aboard TOFC flats or in lots. The movement of illicit drugs across the international boundary presented other problems at Port Huron and Detroit. All of it posed a constant challenge for James W. Aldrich and the Grand Trunk Police Department. Aldrich noted that the role of railroad police in the 1980s had become more technical and more dangerous, and that patrolmen were vexed by growing fears of litigation and liability. Still, there were important victories. General Motors, for example, was especially pleased to commend GTW security personnel for "their desire to protect our vehicles" and "management's commitment to stopping theft and vandalism."[38]

In 1986, the general claims department was renamed the safety and accident investigation department. This was not semantic sleight of hand. As Earl C. Opperthauser observed, the "new" department was authorized to initiate "a comprehensive program to reduce the risk . . . of liability . . . and thus minimize financial impact on the company." Risk management, he clarified, meant "preventing a legal problem, not getting us out of a problem." Included in Opperthauser's program were grade crossing education and means by which to combat onerous liabilities under the Federal Employers' Liability Act (FELA), a turn-of-the-century law for railroads and railroad employees unmodified by later legislation providing no-fault workmen's compensation programs at the state level. Under FELA, an employee is obligated to prove employer negligence through suit. By the late 1980s, FELA awards consumed almost 3 percent of American railroad revenues and, despite sharply lower employee numbers, promised to escalate dangerously in the next decade.[39]

154

GTW's financial performance during the final five years of the 1980s was depressing. The road had operating revenues of $1,626 billion, but operating expenses of $1,655 billion—resulting in an operating ratio of 101.78. GTW earned net profit in four years out of five, but an $8 million loss in 1986 resulted in a profit of only $8.4 for the half-decade.[40]

Grand Trunk Police Department held responsibility for security in yards and elsewhere. Their's was a difficult and dangerous assignment. Photograph courtesy of Grand Trunk Western Railroad.

Neither was the circumstance of Central Vermont a rosy one. As he gathered up railroads for his Guilford collection, Timothy Mellon, scion of the Pittsburgh-based Mellon family, approached CN on at least two occasions about acquiring CV. CN was willing to sell, but only if Mellon would give it perpetual running rights. Mellon would have none of it. In the end, Mellon purchased the largely parallel Delaware & Hudson, a historic competitor for Montreal/New England-New York business.[41]

Canadian National took a "wait and see" attitude as to CV. Maas was impatient, noting that CV's operating ratio was "still unacceptable." An expanded traffic base was essential. Maas and

Earl C. Opperthauser. Photograph courtesy of Grand Trunk Western Railroad.

General Manager Phillip Larson pinned their dreams for such development on the successful establishment of what they called the "New England Auto Terminal," a major automobile distribution center designed to handle vehicles billed from Michigan and Ontario assembly plants and moved to destination, they firmly hoped, on CV via GTW and CN. In this way remunerative traffic would be captive to the parent and two of its GTC roads. Alas, the project perished when a site on another railroad was chosen. It was "a major disappointment," said a dejected Maas, and intensified "the need for the company to develop a permanent solution to its underlying weaknesses." Burdakin in 1985 had pondered the wisdom of seeking an "independent study of CV's viability," and Maas later acted by commissioning an analysis by Temple, Barker & Sloane. Whatever the recommendations, they would not be carried out by Larson, who left CV for a position on the Wheeling & Lake Erie, a newly formed regional using an ancient moniker.[42]

The consultants pointed out that CV's historic function as a bridge carrier had passed and that now CV was primarily a terminating

155

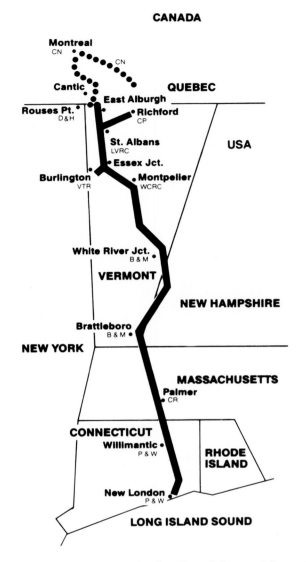

needed revenue. In addition, slow track—down to ten miles per hour—on the jointly operated Connecticut River section also delayed lading, frustrated shippers, and added appreciably to CV's operating costs. All of this added troubles to an already problematic operation. In short, what the analysts found was a regional railroad with costs of a class-one carrier. What medications were prescribed? Three, in the short term, including: increasing CV's traffic base, freezing wages, and reducing employee numbers. In addition, consultants urged significant changes in marketing with a major thrust into haulage agreements with volume and incentive commitments as well as more direct and energetic management of CV's non-rail assets. Even then Temple, Barker & Sloane worried that CV faced an uncertain future.[43]

Christopher J. Burger, 49, who succeeded Larson as general manager at CV on 1 December 1989, certainly had his hands full. A native of New York, educated at Providence College, Burger began his railroad career on the New York Central in 1967 but moved to the Chicago & North Western where he rose through the chairs to become assistant vice president-transportation, and general manager.[44]

Christopher J. Burger. Photograph courtesy of Grand Trunk Western Railroad.

carrier continuously buffeted by swift and unpredictable currents. For instance, Guilford's stewardship of New England roads was questionable, typified by poor track maintenance and acute labor unrest. Shippers deserted Guilford rails in droves with resulting lower traffic for CV which historically moved large blocks of business by way of the Boston & Maine (B&M), a Guilford property. And labor unrest unfortunately spilled over to CV, innocent victim of a secondary boycott when B&M was struck in 1986. Only truckers were winners. On that segment of the Connecticut River line owned by B&M and used by CV poor track condition also frightened Amtrak which in 1987 canceled its *Montrealer*, costing CV much-

CV, like GTW, utilized an annual Santa Train excursion to maintain a sense of family with employees—many of whom were second, third, and even fourth generation railroaders. Photograph courtesy of Central Vermont Railway.

One of many problems that predated Burger's arrival, and would continue to nag, was the Connecticut River line, 49 miles in Vermont and New Hampshire between Windsor and Brattleboro. That trackage, owned by Mellon's Boston & Maine but operated jointly with Central Vermont, was B&M's outlet to the south and west from Wells River and was, of course, part of CV's main route from the international border to New London. B&M under Guilford did not view this route as primary and maintained it accordingly—to the great chagrin of CV and Amtrak, neither of which was successful in persuading B&M as to proper grooming. GTC's managers, especially Robert Walker and Washington attorney Basil Cole, wrestled with the matter and, early in 1988, approved a straightforward approach for CV to buy the line from B&M. Failing that, CV was authorized to work with Amtrak in acquisition. Guilford, which had little use for the line on its own behalf, proved obdurate nevertheless. The state of Vermont chose to involve itself, and together with, CV and Amtrak, agreed to attack in concert. In April, Amtrak asked the Interstate Commerce Commission to condemn the line and to allow Amtrak to purchase it. Despite Guilford's disputations, the ICC

ruled in favor of Amtrak and on 13 September 1988, the line was conveyed to Amtrak which thereupon sold it to CV for the same price ($2.3 million, a part of which came from the state). Rehabilitation started two days later using $3.1 million in federal funds jarred out of Congress by Senator Patrick J. Leahy (D-Vermont). The Herculean task of bringing train speeds from 10-miles-per-hour to 40 for freight and 59 for passenger ended on 20 December with appropriate ceremonies. Amtrak restored its *Montrealer* on 18 July 1989 and, in fact, rerouted it modestly to utilize CV all the way from New London. To advertise that fact and to emphasize the scenic beauty of *Montrealer's* route, Amtrak commissioned illustrator Gil Reid to do a watercolor of its train passing over CV's picturesque Lake Champlain trestle at East Alburg, Vermont. The watercolor graced Amtrak's wall calendar for 1990. Guilford took mighty exception to the condemnation and sale, and pressed the matter in federal courts where it won several battles but eventually lost the war.[45]

The failed New England Auto Terminal project, the unfortunate 24-day secondary boycott levied against CV as a consequence of the strike against Guilford, and trouble with Guilford in the Connecticut Valley—all were body blows for CV. All of these incidents represented lost traffic—in the case of the auto terminal lost *potential* traffic and in the case of the boycott and Connecticut Valley *real* traffic that truckers eagerly grabbed and that Conrail won for its Huntingdon gateway through energetic salesmanship. Robert Rixon and the others responsible for CV's marketing were not about to roll over and play dead, however. Indeed, in 1986 CV won another Golden Freight Car Award for "Rent a

157

Amtrak re-established the *Montrealer* seen here departing White River Junction in June 1990. Photograph courtesy of Charles Bohi.

With the *Montrealer* now moving the entire length of CV from New London to the international boundary, Amtrak commissioned Gil Reid for its wall calendar. Reid illustrated the train crossing the lengthy trestle at East Alburg, Vermont. Photograph courtesy of Amtrak.

Despite its ownership of CV through GTC, CN did not necessarily favor CV over other routing options. In the Connecticut River Valley, near South Charlestown, N.H. Photograph courtesy of John Gruber.

Train," an arrangement with Quaboag Transfer Company whereby the shipper acquired and produced locomotives and equipment plus ramps and the railroad merely provided crews and thoroughfare. "Rent a Train" was devoted solely to the movement of lumber products on trailers, was operated with two-person crews making three round trips weekly between St. Albans and Palmer, and proved profitable for CV. Unfortunately, the trains died in 1988 because of slow running on the Connecticut River line. Adding to that was the continued erosion of CV's overhead traffic. By 1988, 60 percent of business handled from CN terminated on CV. Much of the remaining 40 percent moved via the Palmer gateway with Conrail, which then surpassed the historic connection with B&M at White River Junction in importance for surviving southbound overhead business. Rixon and Burger explored all avenues. Both believed that intermodal service could be profitably reinstituted and both saw advantage in haulage proposals that would give CV new opportunities without being a direct party to divisions and rates.[46]

Burger, like Larson before him, also faced the need to increase productivity. CV had a crew

consist agreement dating from 1983, but negotiations had begun in 1984 seeking agreements that would be less costly than national contracts. But it was slow going. The lengthy work stoppage in 1986 muddied waters and it was not until late 1988 that CV gained additional flexibility in the use of train and engine employees and improved ability to use computers and data terminals. Results were slow to appear, but in 1990 Burger could report that labor expense had been reduced by $2.1 million compared with the previous year. Employee numbers reflected this—208 in 1990, down from 241 in 1989 and 300 in 1985. The process of trimming jobs was sadly painful, but quite necessary.[47]

CV managers also looked for nonoperating income. In 1986, U.S. Sprint leased 225 miles in CV's right-of-way for fiber-optic installation. In addition to leasing revenues, noted Thomas J. Faucett, CV's chief engineer and manager of real estate, the company received free use of more than 100 channels with concomitant savings in communications expense. Further income and savings came from abandonment of part of the Richford branch, 9.4 miles from St. Albans to Sheldon Junction, site of a nasty derailment by a

B&M detour train that tore out a bridge in 1984. Sale of scrap yielded revenue and the state of Vermont acquired the right-of-way for a recreation trail. The rest of the branch, from Sheldon Junction to Richford, remained under lease to the Lamoille Valley Railroad until the fall of 1991 when CV began abandonment proceedings.[48]

By far the greatest opportunity to generate non-operating income was along the shores of Lake Champlain at Burlington, Vermont, where CV owned land that was no longer required for railroad purposes. These lands were appraised in 1981 at $3.5 million if used for development of condominiums. Unfortunately for CV, however, there was much local grumbling over the private use of waterfront property. The company held back, studying options, looking for the proper approach. Finally, after lengthy and expensive study, CV in 1988 proposed a plan with private and public benefit— $170 million to build marinas, a hotel, a restaurant, condominiums, apartments, offices, and stores. That plan, however, received a hostile response. The city of Burlington countered with its proposal for a waterfront park and the state of Vermont and then the city of Burlington both made outright claims on the land. The matter moved to the state legislature and then into the courts. CV faced a dilemma. On the one hand, its financial needs were clear enough but, on the other, the company had no wish for continuation of this public relations nightmare. Ultimately, the case went to arbitration with the railroad responsible for one appraisal and the city oblig-

ated to provide another. The railroad claimed value of $9.4 million, but the city's appraiser weighed in with a mere $1.6 million. Under very curious rules, a third appraiser would make final determination— but he could move no more than 20 percent above the city's figure or no lower than 20 percent below the railroad's claim. As it turned out, the third appraiser felt the property's true value was closer to the city's estimate than to CV's. Settlement occurred early in the fall of 1991. CV licked its wounds, pocketed the paltry settlement, and retained the right to serve local shippers and to maintain connection with Vermont Railroad at Burlington.[49]

The lakefront property case seemed a microcosm of CV's circumstance. The road produced modest net profit in 1986 and 1988 but lost $2 million for the cumulative period 1986-90. In the same years CV's operating ratio was a dismal 110.5. Would the past be prologue? "What to do with Central Vermont?" remained a profoundly disturbing question at both GTC and CN.[50]

The star in GTC's financial crown remained the otherwise unremarked Duluth, Winnipeg & Pacific. "Keep the property strong, achieve maximum efficiency and the DW&P will continue to generate nice income and cash," John Burdakin had forecast in 1984. "In reality," said Burdakin, DW&P "has replaced CN as the financial backbone of GTW." To be sure, DW&P earned net of $12.7 million for the years 1986-90, and its operating ratio averaged 79.9[51]

DW&P was also used as a training ground for those whom John Burdakin and Gerald Maas felt

Richard L. Neumann became general manager of DW&P in 1987. Photograph by Don L. Hofsommer.

would have promising careers within the GTC organization. Early on Phillip Larson moved to Central Vermont and was followed as general manager by Jerome F. Corcoran, Marc H. Higginbotham, and Gene Shepherd—all of whom moved back to Detroit and up the ladder at GTW. Richard L. Neumann took up his duties as general manager in 1987. Born in Lafayette, Indiana, and educated at Purdue, Neumann served as a junior officer in the navy before joining Central Vermont in 1974.

Neumann's challenges on the DW&P were very different from those faced by Burger at CV and Maas and Wilson at GTW. Managers on all three GTC roads were involved in the paradoxical business of trying to inspire a sense of loyalty and cooperation among all levels of employees while at the same time trying to reduce the size and scope of each property; all of them understood that gaining cooperation in the workplace was especially delicate for managers of shrinking companies. At GTW, and especially at CV, it was easy to demonstrate the ravages of competition. On DW&P, however, annual gross ton miles remained essentially constant, average tons per train remained relatively high, and the property was clearly profitable, so employees were less

understanding about cutbacks. They were well aware that employee numbers on their railroad had dropped from 278 in 1985 to 196 in 1990—while gross-ton miles remained roughly the same. But the very fact that tonnage remained flat throughout the 1980s was enough to be concerned about according to Neumann. Moreover, DW&P's revenue per car also had remained stable. Meanwhile, the costs of fuel and labor—operating costs generally—had *not* remained stable, but had gone up appreciably during the same decade. Consequently DW&P, no less than GTW and CV, was obligated to seek greater productivity.[52]

In nearly all cases Neumann found it necessary to spend money in order to make money. Attrition as well as separation programs allowed reduction in personnel but, when DW&P operated its first cabooseless trains in 1988 expenditures were required to upgrade passing tracks with power switches and approach lights and for voice synthesized radio transmissions from hot box detectors to replace digital display boards. At the northern apex of the road, the lift bridge at Ranier was converted in 1989 to remote control with operation directed by dispatchers at Pokegama. Neumann noted in 1988 that DW&P was a Class II railroad bound by Class I labor agreements. That began to change a year later when agreements were signed giving greater flexibility in assignment of various crafts. And on 1 May 1991, an agreement with the United Transportation Union allowed bargaining with that important organization to "negotiate a new local agreement that best suits DW&P/UTU needs." The immediate impact was to eliminate second brakemen on all trains and to eliminate work rule restrictions and arbitrary payments. A separation agreement was also part of the package. Despite the trauma of change, morale remained high among those who labored on behalf of DW&P— "located just south of the Arctic circle," as a Detroit writer put it. DW&P earned additional Harriman safety awards in 1984 through 1987.[53]

Traffic patterns changed by degree. Lumber and potash remained the primary commodities in DW&P's traffic mix with nearly half of all loads in most years. Paper and wood pulp also remained important but real growth took place in grain, machinery, automobile, chemical, and intermodal business. By 1990, "all other commodities"—everything other than lumber, potash, wood pulp, and paper—

accounted for a very pleasant 35 percent of the mix. Local billings and deliveries also improved. In 1990, nine local customers received 875 cars (propane, limestone, methanol, and chemicals) and one customer, Potlatch Corporation at Cook, dispatched 1,324 cars of oriented strand board or "oxboard." In addition, Boise Cascade at International Falls was responsible for more than 3,500 cars (paper and chemicals) via its Minnesota, Dakota & Western Railway (MD&W) connecting the plant with DW&P at Ranier. At Pokegama/Superior, Burlington Northern remained the primary connection, followed by Chicago & North Western, Soo Line, and Wisconsin Central. And, Neumann beamed, after 15 August 1991, traffic moving to and from these connections arrived over an all continuously welded rail route between Ranier and Pokegama.[54]

The nature and circumstance of DW&P's service and operation seemed firmly set as the road rolled into the decade of the 1990s, but fluidity characterized the region's overall railroad landscape. Burlington Northern maintained primacy among players at the Lakehead, but future strategy of Chicago & North Western and Soo Line in that part of the world re-mained blurry. The joker, Neumann observed,

The nature and circumstance of DW&P's service and operation seemed firmly set as the road rolled into the 1990s. Photograph courtesy of Duluth, Winnipeg & Pacific Railway.

162

might prove to be the spritely newcomer, Wisconsin Central Ltd., which was sure to bid for passover business moving between the Lake-head and Chicago. Even tiny Minn-esota, Dakota & Western toyed with expansion. In 1989, MD&W explored the idea of trackage rights over DW&P from Ranier to Poke-gama using Roadrailer trains. DW&P did agree to participate in a test run with RoadRailer, but Boise Cascade and Burlington Northern ulti-mately chose domestic containers moving from MD&W over DW&P in dedicated trains to BN for breakup at Northtown (Minneapolis). BN, inciden-tally, maintained its trackage rights between Pokegama and Ranier for other business.[55]

As books were closed on the 1980s, GTC proper-ties were in good physical condition and were man-aged by a team that had directed the holding company to profit in four out of five years in the last portion of the decade; GTC enjoyed $36,264,000 in total income for the years 1985 through 1989. In addition, these managers had a two-decade frame of reference—the cumulative experience and legacy of Bandeen's experiment—to assist them as they charted a course for the 1990s.[56]

NOTES

1. CN, Annual Report (1976): 1; Ibid. (1977): 3, 5; Ibid. (1978): 3-4; Ibid. (1980): 7-8.
2. Ibid., (1981): 7; Tabular data from CN annual reports, 1974-81.
3. Ibid., (1982): 6-7; Ibid. (1983): 6-7; Ibid. (1984): 6-7.
4. Ibid., (1985): 4-6; Ibid. (1986): 6.
5. Ibid., (1986): 6; *The Globe and Mail*, 21 October 1986; GTW, Minute Book No. 10, 511.
6. *Transportation in America: A Statistical Analysis of Transportation in the United States—Supplements, Updates and Correction*, 8th ed. (Westport: Eno Foundation, 1990), 8; CN, Annual Report (1989): 10; Gus Welty, "The Search for Productivity," *Railway Age* 185 (November 1984): 31-34; Frank N. Wilner, *Railroads and Productivity: A Matter of Survival* (Washington: Association of American Railroads, 1985).
7. Bruce Wigent to J. F. Corcoran, 6 June 1986; J. F. Corcoran to B. R. Wigent, 26 June 1986 (PF 790).
8. GTC, Annual Report (1986): 3, 13; *Railway Age* 187 (November 1986): 23; *Modern Railroads* 41 (October 1986): 14-15; GTW, Executive Committee Book No. 9, Executive Minute No. 675.
9. GTC, Annual Report (1987): 13; Donald E. Gagen to All Labor Leaders, 7 January 1987 (PF 790);
10. *GTC Reporter*, April 1987, 1; Detroit Free Press, 20 July 1988.
11. *Traffic World* (25 July 1988): 11; *Modern Railroads* 43 (August 1988): 14; G. L. Maas to John H. D. Sturgess, 19 October 1988 (PF 791); Ronald E. Lawless to G. L. Maas, 20 July 1988 (PF 790).
12. GTW, Minute Book No. 10, 571: *GT Focus* (March/April 1989): 1-3; GTW, Minute Book No. 10, 552.
13. GTC, Annual Report (1989): 6, 9; *GT Focus* (October-November 1988): 1-2; GTC, Annual Report (1989): 6, 11.
14. GTC, Annual Report (1972): 28; Transportation Problem Solving Presentation (Summary of Afternoon Session), 17 April 1984; TPS Handbook, n.d. [1986?]; *GT Reporter* (April 1986): 4; J. K. Krikau, interview, 11 August 1989.
15. GTC, Annual Report (1972): 27; Ibid. (1982): 9; *GT Reporter* (August 1983): 5; *GT Reporter* (June 1984): 7; GTC, Annual Report (1988): 6; *Rail News Update* No. 2550 (6 June 1990): 2.
16. GTC, Annual Report (1986): 2, 16; Ibid. (1988): 6.
17. Ibid., (1985): 9.
18. Walter H. Cramer, interview, 11 August 1989; Elaine Lyons, interview, 11 August 1989; Thomas Brady, interview, 8 March 1990; GTC, Annual Report (1989): 9.
19. William K. Smith, interview, 24 September 1989; *Wall Street Journal*, 17, 24 January, 30 March, 23 May, 28 July 1989.
20. Tabular data from GTC annual reports, 1985-89; *Wall Street Journal*, 15 February, 16 October, 14 December 1989; General Motors Corporation, "Integrated Rail Strategy," 7 June 1989.
21. Richard Haupt, interview, 6 March 1990.
22. Ford Motor Company, 1980-84 (data); G. R. Bakke to P. L. Manion, 18 February 1987; D. E. Dombrowski to G. L. Maas, 7 December 1987; E. L. Porath to G. L. Maas, 17 December 1987 (PF 123).
23. C. F. Wilkins to W. H. Cramer, 30 October 1986; W. H. Cramer to C. F. Wilkins, 1 December 1986 (PF 500).
24. Mazda, Annual Report (1983): 1; *Journal of Commerce*, 3 December 1984; GTC, Annual Report (1989): 8; *Business Week* (9 September1985): 94-95.
25. *GT Reporter* (March 1985): 1; G. L. Maas to Kunio Ochiai, 20 February 1985; K. Ochiai to G. L.

Maas, 12 July 1985; G. L. Maas to K. Ochiai, 12 July 1985 (PF 135): Walter Cramer, interview, 21 November 1991.

26. Mazda, Annual Report (1987): 3-4, 26-29; T. Kunita to Y. G. Bourdon, 9 July 1985; R. D. Flaig to G. L. Maas, 20 September 1985 (PF 135); GTC, Annual Report (1987): 8.

27. GTC, Annual Report (1986): 14; Temple, Barker & Sloane, GTW Intermodal Profitability Study, 1 July 1986; W. H. Cramer to G. L. Maas, 14 July 1986; W. H. Cramer to G. L. Maas, 13 August 1986 (PF 504).

28. W. H. Morin to G. L. Maas, 23 March 1987; G. L. Maas to W. H. Morin, 16 April 1987 (PF 500).

29. *Modern Railroads* 42 (August 1987): 14; Ibid. 43 (January 1988): 22; GTW, Minute Book No. 10, 575-76; *Modern Railroads* 43 (July 1988): 12; G. L. Maas to Richard Oliver, 6 June 1989 (PF 500).

30. GTC, Annual Report (1989): 11; Bill Rowe, interview, 30 August 1991.

31. Tabular data from GTC annual reports.

32. GTC, Minute Book No. 9, 479-80, 484; GTC, Minute Book No. 10, 500.

33. Ibid., 448-49, 461, 474, 478-79; GTC, Minute Book No. 10, 516; GTW, Locomotive Requirement Study, 1986-90 (PF 900); GTW, Locomotive Roster, 4-23-91.

34. GTW, Minute Books 7-10, passim.; *GT Reporter* (November 1982): 5.

35. *Trains* 50 (November 1990): 46-47; GTW, Statement of Trackage, n.d. [1991], Engineering department; *GT Reporter* (October 1986): 6; GTW, Minute Book No. 10, 604-5.

36. Robert A. Walker, interview, 7 March 1990; GTC, Annual Report (1989), 27; GTW, Minute Book No. 10, 516-17, 525-26.

37. GTW, Executive Committee Minute Book No. 9, Executive Minutes 662-64, 667-69; GTC, Annual Report (1985): 16 and (1989): 4; GTW, Executive Committee Book No. 9, Executive Minute No. 678.

38. James A. Aldrich, interview, 24 October 1990; R. E. Hatfield to G. L. Maas, 3 March 1986; G. E. Bodrie to G. L. Maas, 25 March 1987 (PF 122).

39. GTW, Board Meeting, 10 November 1989, Risk Management Activities Report, Law Department.

40. GTC, Statistical Highlights 1981 through 1990, 4.

41. David Thomas, "Tough Enough to Hurt," *Canadian Business* 55 (November 1982): 34.

42. Yvon H. Masse, interview, 24 May 1989; CV, Minute Book, 119, 123, 128; Howard Nicholas to John Burdakin, 7 March 1985 (PF 102).

43. Temple, Barker & Sloane, "Strategic Plan for the Central Vermont Railway: Executive Summary," 14 September 1989; William J. Rennicke to Robert A. Walker, 20 September 1989 (PF 102.10).

44. *St. Albans Messenger*, 6 December 1989; *Who's Who in Railroading and Rail Transit,* 12th ed. (New York: International Thomson Transport Press, 1985), 43-44.

45. GTC, Annual Report (1987): 24; GTC, Minute Book No. 3, 245-46, 259-60; Statement of Boston & Maine Corporation, National Railroad Passenger Corporation, and Central Vermont Railway, Regarding Implementation of the Commission's Decision and Order Dated 4 August 1989; ICC Finance Docket No. 31259, 14 September 1988; *GTC Today* (Spring 1989): 6; *Modern Railroads* 44 (January 1989): 1, 5; *New York Times,* 24 July 1989; Ira Rosenfeld, "Guilford Seeks Justice Department Probe, ICC Refuses to Overturn Arbitration," *Traffic World* 223 (20 August 1990): 19-23.

46. R. E. Lawless to Richard Haupt, 19 May 1989 (PF 102); Robert L. Rixon, interview, 9 August 1989; *Modern Railroads* 41 (June 1986): 25-26; GTC, Annual Report (1986): 19; Ibid. (1988): 13; Chris Burger to John D. Guppy, 20 December 1990 (PF 102.24).

47. GTC, Annual Report (1986): 20; Ibid. (1988): 13; Ibid. (1990): 14.

48. *GTC Reporter* (October 1986): 3; CV, Directors Minutes, 137.

49. GTC, Annual Report (1988): 18; *Burlington Free Press,* 9 June 1990; Chris Burger to R. M. Gillis, et. al., 21 February 1991 (PF 102.25).

50. GTC, Statistical Highlights 1986 through 1990, CV-5.

51. John H. Burdakin to J. M. LeClair, 19 October 1984 (PF 105); Tabular data from GTC annual reports, 1986-90.

52. Richard L. Neumann, interview, 26 August 1991.

53. GTC, Annual Report (1987): 19, 21; GTW, Minute Book No. 10, 598; GTC, Annual Report (1989): 15; DW&P, Press Release, n.d. [April 1991]; *GT Reporter* (February 1987): 5.

54. Tabular data from GTC annual reports, 1984-90; Richard L. Neumann, interview, 26 August 1991.

55. *Traffic World* 227 (15 July 1991): 22; E. L. Braaten to Richard L. Neumann, 18 May 1989; Walter Cramer to R. L. Neumann, 10 October 1989 (PF 103).

56. Tabular data from GTC annual reports, 1985-89.

9   GT   THE IDES OF MARCH

> We have set Grand Trunk on a path toward self-sufficiency, profitability and long term viability.
>
> Gerald L. Maas, 18 November 1988, to Management Employees.

Six-feet-two-inches in height, broad in the shoulders, ample of girth, Gerald L. Maas presented an imposing figure. And he meant to burn his own imposing brand on the Grand Trunk Corporation. This rapid-talking, fast-moving, fourth-generation railroader would prove to be a risk-taker—not merely within the traditional railroad framework, but within a broader business context.

Relocation of GTC/GTW headquarters to a new building represented the most profound manifestation of Maas's approach. The general office facility at 131 West Lafayette had been acquired for $1 million in 1951, was inadequate in terms of space after DT&I and D&TSL became part of the family, and presented employees with irksome parking problems in a downtown suffering rapid deterioration. Robert Bandeen thought he had never seen a more dark, depressing workplace. Several floors had been remodeled, however, and the handsome GT sign from the former Brush Street Station boldly proclaimed Grand Trunk's ownership from atop the ten-story struc-

ture. Despite these improvements another location was clearly desirable. Even before creation of GTC in 1971, CN had considered moving headquarters functions to Battle Creek or to some suburban community and Burdakin and Bandeen later toyed with the idea of presenting the Detroit building to a nonprofit institution. It was not until Maas became president, however, that a fully acceptable package was crafted. During the summer of 1986, developers of the former Stroh Brewery site on the edge of downtown Detroit extended a tantalizing offer for the ten-year lease of a one-story building originally designed as an office-showroom structure. Meanwhile, a buyer offered $1.7 million for GTC's building on West Lafayette. Maas saw in the combination a means to generate cash and reduce overhead costs while at the same time providing a modern, attractive work environment for headquarters personnel. GTC board members saw it similarly.[1]

The handsome new facility was dedicated on 16 October 1987. "Moving to a new home is both an exciting and challenging experience," enthused a smiling Gerald Maas. He was quite correct. The 144,000-square-foot structure was nicely appointed, completely fitted out with new furniture, featured advance design voice and data transmission capacity, and was adequate for

550 employees who moved in from the old headquarters and two other downtown locations. There were intangible benefits, too. Employees in the new environment took more pride in themselves, in their work, and in their employer. In addition, Maas perceived that the new building enhanced teamwork and instilled a new feeling of professionalism.[2]

Maas personally embraced and fervently preached a "we can do it" philosophy. He underscored the word "we." Only by working together, Maas argued, could "a profitable future be assured." And without profitability there would be no future for *anybody* at GTC. Maas's managerial philosophy for GTC was framed, then, by his belief in the need for sustained profitability and by his unshakable faith in the value of teamwork. His would be a style of "empowerment," of "openness," of creating an atmosphere in which managers and contract employees could more successfully wrestle with the trauma of change—change, he was convinced, that was both necessary and sure to come.[3]

"Empowerment" for Maas meant, in part, a delegation of authority. "People need a voice and the security to say what they think." That could be achieved only in an environment with "no kingdoms"—in an environment fostering more effective coordination among departments. As president, Maas would review all employment, salary, and promotion decisions as well as authorities for expenditures. He would also orchestrate overall plans and directions. But the vice presidents and general managers—Walter Cramer (marketing), David Wilson (operating), Paul Tatro and then Jerome Corcoran (finance), Robert Walker (corporate planning), Richard Neumann (DW&P), and Phil Larson and then Chris Burger (CV)—were expected to be activists. Maas desired lively and innovative discussion and debate followed by vigorous action from this small band of senior managers. He would empower them, yes, but he would hold them accountable.[4]

GTW's office building on West Lafayette in downtown Detroit. Bandeen thought he had never seen a more dark, depressing workplace. Photograph courtesy of Grand Trunk Western Railroad.

166

Not surprisingly, Maas would involve his top assistants in the crucial matter of strategy. The holding company concept remained, they knew, a continuing experiment in the eyes of the parent. Thus, in a real way, their task was to give Canadian National as much time and flexibility as possible for it to select options regarding all properties south of the border. That meant, in a disturbing way, that they should be available when potential suitors came calling. Nothing new in that, of course; several railroads had looked at GTW over the years. In the early 1980s, Missouri Pacific considered acquisition, GTW had brief conversation with Louisville & Nashville (Family Lines), Santa Fe, and Southern, and Timothy Mellon indicated passing interest in both Central Vermont and Grand Trunk Western. At mid-decade, Norfolk Southern, CN's second most important connection for inbound traffic behind the GTC roads, looked at GTW. Later, in 1989, Chicago & North Western's chairman, Robert Schmiege, told his employees that GTW might be a good merger partner for that road, but he foresaw "problems in negotiating with the Canadian government" for such acquisition. During the same year the Henley Group expressed interest in GTW and CV.[5]

Perhaps the most intriguing proposal came from Wertheim Schroder & Company, which suggested a leveraged buyout of Canadian National's Grand Trunk Corporation (and its three railroads) and Soo Line, in which archrival Canadian Pacific had more than a 50 percent

Employees in the new environment took more pride in themselves and in their work. Photograph courtesy of Sam Breck.

stake. Wertheim Schroder urged formation of a new company designed to take over and operate all of these assets—with possibly CN or CP, or even both of them, taking minority investment positions. There was much to commend the idea from a strategic point of view. Soo trackage could provide a link between GTW and DW&P (Chicago to the Lakehead), to CN's advantage; CP for its part, could use GTW between Chicago and its Ontario portal at Detroit, could gain access to the Cincinnati gateway over the former DT&I, and could gain entree to much of New England via CV. With both CN and CP throwing their southbound traffic to the new road and with savings resulting from retirement of redundant capacity in the antecedent properties, the financial picture for the proposed road looked good. CN analysts pointed to potential problems, however. Of special concern was DW&P which gave CN direct access to important competitive connections at Pokegama/Superior. Additionally, CN marketing forces fretted that a combined GTC/Soo would upset the generally cordial relationship with Burlington Northern; if that relationship soured, BN could move toward a dangerous alliance with CP. For their part, CN engineering officers pointed to what they called, "an accumulated deferred maintenance overhang" at Soo. The major rub for CN, however, was the short, profitable, and strategically located DW&P, and the competitive edge it gave CN; without DW&P the Wertheim Schroder package lost luster. It died accordingly.[6]

All of this was defensive in character, but there was little GTC managers could do to advance an offensive campaign to expand CN's operations in the United States. Yes, GTW had gained DT&I and the Shore Line, but in the Milwaukee case GTC—and thus CN—missed the brass ring. GTW also lost in 1984 when Chesapeake & Ohio snapped up the short but profitable Port Huron & Detroit Railroad—right in GTW's backyard. With the parent unable or unwilling to promote further expansions, GTC managers were forced to examine other means of protecting CN's investments in the United States.[7]

That meant annual review or revision of five-year business plans. These must be fluid, Maas insisted, "indicating the direction—but not necessarily the route" GTC would take. Indeed, these plans were altered year by year to reflect an ever-changing business landscape and Maas's growing imprint on GTC affairs. During the mid-1980s, these plans focused on GTC's attempt to deal with deregulation and put forward strategies of geographic market expansion and plant rationalization. Maas was pleased at the progress made in these areas—noting that such progress reflected plans to place GTC "on a path toward self-sufficiency, profitability, and long-term viability." The task for the next decade however, would be to "achieve prosperity." To that end, said Maas, the thrust in the 1990s would be "to build on the more productive and competitive rail base and to pursue limited diversification and expansion in non-rail ventures with high yield potential."[8]

The idea of diversification under GTC's broad umbrella was not new. Bandeen's long-term objective had been to convert GTC into a profitable corporation, the stock of which would trade publicly. Meanwhile, GTC's substantial tax loss shelter could be utilized by acquisition of profitable corporations which, he believed, ought to be related to transportation as much as possible but not involved in it. Early in 1973, Bandeen proposed as much to CN's board which was generally receptive but wanted feedback on the issue from American businessmen on GTC's board. Animated discussion followed. GTC's board, in general, felt diversification of this sort was a good concept with reasonable risk entailed. Moreover, diversification might provide a good way for CN to recoup some of the money it had

sunk into Grand Trunk Western over the years prior to 1971. The CN board then asked for a specific proposal. With responsibility back in its court, the GTC board looked at several opportunities, such as New York real estate, Berwick Forge, and the knitting machine division of Rockwell International. Special attention was paid L. B. Foster Company, a firm principally engaged in wholesaling rail, pipe, piling, highway products, and construction equipment. Nothing came of any of this as Bandeen became preoccupied with matters at CN and as John Burdakin and crew wrestled with the new era of railroad deregulation. GTC did, however, create several corporate vehicles required for diversification: Domestic One Leasing Corporation and three similar cousins.[9]

The next surge of activity came in the mid-1980s when Burdakin and then Maas turned increasingly to Paul Tatro to find diversification opportunities that would allow GTC to achieve long-term profitability and financial independence while at the same time providing a vital adjunct for CN Rail in the United States. To this end, Maas and Tatro pressed the idea of moving

Burdakin and then Maas turned increasingly to Paul Tatro to find diversification opportunities. Photograph courtesy of Grand Trunk Western Railroad.

GTC into limited partnership arrangements. These would be, they said, non-rail ventures, and would utilize GTC's net operating losses and investment tax credits. GTC's prime focus would remain on its three railroads but, as Tatro noted, diversification would improve GTC's financial strength and in that way enhance "performance of the basic rail transportation function."[10]

Diversification took real form in 1987, when GTC acquired the outstanding shares of Relco Financial Corporation (Relco) at a cost of $25.7 million in cash and notes plus $38.6 million in liabilities collateralized by leased assets. Relco, born in 1969, once had financed and leased a wide variety of items but by 1984 had come to concentrate on the lease of automobiles and light trucks.[11]

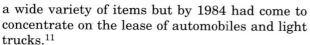

A year later, in 1988, diversification interest intensified greatly as Paul Tatro took the point position in a bold plan to join with others in acquisition of CG&T Industries, which held VMV Enterprises and the Paducah & Louisville Railroad as wholly owned subsidiaries. VMV's function was to rebuild and lease of diesel-electric locomotives and locomotive and marine engines. Its massive plant at Paducah, Kentucky, once had been the main locomotive shop for Illinois Central Railroad and its successor, Illinois Central Gulf (ICG). Paducah & Louisville, too, derived from ICG which, in 1986, determined to retain only a core route from Chicago to New Orleans. Massive line sales followed and included those constituent to Paducah & Louisville. ICG, with reduced need for locomotive maintenance, also sold the Paducah Shop. The package Tatro tailored called for GTC to invest $7.5 million to acquire a limited partnership interest in CG&T (in essence, the Paducah Shop and Paducah & Louisville). The major partner would be First Chicago Venture Capital, a subsidiary of First Chicago Bank. The underlying justification was to maximize return to the partners through earnings that would be enhanced by using GTC's tax benefits. A thorough due diligence followed and the report was generally favorable. GTC backed out at the last

minute, however, apparently because of concern in Montreal over VMV's viability and resistance on the part of one or two of GTC's own board members.[12]

Whether or not GTC made the proper decision in the Paducah matter, Gerald Maas would continue the search for diversification. By the summer of 1990, GTC staffers had looked at "some one hundred acquisition candidates" and the process was continuing. But those staffers did not include Paul E. Tatro, who resigned to take a senior position with the Kentucky operation. In any event, Robert Walker picked up Tatro's baton and warmed to the task of diversification. At the summer board meeting in 1990 he affirmed his interest in diversification by reminding directors that it was important for GTC to find ways "to even out ups and downs." This could be accomplished in part by using investment tax credits from the purchase of capital equipment that could be carried forward. GTC had so many of these, he argued, that several would expire before they could be used.[13]

The strategy developed by Maas, Walker, and Bonnie Reyes—GTC treasurer—was straightforward. GTC would look for companies with the following characteristics: a history of strong earnings; traditional in focus and scope; strong management teams that could stay in place; and the capacity to finance and service their own debt.

Such acquisitions, said Maas, would not show debt on the books of GTC or CN, and would not be considered unless GTC could formulate an acceptable "exit strategy" that would define on what basis GTC would drop the business—usually in three to five year. GTC's raison d'etre, Maas earnestly affirmed, was its rail operations—now and in the future—but rational diversification would be "helpful financially" since GTC would invest and share in profits and would apply credits against profits deriving form non-rail investments.[14]

GTC's diversification holdings in the summer of 1990 included the following (mostly limited partnerships):

Diversification plans would go forward, but GTC's focus would remain on its three rail operations. #392 at South Bend, Indiana. November 1989. Photograph courtesy of David Korkhouse.

1. Relco Financial—leasing motor vehicles.
2. McDonnell Douglas Financial—leasing computer equipment.
3. GT InfoTech—French software.
4. Apache Plastics—plastic pipe. GTC's largest non-rail investment, 60 percent limited interest.
5. Helm Locomotive Leasing—acquisition and leasing of locomotives and rail cars.
6. Railease Associates—advertising display using GTC land properties for placement.
7. Corporate Flight Inc.—licensed charter aircraft at Detroit Metro.

One of the most interesting of these holdings, and one that clearly fit Bandeen's early idea of buying entities related to but not involved in transportation, was Helm Locomotive Leasing. During the mid-1980s, GTW entered into sales/leaseback programs to rebuild locomotives. Taking advantage of the sale of tax benefits, GTW found that economies were far more beneficial than would accrue from the acquisition of new units. So financially beneficial, in fact, that in the summer of 1987, GTW—utilizing GTC's Domestic

Three subsidiary—entered into a joint venture partnership with Helm to purchase forty-four used GP-38-2 locomotives. The arrangement gave GTW the right to purchase this motive power from the joint venture and thus replace its fleet at very favorable prices. Work would be done at GTW's shop in Battle Creek. Moreover, rentals would produce attractive income, and the enterprise would be financed completely from outside sources with minimum risk. The joint venture with Helm for the acquisition, remanufacture, sale, and lease-back of locomotives proved to be one of GTC's most impressive accomplishments in diversification.[15]

Gerald Maas was even more energetic in the trying matter of employee productivity—an acute problem at GTW, troubling at CV, if a modest issue at DW&P. John Burdakin, Robert Adams, Gerald Maas, and David Wilson all made gains at GTW over the years, but much remained to accomplish. The problem was magnified during the 1980s when truckers became more aggressive, railroads gained vitality under the Staggers Act, and customers demanded a higher-quality transportation product at a lower price. Maas and Wilson thus found themselves in a grueling

Remanufacturing would be accomplished at the Battle Creek shops. Photograph courtesy of the collections of Sam Breck.

race to bring down labor costs faster than competitive forces drove down rates. This was an issue for all rail carriers in the United States and Canada, of course, but it was a matter crucial to GTW and, by extension, to the Grand Trunk Corporation experiment.[16]

"What makes Grand Trunk Corporation work?," asked Gerald Maas in a rhetorical question directed to employees of the GTC roads. Yes, track, locomotives, and cars were essential, "but they really aren't what makes Grand Trunk *work*," said Maas. "People are." By that he meant the employees of GTW, CV, and DW&P—employees who were, he proudly pointed out, constantly learning and adapting. Such skills were vital since these employees and their employers alike faced a world that was constantly in flux. Then he dropped the other boot. "To adapt, railroads must rely on the newly acquired skills of a smaller, more flexible work force." Maas was not being coy. He firmly believed that GTC's employees were its greatest asset. Yet he also knew that that work force was going to have to produce more customer-oriented transportation and do so more efficiently than ever before.[17]

Maas, together with Walker and Wilson, was devoted to the goal of changing the corporate culture of the GTC roads—at least in terms of communication between management and contract employees. Thus his tenure was typified by energetic efforts to foster "employee ownership in a corporate strategy" by ensuring that those employees were kept "informed and involved in significant corporate issues." Maas was successful in this campaign because he clearly believed the message and was good at delivering it.[18]

The impetus for change was, in a sense, thrust upon GTC's senior managers in 1987 when the United Transportation Union (UTU) and the Brotherhood of Locomotive Engineers (BLE) challenged them to show how they would run Grand Trunk Western with new work rules and to demonstrate what new business would be generated with such new work rules in place. Maas leapt to the challenge. The threat to GTW's—and thus GTC's—survival was not from organized labor, he insisted, but from a corporate culture that insisted on doing business in the same old tired ways. Rather, hands at all levels had to recognize the need for and to accept a new market-driven mentality—one that *really* understood the shippers' needs and their transportation alternatives. The only way to survive—let alone prosper—Maas lectured, was to craft a high-quality, cost-competitive service at each of the GTC properties. Easily said. But railroad managers and railroad labor tended to be controlled by the past, not instructed by it. Maas and his fellow senior managers would have their hands full.[19]

"Tell it like it is," was Maas's credo. That meant telling employees how GTC properties compared to competing railroads and other transportation providers. Focus was on GTW, although it might have included CV as well. "*We're* in trouble!," Maas warned, because on a comparative basis, GTW spent a larger portion of revenue on labor, because its trainmen and enginemen wages per train mile were higher than on competing roads, because GTW had the highest switch crew rates per yard hour, and because GTW suffered from unfortunately elevated costs of gathering and distribution. In sum, GTW had the highest expense per ton mile. This, in turn, imperiled service levels. For instance, GTW held trains for tonnage or maximum length because its wage rates precluded operation of more frequently operated shorter trains. That, of course, hamstrung Walter Cramer's ability to gain or even hold business. Was there hope? Yes, but haste was imperative. "The longer we wait the worse the situation becomes and the farther behind we will be," warned Maas.[20]

Gerald Maas was hardly the only railroad manager ballyhooing the need to change corporate culture. Indeed, the idea was much in vogue on most if not all major railroads. Earlier efforts to effect such basic change had been greeted negatively; responses from entrenched management and labor alike usually ranged from "ho hum" to "oh yeah?" But managers and workers in the 1980s gradually, if grudgingly, agreed to substantial alterations in modus operandi.

Maas and the vice presidents worked as a team in this campaign, scheduling annual travel to talk with employees on each property. "All of us need voice," said Maas, "all of us need the ability to influence." Maas would engage in "grassrooting"; he and his team would listen to what employees had to say, and they would respond directly to questions regarding "the future of the company." In all cases Maas would preach the need for a " surprise-free environ-

ment." In the same vein, GTW employees received by mail each year a copy of *Straight Talk* containing commentary from Maas, Walker, and others plus a tear-out "What are your ideas?" form that employees could return to the Detroit headquarters.[21]

GTW managers gained credibility with employees and their unions. Late in 1989, BLE ratified an agreement giving GTW the right to train new engineers at the carrier's discretion using a locomotive simulator and other teaching aids; enginemen already on the seniority roster would receive a $14,500 payment and rights under a 401-K savings plan. Then United Transportation Union agreed in 1990 to eliminate the second brakeman on road trains and to discontinue the practice of stopping trains en route for meal breaks. In return, UTU gained severance payments and productivity bonuses as well as cost-of-living allowances. Other productivity-enhancing agreements covered nonoperating employees represented by the Transportation Communications Union. All of these agreements were negotiated locally, apart from national bargaining. By the end of 1990, David Wilson could forecast a 15 percent reduction in road crew costs per train for that year alone. Indeed, the total number of GTC employees declined by 39 percent during the 1980s—impressive, to be sure. Maas pointed to the obvious. These gains in productivity allowed the GTC roads to price service in a way that would improve competitive position.[22]

As Maas and the operating managers labored to bring down costs of moving traffic, Walter Cramer and the marketing/sales group continued with their endless quest to win and hold business with rates and service agreements that would compensate the effort. Intermodal provided an exciting if volatile case in point, especially at GTW where financial performance sometimes drove innovation. Detroit's MoTerm facility was again expanded and improved to handle trailers and containers for GTW's account, but increasingly for Atchison, Topeka & Santa Fe Railway (AT&SF), BN, CN, and CSX Transportation (CSXT), as a common-user or hub center; GTW, in effect, wholesaled its service between Detroit and major gateways. GTW also invested in a new terminal at Battle Creek to serve the needs of Ralston Purina, General Foods, Kellogg, and Nippondenso, all of which had come to favor shipping cereal products in trailers over boxcars.

The North American automobile industry found itself in pain throughout 1991. GTW suffered accordingly. Photograph courtesy of Grand Trunk Western Railroad.

GTW made proposals to several other rail carriers, pledging Battle Creek as a "neutral intermodal terminal" with haulage agreements similar to those with roads using MoTerm.[23]

Early in 1991, GTW along with Union Pacific, Southern Pacific, and the National Railway of Mexico agreed to move Ford's auto parts by dedicated intermodal train (double-stack containers) in both directions from a plant in Hermosillo, Mexico, and those in Michigan and Ontario. This "one-stop shopping" arrangement reflected the auto industry's growing interest in intermodal as opposed to boxcars for parts, and it also reflected GTW's historic relationship with North American motor vehicle manufacturing. That mainstay industry, however, found itself in profound flux and urgent stress going into the decade of the 1990s. Fifty years earlier, in 1941, as the United States geared up for participation in World War II, B. C. Forbes of *Forbes Magazine* considered the automobile industry the best managed in America. *Forbes* writers in 1991 made no such bold pronouncements. Indeed, wrote one, the North American automobile industry was "in pain" experiencing "the worst of times." Another writer, at *Fortune*, wondered: "Can American

cars come back?" All of this, of course, was of great concern to those of GTC persuasion. "When the Big Three sneeze, we don't catch a cold; we contract pneumonia!," reminded GTW's Edward J. Stasio.[24]

There was ample reason for concern. During the years 1987-90, the Big Three shuttered eight assembly plants and opened but one. Employment suffered accordingly; the United Auto Workers lost a half-million members during the 1980s. Moreover, market share declined, product development lagged, and many consumers found themselves more satisfied with foreign-made vehicles. These problems were magnified by an increasingly soft economy that tilted dangerously toward recession; spending slowed, production of durable and capital goods declined, and white collar workers joined their blue-collar brethren in the ranks of the unemployed. Those who had jobs paid down their debt instead of buying new goods. Problems of the North American auto industry deepened exponentially. The auto market in the United States for 1990 was the worst since 1983; 1991 would prove even more frightening. Rail shipments of motor vehicles and equipment during the fall of

173

1991 were 9 percent under the year before—also an unimpressive season.[25]

As always, GTC managers took particular interest in the financial health and special needs of General Motors. And always, GM managers were interested in the health and needs of GTC properties. The result was a strong symbiotic relationship that was at once historic and contemporary. "We form partnerships with transportation providers," said one GM logistics officer. Among the railroads used by GM, he pointed out, GTW ranked "from fourth to sixth" in terms of dollars expended. For GTC, traffic from GM was crucial—supplying an average of 29.75 percent of all revenues for the years 1987-90. Small wonder that each company studied the other. GM praised Grand Trunk Western's service on inbound materials and called GTW's handling of setup automobiles "as good as anybody." GM was not altogether satisfied, however, noting that railroads still spent much of their energies competing with each other, seeming to ignore GM's insistence that they work harder on high-quality, reliable, and efficient door-to-door delivery. "Railroads still seem reluctant to work collectively," another GM staffer complained. Consequently, the percentage of GM's transportation bill going to rail slipped to 45 percent by 1989. Turning again to Grand Trunk Western, GM transportation managers admired its cooperative attitude, its willingness to innovate, and its ability to respond quickly to issues of pricing, but wished that GTW was a "healthier, more productive" company. They also wondered about the relationship between Canadian National and its properties in the United States. "I don't have the feeling that CN goes out of its way to support GTW," said one GM manager.[26]

Walter Cramer, Robert Zaleta, and others responsible for automobile marketing worried about the health and direction of the giant automaker, but they took heart as Robert G. Stempel, GM's new chairman, pledged to increase his company's quality control, to demand attractive and efficiently designed products, and to win back public confidence. He would also address GM's excess production capacity. Late in 1991, Stempel announced that GM would close 20 plants, cut 74,000 jobs, and trim capital spending. Specifics followed two months later. GM, said Stempel, had lost $1.99 billion in 1990 and $4.45 billion in 1991; "we

must accelerate fundamental changes in the way General Motors does business." Among facilities scheduled for closing was the V8 engine plant at Flint, served by GTW. Zaleta, in charge of automotive marketing at GTW, breathed easier; the news might have been much worse. Zaleta knew, however, that GM remained saddled with considerable counterproductive tradition, several inefficient factories, a huge workforce used to inflexibility, and a powerful union that threatened strikes if GM sought labor concessions. Tough medicine would be required on a protracted basis. Nevertheless, GM's plan, Stempel assured, was "for the long term to get GM lean and viable." That could only bode well for GTC.[27]

The entire matter, however, posed a monumental question for GTC planners. If GTW and thus GTC were dependent on the motor vehicle industry, did it follow that General Motors, Ford, and the automakers generally were dependent on the GTC roads? The answer, most emphatically, was no. Cadillac's new plant at Hamtramck had been designed with rail docks for inbound parts; when completed, though, the facility was devoid of such docks and was totally dependent on truck delivery for parts. Even "captive" plants—those served by GTW as the sole railroad—were not safe. Trucks could "invade" with parts or even haul away finished products to destination or to loading ramps of competing railroads—to CSXT at New Boston, Michigan, or to Norfolk Southern at Melvindale, Michigan. And GTW could be frozen out completely, which happened when Chrysler determined late in 1990 to consolidate all Detroit-area loadings and thus terminate use of GTW's Highland Park facility. For that matter, did the motor vehicle industry have to rely on the railroad industry for anything? The answer, again, was no. Maas and his cadre would be obliged to make strategy accordingly.[28]

To help assess the strengths and weaknesses of the GTC roads, especially GTW, and to suggest potential changes in direction, Maas called in consultants in mid-1990. The findings were mixed; there were some surprises and a few disappointments. Surveys confirmed that GTW was doing "a good job of developing positive, personal relationships with its customers." But customers pointed quickly to GTW's Achilles' heel: its "lack of geographic access." Said one shipper: "GTW is a regional carrier. It can't get the long hauls, so it has to work through joint line moves." Said

Grand Trunk Western Railroad Co.

Expedited Train Services
Distribution Terminals — Trailer & Container Services
Best Connections for Intermediate Rail Service
between the U.S. and Canada

Chicago Connections:

ATSF	IC
BN	IHB
BRC	MJ
CC	MP
CNW	NSS
CR	SOO
CSXT	SP
CRL	SSWN
GWWR	WC
IAIS	WICT

Detroit Connections:

CN	CSXT
CP	DC
CR	NSS

Toledo Connections:

AA
CR
CSXT
NSS

Cincinnati Connections:

NSS
CSXT
CR

Marketing Services
November, 1990

GT

CUSTOMER ASSISTANCE

1-800-521-6900

Facsimile 313-396-6118

Grand Trunk Western Railroad Co.
1333 Brewery Park Boulevard, Detroit, MI 48207-2699

another: "For my type of business, GTW needs to get bigger and serve more destinations." Others echoed the same theme. "Grand Trunk Western needs to find a partner railroad, and put together a series of joint moves that can better serve the customer." Did that imply Canadian National as the "partner railroad"? Not necessarily. Only a few mentioned it. Shippers, in fact, were mystified by the working relationship of CN with the GTC roads. "It almost seems as if CN has a better arrangement with Norfolk Southern than with Grand Trunk Western," observed one bemused traffic manager.[29]

Consultants also interviewed GTW commodity managers—personnel from the company who had direct interface with customers. In some cases the views of commodity managers and customers meshed. "GTW is small so we can react promptly

to customer concerns; because we are closer to our customers we can work with them," noted one manager in identifying GTW's main strength. The principal weakness, said a majority, "is that we don't go anywhere. We need to get the destination and origin of our customer, not just one or the other."[30]

Consultants also unearthed a distressing level of frustration and, in fact, disenchantment among commodity managers. Half of them complained of a lack of direction from senior management. Several asserted that top managers talked much about a market-driven company, but practiced it little. Was Maas, so effective in communicating his vision to contract employees and their unions, less effective in getting the vice presidents to pull in harness? Another prevailing theme centered on the size and nature of the

175

management team. "We run this railroad like a Conrail, as opposed to a short line railroad, which we are," said one. "The company is too top heavy," concluded another. Others offered suggestions in the form of questions. "Why can't GTW become a large DW&P?," was the most provocative.[31]

The consulting team probed elsewhere. Was GTW pricing its service properly? Yes. What could be done to improve operating profit? Increase volume and/or reduce high fixed costs. How could volume be increased? Engage in more "common user rail service" by becoming a provider of transportation for other carriers through haulage agreements, and by consolidating yard and terminal operations of otherwise competing railroads. What about trimming fixed costs? This could be accomplished only by reductions in staffing.[32]

The consultants handed Maas a frightfully dry-eyed assessment. Frankly, they felt GTW could look forward to "few, if any, opportunities for significant growth." GTW could, they thought, achieve a break-even position on operations "with a major effort in cost reductions." Gerald Maas and the vice presidents leaned back in their chairs and breathed deeply. They had already seen to the rationalization of GTW's plant, had secured impressive productive gains from the labor force, and had cut layers out of management. Dealing with GTW, they concluded, was like running on a treadmill; you ran hard, but the scenery changed not at all. Yet break-even was about all that ever could be expected at GTW. It was the same at CV. But there was the promise of net income from DW&P, and potential in tax loss carry forwards and in diversification. That, of course, taken collectively, had been the thinking behind the Grand Trunk Corporation experiment all along.[33]

It was not in Maas's nature to be pessimistic and he took pride in what he had accomplished at GTC. He had promoted open communication at all levels—especially between management and labor—at GTW and, by extension, at CV and DW&P. He had a broad vision of where to position GTC for the rest of the decade, he was a fine cheerleader, and he remained committed to creating an atmosphere that could change the culture of the GTC roads. His successes gave him confidence. Moreover, the recession in Canada and the sluggish economy in the United States

since late 1989 had surprisingly little impact on GTC's income statement. In fact, revenues often ran ahead of forecasts. Challenges remained great—a constant for any manager at any time, and even more so at GTC—but if the economy got no worse Maas could press forward in his usual style.[34]

It was not to be. "The bottom dropped out" was a refrain heard late in 1990 at all GTC roads, even at the usually prosperous DW&P, and especially at GTW. The automakers cut deeply into fourth-quarter production schedules leading Walter Cramer to conclude before Christmas that GTW would be deprived of 4,000 anticipated carloads. That, as it turned out, was the good news. General Motors told Cramer and then announced publicly that it would temporarily shut down three assembly plants served by GTW for "major model changeovers." Those decisions, Cramer gloomily predicted, would cut GM's shipments on GTW for 1991 by some 18,000 carloads ($16.9 million in revenues). What of the overall outlook for 1991? Jerome Corcoran somberly predicted a

Jerome F. Corcoran, GTW's vice president-finance, somberly predicted a massive pre-tax loss that would exceed GTC's lines of credit. Photograph courtesy of Grand Trunk Western Railroad.

Clouds gathered on GTC's horizon. Near West Delta, Ohio. Photograph courtesy of Sam Breck.

massive pretax loss that would exceed GTC's lines of credit—an unacceptable circumstance by any measure. Senior managers huddled at year's end to review the budget line by line. Cuts were necessary, but how deep? After all, assuming that this downturn was cyclical and of short duration, GTC did not want to impair long-term revenues by reducing service in a way that would drive off business. Maas was loathe to change directions in any dramatic way. He would stay the course—as much as possible.[35]

Nothing was possible for Maas, as it turned out. The dreary news that GTC had suffered an unexpected loss of $3.65 million in 1990 and that its performance in 1991 was certain to be appreciably worse was hardly good news in Montreal where CN Rail lost more than $100 million in 1990 and CN's consolidated net was a paltry $7.7 million. The distress was palpable when Maas attended CN's rail management committee meeting late in February 1991, and that distress deepened in the coming weeks. Maas held strongly to his view of an independently managed company holding CN's assets in the United States—a view that had been tolerated by CN's senior managers during times when GTC turned profit or held steady, but a view that had been in flux at Montreal since the very minute Bandeen breathed life into his dream. That dream, admittedly, had always been an experiment and now many CN managers thought the time had come for change. When Maas dug in his heels a collision was inevitable. He resigned late in March for "personal and philosophical reasons." Ronald E. Lawless praised Maas, saying that he had "guided the [GTC] companies through a period of restructuring, and leaves a legacy of strong commitment to customer service through employee teamwork." At Detroit and abroad the GTC properties there was shock at Maas's abrupt departure and distress at the directional void that his absence implied. "We are leaderless," exclaimed one astonished manager. Lawless sought to soothe matters, announcing that the selection of a successor "is in the mill now." Meanwhile, Lawless invested the four vice presidents (Corcoran, Cramer, Walker, and Wilson) with day to day authority.[36]

NOTES

1. *GT Reporter* (March-April 1973): 2; *GT Reporter* (November-December 1973): 2; Overview—Grand Trunk Western (Montreal: 1966), 62; GTW, Minute Book No. 7, 298; GTW, Minute Book No. 10, 504-5, 517-18; *GT Reporter* (October 1986): 1; GTC, Annual Report (1986): 16.

2. GTC, Headquarters Dedication (booklet), 16 October 1987; GTC, Annual Report (1987): 5, 19.

3. GTC, Annual Report (1987): 5; Gerald L. Maas, interview, 9 February 1990.

4. Gerald L. Maas, interview, 9 February 1990.

5. Robert A. Walker, interview, 7 March 1990; John H. Burdakin, interview, 5 March 1991; *North Western Lines* 16 (Spring 1989): 6; Harold W. Buirkle to Pierre J. Doumet, 17 May 1989 (PF 105).

6. Wertheim Schroder & Co., "Transaction Detroit" (1989); CN, Evaluation of a Proposal for the Sale of GTC (PF 105).

7. John H. Burdakin to R. A. Walker, 8 October 1984 (PF 950); *Traffic World* (1 October 1984): 46.

8. Gerald L. Maas to Management Employees, 7 January 1986. Part of GTC, Five-Year Business Plan and Strategic Narrative, 1986-1990; G. L. Maas to Management Employees, 18 November 1988; Part of GTC, Planning for the '90s, (PF100-8).

9. GTC, Minute Book No. 1, 32-35, 38-40, 50-51.

10. Ibid., 251.

11. GTC, Annual Report (1987): 35.

12. P. E. Tatro to J. Brouwer et al., 7 October 1988; Emmett R. Kronauer to Paul E. Tatro, 14 October 1988; Mike Desmet and Jay Horine to Paul E. Tatro, 14 October 1988; Paul E. Tatro to Y. H. Masse, 18 October 1988; Coopers & Lybrand, Preacquisition Review CG&T Industries Inc.— Draft, 28 October 1988; G. L. Maas to Paul R. Wood, 4 November 1988; GTW, Minute Book No. 10, 561; Frank Malone, "Paducah & Louisville: The Making of a Winner," *Railway Age* 190 (November 1989): 40-42; *Railway Age* 190 (May 1989): 14.

13. GTW, Minute Book No. 10, 571; Video presentation for GTC board, summer meeting, 1990.

14. GTC video.

15. GTW, Executive Minute No. 677; GTC, Preparing for the '90s, 9. PF 100-8; GTW, Minute Book No. 10: 559, 563-64, 589-92; GTC, Minute Book No. 4: 317; Bonnie M. Reyes to Jerome F. Corcoran, 5 February 1990 (PF 100).

16. *Railway Age* 191 (January 1990): 4.

17. *GTC Today* (Winter 1991): 1.

18. GTC, 1990-1994 Plan, 1(PF 100-8); *Keeping Track* 25 (June 1990): 1, 6-8.

19. GTC, Meeting the Competitive Challenge: Grand Trunk's Plan for the Future (25 August 1987), I-1.

20. Ibid., II-28-30; Gerald L. Maas, "No Sugarcoating, No Stonewalling," *Modern Railroads* 44 (November 1989): 8.

21. Gerald L. Maas, interview, 23 January 1989; *GT Focus* (January/February 1989), 1.

22. *GT Focus* (November/December 1989): 1-2; GTC, Annual Report (1990): 11; *GT Focus* (November/December 1990): 1; Ibid. (May/June 1991): 3; GTC, Annual Report (1990): 2-3; GTW, Minute Book No. 10, 608; *Traffic World* 222 (14 May 1990): 25.

23. *Modern Railways* 45 (March 1990): 44-46; *GT Focus* (September/October 1990): 1-2; GTW, Minute Book No. 10, 610-12; GTC, Annual Report (1990): 12-13; *Progressive Railroading* 34 (August 1991): 24.

24. *Journal of Commerce*, 17 March 1991; *Forbes* 148 (14 October 1991): 241 and (28 October 1991): 59; *Fortune* 121 (20 February 1990): 62; Edward J. Stasio, Presentation before the ARDA in Philadelphia, 24 May 1991.

25. *Wall Street Journal,* 16 February 1990; *Washington Post*, 30 September 1990; *Wall Street Journal*, 7 January and 26 November 1991, 9 January 1992; *Traffic World* 228 (21 October 1991): 18-19.

26. GTC, Annual Report (1989): 23; Ibid. (1990): 23; John J. Baisley, interview, 6 March 1990; J. J. Casaroll, interview, 6 March 1990; J.W. Flanigan, interview, 6 March 1990; *GT Focus* (July/August 1990): 2.

27. *Wall Street Journal*, 4 May 1990, 21 November, 18 December 1991; *Forbes* 149 (20 January 1992): 40-41; *Wall Street Journal*, 24, 25, 26, 27 February 1991.

28. Robert M. Zaleta, interview, 31 May, 11 November 1991.

29. Dan R. E. Thomas to Gerald L. Maas, July 1990 (PF 105).

30. Ibid.

31. Ibid.

32. Dan R. E. Thomas to Gerald L. Maas, 5 October 1990, (PF 105).

33. Ibid.

34. Gerald L. Maas, interview, 9 February 1990.

35. *Wall Street Journal*, 28 November 1990; GTW, Minute Book No. 10., 608-9; Minutes of Executive Committee Meeting, 10 December 1990, (PF 101.6).

36. GTC, Annual Report (1990), 18; CN, Annual Report (1990): 30; Gerald L. Maas, interview, 6 March 1991; *Crain's Detroit Business* 7 (1-7 April 1991): 1, 27; *Traffic World* 226 (8 April 1991): 29.

Canadian National effectively killed the creative initiative of the American employees of GTW by smothering it. What we're trying to do is make this a career place for Americans.

Robert A. Bandeen, quoted in *Detroit News,* 6 October 1971.

Canadian National Railway and its three U.S. roads—Grand Trunk Western; Duluth, Winnipeg & Pacific; and the Central Vermont—have integrated their marketing and operating functions to form CN North America.

CN North America brochure, December 1991.

The departure of Gerald L. Maas as president and chief executive officer of Grand Trunk Corporation coupled with signals from Canadian National that seminal changes would be forthcoming in its relationship with progeny in the United States played out against an extremely fluid business climate in North America—and in the world, for that matter.

Railroads in the United States had recorded major accomplishments during the decade of the 1980s in a partially deregulated environment provided for under the Staggers Act. Indeed, in 1990 the railroads' share of transportation ton miles was the highest since 1981, and Wall Street took note as investors anticipated even greater gains during the next decade. Not all, to be sure, was sweetness and roses. In the years 1980 through 1989 the industry also saw its share of the national transportation dollar drop from 13.1 percent to 9.1 percent. Water and pipeline shares dropped also, but air rose from 1.9 percent to 3.6 percent and trucks increased their overwhelming supremacy from 73.9 to 77.8 percent. The Interstate Commerce Commission (ICC) reported that for 1989 only Burlington Northern and Norfolk Southern were "revenue adequate" (their rates of return on investment were at least matched by the cost of capital). Grand Trunk Western ranked last among class one railroads by this index.[1]

In pursuit of increased market share and revenue adequacy, American carriers persisted in the mega-merger movement. During 1987, Chesapeake & Ohio vanished into CSX and Seaboard System also was merged into CSX; in 1988, Rio Grande Industries (which already owned Denver & Rio Grande Western) acquired sprawling Southern Pacific, and Union Pacific gobbled up Missouri-Kansas-Texas; in 1990, the ICC approved a petition by Blackstone Capital Partners, L.P., to control Chicago & North Western as well as former United States Steel carriers held by Transtar, a Blackstone affiliate

179

(Union Pacific took a substantial position in C&NW); and in 1991, Wabash, long leased by Norfolk & Western, was merged into that company—which was held by Norfolk Southern. Industry watchers contemplated still greater amalgamation and offered possibilities such as Conrail with Union Pacific, Burlington Northern with Norfolk Southern, CSXT with Santa Fe, leaving Southern Pacific for dismemberment.[2]

In the service areas of Grand Trunk Western and Central Vermont, the primary rail variables, although very different one from each other, were Conrail and Guilford. In 1980, Conrail had been a ward of the federal government; a decade later it was a slimmed down but muscular private company turning annual net profit. Shippers pointed with satisfaction to Conrail's innovative and aggressive marketing, its devotion to quality service, and its pronounced desire to be "the carrier of choice." GTC planners watched nervously and with good reason. Conrail successfully wrested grain shipments from GTW/CN in the Chicago-Buffalo corridor, offered a constant threat to GTW's vital motor vehicle and parts business, and threatened Central Vermont's life by assiduously courting CN's traffic from eastern Canada via Huntingdon, Quebec, and away from CV. In fact, CN in 1989 sold Conrail its line from Massena, New York, to Huntingdon, and even gave Conrail operating rights into Montreal. Elsewhere, Conrail's new double-stack hub at DeWitt Yard near Syracuse was posed to offer powerful intermodal service in upstate New York and throughout New England.[3]

If Conrail was the awakened giant striding boldly across the northeastern American landscape, Guilford Transportation Industries proved to be the joker in the deck. A holding company formed in 1980 by Timothy Mellon, Guilford had quickly acquired Maine Central and Boston & Maine (B&M). CV, on its own account and as a surrogate for CN, had protested Guilford's claim to B&M saying that issues in the case were much broader, that the ICC should examine the entire difficult New England scene, and that if Guilford were allowed to combine Maine Central and Boston & Maine it would hurt CV while at the same time depriving CN of revenue adequate to justify operation of CN's historic but marginal line to and from Portland, Maine. To no avail. The ICC perceived that Guilford was the only

agent able to save the fragile New England rail network and the deal went through. Furthermore, the state of New York—fearful that tottering Delaware & Hudson (D&H) would perish, urged that Guilford add that property to its collection. Again CV protested, and again to no avail; D&H, which competed directly with CV for traffic out of eastern Canada, became part of Guilford. But prosperity for Guilford proved elusive. Guilford reduced service, dried up certain lines, and alienated shippers, connecting carriers, labor, and politicians. On 20 June 1988, Guilford placed D&H in bankruptcy, a trustee was named, and the ICC designated Delaware Otsego's New York, Susquehanna & Western as emergency service operator. One year later the trustee requested bids for D&H assets.[4]

Robert Walker carried out an investigation to determine what stake CV and thus GTC might have in the fate of D&H. Analysts concluded that D&H was of little value to GTW, of moderate value to Canadian National, "but vital to the future of Central Vermont." If powerful Conrail, which already handled the lion's share of CN business to and from Quebec, were to acquire D&H and its short-mile route, the impact on CV would be devastating. Even if a neutral carrier such as New York, Susquehanna & Western were ultimately to acquire D&H, the impact on CV would be telling. The sad fact, said analysts, was that the volume of business in the region did not justify four existing routes (CV, D&H, Conrail, CP/B&M). What path should GTC pursue? One option was for GTC to bid on D&H, but analysts did not recommend it: "The opportunities for traffic growth are," they concluded, "nearly matched by the risks of traffic loss." Perhaps an approach with combined interested parties would be best; CV, for instance, might utilize D&H southward from Rouses Point while New York, Susquehanna & Western, for example, could utilize the Buffalo to Binghamton route. But what were the views of Canadian National in terms of D&H? "In many ways," GTC analysts concluded, "the Canadian roads hold the key to resolving the disposition of D&H."[5]

Canadian Pacific Limited, owner of one of those Canadian roads—CP Rail—was presently in the process of refocusing its directions and energies. When CP celebrated its centenary in 1981, it held assets valued at $16.3 billion and owned a solid reputation for earning net income

180

If even a neutral carrier acquired D&H it would be devastating to CV. Crossing the White River near White River Junction, Vermont, October 1989. Photograph courtesy of Charles Bohi.

and paying dividends. For CP, the 1960s and 1970s had been typified by expansion and diversification. By 1985, however, CP's senior management determined to have another look. Consequently certain assets were written down and others—Canadian Pacific Air Line, for example—sold. CP managers continued to refine focus; CP's substantial interest in Algoma Steel was dumped in 1988.[6]

Predictably, CP's flinty-eyed managers in Montreal turned eventually to the company's sizable stake in Soo Line Railroad. That company had derived from the 1961 merger of Duluth, South Shore & Atlantic Railroad; Minneapolis, St. Paul & Sault Ste. Marie Railroad; and Wisconsin Central Railroad. CP held more than a 50 percent interest of the newly defined Soo. During the next twenty years Soo earned a sound reputation as a steady performer with a traffic mix oriented toward the agricultural, housing, and paper product sectors of the economy. Its operating ratio was enviable, it spent judiciously to improve plant, and its dividends were attractive. When Milwaukee Road shuddered onto the rocks, Soo concluded that acquisition of Milwaukee's core would result in a more balanced

traffic mix with an improved revenue base and, of course, finally won that property.

Soo, however, was ill-equipped to refine the Milwaukee merger to its greatest reward. "The process will take time," shareholders were told. Soo's debt had quadrupled because of assumed Milwaukee debt and the result of loans required to finance the cash portion of the purchase price. Soo stumbled. Dividends were trimmed in 1986 and eliminated in 1987. In the latter year Soo also sold nearly 1,800 miles of line, located principally in Wisconsin and Michigan, to a new concern—Wisconsin Central Limited—which instantly became a major regional carrier. Prospects seemed to brighten. Soo showed a profit of $15.6 million in 1988, and its operating ratio dropped from 96.8 in 1987 to 90.5 percent in 1988.[7]

Meanwhile, Canadian Pacific, with approximately 56 percent of Soo's common, became impatient and even scornful of Soo's fortunes. CP icily and ominously reminded Soo that their historic joint traffic agreement (in place since 1944) could be broken by either party with one year's notice. Then, early in 1989, CP bluntly announced that it would seek "to dispose of its

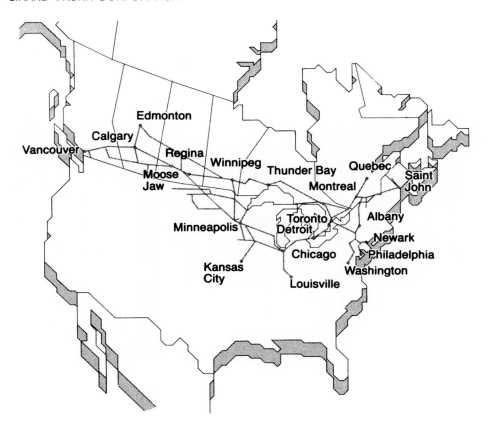

CP, by 1991, had undergone a strategic consolidation and a strategic expansion; it would be a most formidable competitor—not just in Canada, but throughout much of the United States. Photograph courtesy of CP Rail System.

the Minneapolis headquarters building and Soo was integrated into the marketing and operating schemes of its parent. Branches and secondary operations were sold or shopped around demonstrating CP's long-term interest only in Soo operations from Portal (North Dakota), Noyes (Minnesota), and possibly Superior (Wisconsin) through Minneapolis and St. Paul to Chicago (over former Milwaukee Road) and thence Windsor, Ontario (via trackage rights from CSXT to Detroit), plus Soo's access to Kansas City and Louisville gateways. By fully absorbing Soo, CP Rail became the seventh largest railroad system in North America with more than 20,000 miles of track.[9]

Canadian Pacific Limited, it seemed, had rediscovered its railroad heritage. Even earlier, in 1987, it had merged the tiny but strategic Toronto, Hamilton & Buffalo into CP Rail, and two years later it had strengthened its transcontinental route in the West by opening a new Rogers Pass line featuring a splendid 9.1-mile tunnel. Internally, CP Rail realigned its marketing and operating functions into two business units—one based in eastern Canada to develop intermodal freight systems (traffic susceptible to trucks) and the other located in the West to concentrate on heavy haul freight (bulk products). CP Rail also created a new corporate entity, Canadian Atlantic Railway, into which it dumped most Maritime lines—lines that, on a comparative basis, were less profitable than those west of Montreal. Did that mean CP had lost interest in rail operations on its eastern flank? No—at least not if East was defined as the eastern seaboard of the United States.[10]

interest in Soo Line," as that property was "not part of the company's long range North American railway strategy." Yet CP found little interest among prospective purchasers of Soo securities, and a joint management-labor team at Soo failed to locate capital adequate for a buyout. Then, in a most adroit turnabout, CP mounted a tender offer for all Soo Line shares. Canadian Pacific Limited, not surprisingly, soon owned "essentially all shares of Soo Line Corporation." Henceforth, said CP, Soo would have "a closer working relationship with CP Rail, thereby permitting both railways to take advantage of increasing north-south flows . . . ."[8]

Closer indeed. "A newly strengthened executive team," reported CP, "is in the process of implementing a comprehensive business plan aimed at returning Soo Line to substantial profitability and realizing the inherent synergies between the two railways." Soo was quickly "CP-ized." Senior local management disappeared from

182

Indeed, CP Rail raised many an eyebrow when it became one of many bidders for Delaware & Hudson assets. Service levels on D&H and the road's physical plant had deteriorated badly and shippers often dolefully referred to D&H as "Delay & Hesitate," but CP analysts detected great potential in the road. CP had lost market position in the region because of Guilford's slack standards, but by acquiring D&H CP could reaffirm its traditional strong presence in New England. More than that, D&H would give CP access to port facilities in and about New York City and Philadelphia with incalculable opportunities for increased intermodal—especially international container—traffic. (Containers might otherwise move over CP from Saint John, New Brunswick, but that port suffers by comparison to Halifax on CN because Halifax is closer to the Great Circle Route. It also suffers in comparison because of unpredictably vicious tides that often delay docking. Moreover, container ships increasingly call in the United States over Canadian ports.) Additionally, D&H would give CP direct connection with CSXT at Philadelphia (Park Junction) and CSXT and Norfolk Southern at Potomac Yard in Washington, D.C.—in the process forging an extremely impressive linkage for north-south movements. Regional and federal government agencies favored any agreement that would give competition to Conrail—ironic, given Conrail's curious past—and CP's financial strength could only help its brief.[11]

The D&H case held broad strategic implications for Canadian Pacific. The D&H case similarly held broad strategic implications for Canadian National, not just in the sense of what might happen to Central Vermont as a consequence of resolution, but truly in terms of the accelerating volume of business moving between Canada and the United States. At stake also was the great potential in container traffic. D&H in the hands of CP would clearly endanger CN's container traffic at Halifax as well as its investment in CV. CN, nevertheless, chose a timid course. No bid for D&H was entered on behalf of CN, although CN did join with an investment group associated with Wertheim Schroder & Company to submit an alternate proposal after the trustee gave his nod to CP. That coalition evaporated, however. Canadian Pacific, too, had second thoughts and withdrew its bid when Conrail—which correctly saw Canadian Pacific's

effort to acquire D&H as a competitive threat of the first order—failed to grant CP trackage rights from Harrisburg, Pennsylvania, to Hagerstown, Maryland, that would have yielded CP a handsome connection with Norfolk Southern. The D&H trustee was predictably dismayed at CP's decision and threatened liquidation of D&H—a fine idea, thought Gerald Maas, who considered D&H "essentially a surplus carrier." CN managers held similar, if private, views.[12]

Delaware & Hudson may have been "surplus," but only in an academic sense, as it turned out. Canadian Pacific returned with a lower bid absent demands to reach Hagerstown and the deal was finally made. CP assumed operation on 1 August 1990, and took title several months later. Massive improvements to property followed.[13]

In a very short time CP Rail had undergone a strategic consolidation (Soo Line) and strategic expansion (D&H). CP's reach now extended directly to important gateways in the United States (Chicago, Louisville, Kansas City, New York, Philadelphia, and Washington) and at once to some of the country's most populous areas. CP marketing could sell transportation on a north-south axis (containers, for instance, moving from New York-New Jersey or Philadelphia to Toronto and Montreal via D&H), as well as a west-east axis (lumber, for example, from British Columbia to Washington, D.C., via CP, Soo, D&H).

All of this was timely in the extreme since Canadian Pacific and, for that matter, Canadian National and all other Canadian railroads as well as their customers, now were able to anticipate greater competitive opportunities under deregulation as well as greater volumes of cross-border business, the result of free trade agreements embraced by Canada, the United States, and Mexico.

Deregulation in Canada took the form of the National Transportation Act and became effective on 1 January 1988. This new legislation brought fundamental change to Canadian rail procedures. It disallowed collective rate making, permitted confidential rate contracts between railroads and shippers, and allowed certain shippers served by only one railroad to interchange with another at the nearest connection at prescribed rates. The act also provided for arbitration of disputes between carriers and shippers.

Coupled with free trade, deregulation augured well for Canadian railroad companies.[14]

Free trade, involving profound traditions in international relations, was a sticky issue for both Canada and the United States, the world's largest trading partners. Canada, with nearly 30 percent of its gross national product accounted for by exports in 1987, already saw more than 25 percent of its rail traffic flow into the United States. Eased trade restrictions could only increase that flow. There was understandable jubilation among those in the business and transportation communities when the landmark United States-Canada Free Trade Agreement took effect on 1 January 1988. It called for removal of tariffs over a ten-year period. A side benefit for railroads took the form of relaxed restrictions on equipment rules allowing freer use of rolling stock and motive power crossing the border.[15]

Deregulation and free trade were bound to drive more business through the Sarnia-Port Huron gateway. Photograph courtesy of Canadian National.

With deregulation and free trade in place, managers at Canadian National and Canadian Pacific turned their eyes to international portals—especially the Detroit River Tunnel between Detroit and Windsor. Completed in 1910 by a subsidiary of New York Central, that twin-tube was used under trackage agreement by Grand Trunk Western after cross-river ferry service by CN ended on 20 February 1975. Ten years later ownership of the tunnel passed to joint ownership by Canadian National and Canadian Pacific when Conrail (ultimate successor to New York Central) sold its 237-mile Canada Southern.

Unfortunately, however, neither of the tunnel's tubes could accommodate tri-level or even bi-level auto racks. These continued to move via cross-river ferry at Port Huron-Sarnia (CN) and Detroit (CP using Norfolk Southern [NS]), slow and expensive operations at best. Moreover, limitations of the Detroit River Tunnel precluded use by double-stack containers which loomed large in the aspirations of both owners. CP also anticipated a growing volume of general business with GTW's competitors via Cincinnati if the tunnel could be enlarged. Such a prospect thoroughly alarmed Walter Cramer: "Enlargement of the Detroit-Windsor tunnel would be a major disaster for GT," he warned. Matters were muddied, however, since both CN and CP had promised to improve the tunnel in the Canada Southern case and since CP had charged CN with foot dragging.[16]

CN's position was plainly defensive—hoping to prevent CP from making further inroads in the U.S. market. GTC's Robert Walker urged a more expansive view. "We should," he argued, "examine what type of service and investment might be necessary to not only maintain our market share vis-a-vis CP in the short run, but how we can enhance our share of the total transportation in the long term." Walker and others in Detroit favored improvement to the CN/GTW Toronto-Sarnia-Chicago route over the CN/GTW Toronto-Windsor-Detroit-Chicago corridor. In other words, Walker counseled, spend money on the St. Clair River tunnel at Port

Size restrictions at both Detroit-Windsor and Port Huron-Sarnia tunnels necessitated expensive and time-consuming water movement across the St. Clair River for auto racks and other high-dimension cars. Photograph courtesy of Canadian National.

Huron-Sarnia which only CN and GTW used instead of the Detroit River tunnel which also served the needs of powerful competitors. If improved, the Port Huron-Sarnia tunnel could handle not only high-level auto racks and conventional trailer-on-flat-car but also double-stack containers.[17]

CN gradually reassessed its position. In typical fashion all issues were studied assiduously. Indeed, a $1 million feasibility study was authorized during the summer of 1991. Before the year was out, however, CN—acting with uncharacteristic alacrity—committed to a new 6,000-foot, $155 (Canadian) million tunnel adequate for "all types of rail traffic" including, CN pointedly announced, tri-level and double-stacked cars. There was ample reason for good cheer in Detroit. CN's decision boldly proclaimed a growing importance for Grand Trunk Western's historic route to Chicago.[18]

Trains moving over that route would not use Chicago's historic Elsdon Yard, however, for it had been abandoned a decade earlier. If they were intermodal trains, they might use RailPort. Most, however, would move directly to or from major connecting carriers—Burlington Northern

(Cicero), Chicago & North Western (Proviso), Indiana Harbor Belt (Blue Island), Santa Fe (Corwith), Union Pacific (Yard Center)—or to the Belt Railway of Chicago (Clearing) which, of course, GTW owned in part. GTW trains would not utilize the Chicago & Western Indiana Railroad, in which GTW also owned a partial stake, for that company and its few remaining assets were sold to a subsidiary of Union Pacific late in 1991. GTW received $2.4 million in that transaction.[19]

As Ron Lawless and his top staffers in Montreal pondered changes in the relationship between Canadian National and its railroads in the United States, they did so against the backdrop of economic distress and political unrest. A recession began in Canada before it hit the United States, reflected a greater trauma within the core elements of the national economy, and stubbornly resisted recovery. At the same time, recurrent demands from the province of Quebec for more autonomy threatened to tear Canada into pieces. Canada was not divided simply along English-French lines. Western provinces, for example, persisted in the belief that they were short-changed in the federal arrangement although Ontario, with about one-third of Canada's population, traditionally paid most of the bills, while the Maritime Provinces eagerly suckled at Ottawa's breast. Increased feelings of nationalism in Quebec simply exacerbated existing tension.[20]

It was not possible to disconnect economic and constitutional problems. The comparatively high cost of doing business in Canada killed some companies while others fled to the United States and elsewhere. Canada lost 180,000 manufacturing jobs in 1990 alone. Many Canadians pointed to the free trade agreement of 1988 seeing it as the villain. But, in fact, Canada had always been a trading nation and was simply making its own painful adjustment to an ever-growing global economy. Canada, simply stated, was trying to find its place in a changed and changing world order.[21]

Canadian National was a microcosm of it all—searching for its niche abroad the transportation landscape of North America and buffeted by powerful political currents at home, by dramatic changes within the continental and even world economies, and by unrelenting demands of sophisticated shippers.

Canadian National remained the largest of Canadian railroads with more than 21,000 miles of track. Much of that mileage produced marginal volumes, however, and some was operated at net loss. To reduce or terminate service and employment remained a political hot potato, but any sober analysis of CN's circumstance pointed to an inevitable conclusion: CN had to slim down to meet rugged competition from Canadian Pacific and powerful railroads in the United States—to say nothing of pressure from other modes of transportation. Lawless chafed when many in Canada clung to the belief that CN's obligatory role, since it was owned by the government, was that of providing jobs. Not so, said Lawless. "Under today's competitive conditions, both domestic and global, all of us have to pull our weight," he bluntly declared. "There is absolutely no room for redundant jobs, redundant plant or redundant anything." CN employee numbers did decline from 61,000 in 1986 to 38,000 in 1990, and CN labored to become a good business instead of simply a good railroad. Nevertheless, it would be a demanding contest requiring that Canadians look at Canadian National in a new way and that

Canadian National see itself in a new looking glass.[22]

Canadian National also found itself obliged to deal with factors over which it had little control—traffic flow being an easy example. In the early 1990s CN's traffic was divided roughly in thirds—one-third wholly domestic, one-third import-export, and one-third originated or terminated in the United States. CN's Mountain and Prairie regions in the West produced about 65 percent of all gross ton miles, while the St. Lawrence and Atlantic regions in the East produced less than 15 percent. Of traffic that originated in the West, less than 20 percent moved to eastern Canada (east of Thunder Bay, Ontario). In other words, the vast bulk of CN's traffic billed in the West—chemicals, grain, wood pulp, sulfur, potash, coal, milled lumber, and wood chips—moved westbound to Vancouver, Prince Rupert, and Kitimat. Imported automobiles moved to the interior from Vancouver and containers moved in both directions. In sum, CN was burdened by traffic imbalances with the West providing the bulk of tonnage (and compensatory business) while the East often provided more expense than revenue.[23]

Directional flows of traffic and imbalances in them were not the only problems; the matter of business volumes or, more specifically, the lack of business volumes at Canadian ports was especially vexing. The issue was simultaneously economic and emotional, thus political. Canadian Pacific had frankly despaired of its oceanic link at Saint John where tides interfered with dockings and transloadings, and had turned its attention through Delaware & Hudson to eastern seaboard ports in the United States. Halifax and CN were threatened by CP's decision to emphasize American ports but also by the fact that container ships generally favored those same ports, in part, because they were closer in distance to the heart of North America (Chicago, for instance). Canadians were predictably dismayed when goods bound to or from Canada moved by truck or rail to and from tidewater at New York, Baltimore, Philadelphia, or even Norfolk. They were further dismayed as Los Angeles, Oakland, Tacoma, and Seattle found favor over Vancouver. In fact, Seattle and Los Angeles together handled more import-export containers than all Canadian ports combined. Canadian railroads suffered accordingly. For example, CN was left to pick up fragments of that traffic—handling, for example, double-stack containers to central Canada from the Pacific rim that landed in Tacoma and moved over roads in the United States all the way to interchange with CN at Buffalo, New York.[24]

To Ron Lawless ultimately fell the duty of wrestling with all of this and of positioning Canadian National for the challenges of the 1990s and beyond. CN already had sold holdings in non-rail enterprises and had reduced its debt. CN, however, remained flabby with too many managers and too many contract employees compared to its competition. CN also labored under its own schizophrenia as a Crown Corporation which the Canadian people expected, on the one hand, to be operated strictly as a business, while on the other hand, demanding that it provide social and public-policy benefits to Canadian society. The inability to pursue private equity financing continued as a most severe handicap as did internal reluctance to change long-practiced traditions. Problems begged for solutions. What CN needed, Lawless eventually concluded, was a fundamental reorientation "to create a new customer-centered culture."[25]

A central ingredient in that prescription—one professed if not always embraced by much of the railroad industry in the United States and Canada—was "seamless transportation." For CN that ingredient took at least small form early in 1991 when it leased GTW's RailPort intermodal terminal in Chicago. The arrangement gave CN "total control . . . over service options" and reflected CN's desire to "offer a single-line rate." GTW, of course, continued to handle CN trains on a haulage (contract with set fee, i.e., wholesale) basis but, insofar as customers were concerned, they would deal with only one railroad—CN. To further the cause of "seamless transportation," CN also forged agreements with other huge railroads—Burlington Northern, Norfolk Southern, and Union Pacific for traditional boxcar business, and Southern Pacific for perishables. These alliances promised to make the boxcar fleets of these carriers more fluid, reduce costs, and allow more effective pricing in campaigns to wrest traffic away from trucks.[26]

A more pronounced implication that CN would fully and vigorously embrace seamless transportation came at the summer meeting of GTC's board of directors in 1991 when Ron Lawless was named president and chief executive officer of Grand Trunk Corporation. In the tradition of Bandeen and LeClair, Lawless was already chairman of GTC and its subsidiaries; he then assumed additional responsibilities. Since Maas's abrupt departure in March, GTC had been overseen by Lawless as chairman and by an executive committee of Cramer, Corcoran, Walker, and Wilson. Lawless, outgoing and friendly, owned a fine reputation as a salesman and consensus builder. He was well respected within and without. One senior subordinate at CN thought him "a natural leader" and a "good communicator"; another considered him a "very good strategic thinker." Robert Bandeen called Lawless "excellent." Thomas J. Lamphier, retired president at Burlington Northern, referred to him as "a fine man." But Lawless was a Canadian, and Bandeen's experiment as affirmed by Maurice LeClair and earlier by Lawless himself had called for American leadership of GTC. What was implied by this change? Many in Detroit recalled that Lawless's appointment at CN was scheduled to run out soon. Perhaps, they thought, his elevation at GTC would prove an aberration.[27]

It was not. Lawless's contract was extended at CN. More changes at GTC would follow. The value of GTW to CN and, to a great extent, the value of GTC to CN were, said CN's John H. D. Sturgess, "studied endlessly," ebbing and flowing according to net income produced by the American holding company. This was reflected in 1989 when CN's Yvon Masse recommended that the parent "take a proactive stance toward our entire involvement in the U.S" and, to that end, CN's marketing wing undertook yet another study although, as Peter Clarke reminded Masse, "today's conclusions may not hold in the long term" since "the North American marketplace is changing so rapidly." CN's marketing study late that year recommended that CN retain each one of the GTC properties, but made several points that urged deeper analysis. GTW, the author of the study pointed out, drew two-thirds of its gross revenue from traffic in which CN did not participate; CN, consequently, should better "utilize GTW's geographic advantages to promote and enhance transborder traffic"—traffic, all hands agreed, that would only increase in future years. CN's marketing managers also noted that while "GTW is an excellent route to Chicago," competitors—Canadian Pacific (via CSXT) and Norfolk Southern—now offered scheduled service

187

to Chicago equal to CN/GTW, and they did it "on a single line basis."[28]

A single line basis. Those words rang with an ominous tone in Detroit. It was true, GTC managers realized, that major shippers were increasingly impatient in dealing with carriers on moves requiring one or more connections. Shippers preferred to work with one, the originating carrier perhaps, on the matter of rates, service, equipment, claims, and the like. But Bandeen's GTC experiment had purposely included an independent posture for the GTC roads, especially GTW, that encouraged creative tension with CN. Walter Cramer and others at GTW, as managers of a stand-alone railroad, were expected to show initiative, sometimes to the consternation of the parent. On the other hand, the parent caused consternation in Detroit when it sought its own best advantage, sometimes at the expense of GTW, CV, or even DW&P. Shippers such as General Motors and Ford which were sophisticated in their knowledge of transportation providers often found themselves bemused by the relationship of CN with the GTC roads. These same shippers, however, now became less tolerant of such curiosities. "The perception of CN and GTW as two separate railroads to our customers and other railway connections places us at a disadvantage," complained one CN marketing manager.[29]

As Lawless and his staff pondered new directions for GTC, managers in Detroit, St. Albans, and Pokegama struggled with reduced earnings on GTW, CV, and DW&P as the recession of 1990-91 stubbornly persisted in the United States and Canada. These managers also had to deal with low morale as salaries were frozen and as GTC went through another round of buyouts and other cuts to reduce expenses. Low morale also was occasioned by the lack of sure direction from the parent, and at GTW by curtailment of capital spending. In that regard, David Wilson was obliged in 1991 to insist that no welded rail be installed on GTW—regardless of need—and ordered that tie replacement and surfacing be held to minimum requirements.[30]

There was much gloom abroad GTC properties, and good reason for it, but there were also occasional reasons to smile. Mazda announced that it would locate an "inland port" (shipments from overseas remaining in bond to destination) operation at its Flat Rock facility; twenty locomo-

tives were rebuilt at the Battle Creek shops and one of these was equipped with innovative microprocessors to improve fuel efficiency; a computerized train dispatching system was installed at Pontiac; a lumber reload center reopened on CV at Sharon, Vermont; safety and operating results were much improved on CV; and on DW&P the Ranier lift bridge was improved to accommodate double-stack containers.[31]

John H. D. Sturgess, CN's senior vice president and chief operating officer, gave strong hint as to CN's evolving position regarding GTC in a speech delivered to a Quebec City audience in the summer of 1991. "When we speak of domestic freight on the railways," said Sturgess, "we do not refer to Canada only. We mean the entire North American market." Already 43 percent of GTC's traffic was interchanged with CN—much more on CV and DW&P, a bit less on GTW; loads received from CN exceeded loads delivered to CN by the GTC roads. Sturgess seemed to imply that in the future CN would place even greater emphasis on cross-border connections. What impact would that have on the GTC roads? After all, CN often favored carriers other than its own American railroads. Conrail was the preferred connection in the east (Huntingdon) over CV, and CN had already turned its back on the historic route to Portland, Maine. That trackage, at least 163 miles of it in the United States, had been sold to Emons Development Corporation in 1989 to form a new short line appropriately styled the St. Lawrence & Atlantic Railroad. CV's place in CN's thinking remained unclear, but as the days passed it became apparent that CN was formulating new plans for GTW and DW&P.[32]

The fruits of CN's analysis were finally announced late in 1991. Ron Lawless told GTC managers on 18 December that primary functions at CN and GTC roads—marketing and operations—would be integrated or coordinated under a broad new corporate canopy: CN North America. These crucial functions for CN North America would be collectively orchestrated in Montreal and that, in turn, would require elemental changes in reporting. The dust settled very quickly. Walter Cramer, who had headed GTC's marketing since 1971, chose to retire; David Wilson hereafter would answer to CN's senior vice president of operations; Robert Walker would remain in charge of functions (other than marketing and operations) remaining

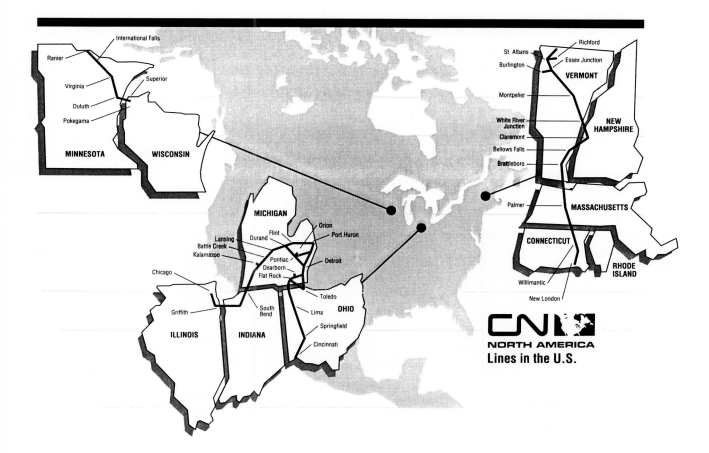

Map labels:
International Falls, Ranier, Virginia, Duluth, Pokegama, Superior, MINNESOTA, WISCONSIN, MICHIGAN, Orion, Port Huron, Flint, Durand, Lansing, Battle Creek, Kalamazoo, Pontiac, Dearborn, Flat Rock, Detroit, Chicago, South Bend, Toledo, Lima, OHIO, Griffith, Springfield, ILLINOIS, INDIANA, Cincinnati, St. Albans, Richford, Burlington, Essex Junction, VERMONT, Montpelier, White River Junction, NEW HAMPSHIRE, Claremont, Bellows Falls, Brattleboro, Palmer, MASSACHUSETTS, CONNECTICUT, RHODE ISLAND, Willimantic, New London

CN NORTH AMERICA
Lines in the U.S.

"We want to talk to our customers as one, not as one, two, or three different companies," said Ron Lawless. CN North America, he maintained, would accomplish that. Photograph courtesy of Canadian National.

in Detroit. Yes, said Lawless, GTC would continue as a wholly owned subsidiary of CN to preserve legal, tax, labor, and other responsibilities and opportunities under its charter.[33]

Thus perished Bandeen's experiment which had viewed GTW, CV, and DW&P as independent American railroads organized for CN under a traditional holding company arrangement. No more. CN North America—"Heading in All the Right Directions"—instead would introduce a "single system" offering customers "seamless transportation." Said Lawless: "We want to talk to our customers as one, not as one, two, or three different companies."[34]

The decision to integrate GTC railroads with CN—to create CN North America as a philosophy and then to implement that philosophy as practice—was not made lightly and was driven by multiple factors that converged collectively.

The growing volume of international business (two-thirds of CN's volume in 1990 was with the United States or to or from overseas markets) clearly loomed large in Montreal. Cross-Canada traffic on CN had remained static following deregulation, but because of free trade agreements CN forecasters freely predicted a continuous escalation of business moving on a north-south axis. Chicago, served by GTW, was the key to CN's participation in such growing volume. That, collaterally, served to direct focus to the St. Clair Tunnel, a "pinch point" inhibiting the free flow of traffic and throttling CN's hopes for a competitive edge. The "tunnel problem" would be obviated, though, with the new bore. In addition, Lawless and others of marketing persuasion at CN were especially sensitive to calls from principal shippers for single-carrier or seamless transport. Finally, the comings and goings of arch rival Canadian Pacific provided yet another acutely important variable. CP had moved adroitly to acquire full ownership of Soo Line and then to integrate its functions even as it successfully pursued Delaware & Hudson to offer shippers what CP called "Savvy Single-Line Service" provided by the "New CP Rail System."[35]

These several and related elements jumped into full relief with the departure of Gerald Mass from GTC. Absent the keeper of the gate, the process of planning a closer association between CN and GTC—a process already under way—could be accelerated. And with revenues down and costs high as the recession tightened, Lawless was convinced that timing was right for Canadian National to make its bold move. So it was.

CN North America clearly implied a change in the independent, stand-alone status of the GTC roads. Photograph courtesy of Don L. Hofsommer.

●　　●　　●　　●　　●

"What goes around comes around" is an ancient bit of American folk wisdom. Indians of the northern Great Plains put it somewhat differently: "The power of the World always works in circles, and everything tries to be round." In both instances, however, the emphasis is on symmetry. Many at GTC in 1992 and after pointed to such symmetry when comparing plans for CN North America and the reintegration of GTC roads into the bowels of the parent—re-establishing, to a great extent, the relationship that existed between the parent and GTW, CV, and DW&P before the advent of Grand Trunk Corporation. Lawless's plan for CN North America, they hinted, turned the clock back to 1971. They further implied darkly that strenuous

efforts over two decades by all parties at GTC had been in vain, that CN executives had learned nothing of railroad operations and circumstance in the United States during the interim, and finally that the GTC experiment had been a failure.[36]

But was Bandeen's GTC experiment in fact a failure? Absolutely not. After all, the word experiment hardly implies permanence, and Bandeen never talked of GTC as something chiseled forever on CN's broad brow. Under Bandeen, CN gave life to GTC on a trial basis. Its leaders—Bandeen, Burdakin, Maas, and Lawless—were men of varying strengths and abilities who, each in his own way, placed an indelible mark on GTC. Collectively these men, those who toiled with them, and the company they led enjoyed successes, suffered disappointments, and made mistakes.

Fortunately, successes outnumbered disappointments and failures. Most important, the GTC experiment stanched the massive and escalating hemorrhage of red ink at Grand Trunk Western. This was accomplished by an aggressive, on-site management team appalled at the drone mentality it found upon arrival in Detroit, and devoted to the goal of carving out a clear and impressive identity for GTW. Then, by adeptly using tax losses at GTW to shelter income at DW&P, the holding company bought time for CN to sort out its options regarding GTW and to a lesser extent CV while simultaneously providing the parent high-quality links to the American market. Through GTC, CN was able to reach the Cincinnati gateway by purchase of Detroit, Toledo & Ironton, and to generate handsome net profit from Helm Leasing and Relco as a part of the holding company's plan of diversification.

190

And, significantly, GTC paid the parent dividends aggregating $30,080,000.

There were, predictably, numerous disappointments and frustrations. In the crucial area of finance, the unfortunate inability to develop a means of external equity participation clearly inhibited GTC's flexibility just as it limited the parent on a larger scale. That problem was inextricably linked to others, such as route expansion. The most serious disappointment psychologically and strategically was failure in the Milwaukee case which, had it been successful, would have given GTW a direct link with DW&P to form an all-CN route through the United States while extending CN's reach to Kansas City and Louisville gateways. A second major disappointment came when the value of DT&I and the Cincinnati gateway lessened as expected friendly connections became integral and then hostile elements of Norfolk Southern and CSXT. Another issue was more amorphous, but crucial, nevertheless: the matter of cost of operation at GTW and CV which, while attacked most vigorously, defied adequate redemption. As a consequence, competitive forces drove down rates faster than managers could reduce costs of running the railroads.

Failures? GTC suffered three major financial mistakes, all in area of diversification: Apache Plastics and Corporate Flight which GTC pursued to ultimate distress, and VMV (locomotive rebuilding) and Paducah & Louisville, which it did not pursue to fruition and should have given the success of those enterprises.

On balance, then, Grand Trunk Corporation proved a successful experiment. And its legacy includes an exciting footnote of opportunity. Just before the end of the nineteenth century and again shortly after the dawn of the next, Grand Trunk leaders had dreamed of forging a connection with Winnipeg west from Chicago. John Burdakin rekindled that dream in the Milwaukee case of the 1980s, and in the early 1990s the dream burned brightly again at CN North America which sought something of a "super VCA" with one or more of four carriers— Burlington Northern, Chicago & North Western, Soo Line, and Wisconsin Central—that operated lines between Chicago and the Lakehead. But in 1992, the idea was more appealing than ever since CN had committed to remove the bottleneck at Port Huron-Sarnia with a modern expansive tunnel. In so doing, CN made the decision to provide the finest rail thoroughfare between Montreal and Toronto to Chicago. Important in and of itself because of Chicago's importance as an entrepôt, improvements to the Montreal-Chicago corridor—coupled with attractive haulage contracts between Chicago and Pokegama—would enhance CN's ability to attract container and other valuable traffic over its line through Pokegama and Winnipeg to Vancouver.

None of it would have been possible had Robert Bandeen's Grand Trunk Corporation experiment not seen life to give Canadian National full title to its options.

NOTES

1. *Rail News Update* No. 2581 (21 August 1991): 1; *Traffic World* 228 (21 October 1991): 25; *Traffic World* 224 (26 November 1990): 11.

2. *Trains* 50 (November 1990): 47; *North Western Lines* 17 (Winter 1990): 9; Norfolk Southern, Stockholder Newsletter (10 December 1991): 10; *Traffic World* 228 (28 October 1991): 4.

3. John Ettore, "Conrail Confronts New Uncertainties," *Modern Railroads* 44 (October 1989): 21-26; Gordon H. Kuhn, "Conrail Striving to be *Carrier of Choice*," *Progressive Railroading* 34 (October 1991): 30-31; Peter L. Schwartz, interview, 7 August 1989; *Traffic World* 220 (30 October 1989): 32; Conrail, Third Quarter Report, 1991, 6.

4. Tom Shedd, "Guilford Gets Rolling in Northeast," *Modern Railroads* 39 (March 1984): 30-34; John H. Burdakin to R. A. Walker, 17 May 1982 (PF 102); Journal of Commerce, 1 November 1982.

5. GTC, The Delaware & Hudson Railway Bankruptcy: A Preliminary Report (1 September 1988), 1, 47-48.

6. CP, Annual Report (1981): 6; Ibid., (1986): 6-7; Ibid., (1988): 5.

7. Soo Line, Annual Report (1983): 3; Ibid., (1984): 2, 7; Ibid., (1987): 11; Ibid., (1988): 1, 3; *Trains* 48 (January 1988): 3-6; Gus Welty, "Regional Railroad Planner's Guide," *Railway Age* 190 (May 1989): 81-84.

8. CP, Annual Report (1989): 2; *Wall Street Journal*, 23 January 1989.

9. CP, Annual Report (1989): 12-13; *Trains* 50 (November 1990): 18.

10. *Trains* 50 (November 1990): 46-47; *Trains* 49 (January 1989): 8-9.

11. *Wall Street Journal*, 29 August, 26 September 1989; William J. Rennicke to Robert P. vom Eigen, 4 December 1989 (PF 102.11).

12. *Rail News Update* No. 2540 (17 January 1990): 2; *Toronto Globe and Mail*, 12 February 1990; *Wall Street Journal*, 14 February 1990; CV, Directors Minutes, 13 February 1990; *Traffic World* 221 (26 February 1990): 1, 36-37.

13. *Traffic World* 222 (21 May 1990): 23; Ibid., (1 October 1990): 13-14; Ibid., (17 December 1990): 9-10; Ibid., (28 January 1991): 32; *Wall Street Journal*, 18 December 1990; *Toronto Globe and Mail*, 27 May 1991.

14. William E. Thoms, "Dereg Comes to Canada," *Trains* 49 (December 1988): 26-27.

15. Andrea Chancellor, "Doors to Canada Swing Even Wider," *Modern Railroads* 44 (May 1989): 34-35; *Washington Post National Weekly Edition*, 3-9 July 1989; *Canadian Reports* 2, no. 3 (1990): 1-16.

16. *GT Reporter* (April 1975): 1-2; W. H. Cramer to G. L. Maas, 31 May 1989; D. K. Nordlund to J. P. Kelsall et al., 9 November 1989; D. K. Nordlund to P. H. Clarke et al., 30 January 1990 (PF 105).

17. R. A. Walker to P. A. Clarke, 19 June 1990, (PF 105); *Traffic World* 227 (12 August 1991): 22-23.

18. John Uckley, "Hundred Year Tunnel," *Rail Classics* 19 (February/March 1990): 25-27, 56-65; *Financial Post,* 5 December 1991; Journal of Commerce, 10 December 1991 and 17 January 1992.

19. *Railway Age* 192 (April 1991): 8; J. H. Park to Board of Directors, 9 November 1988 (PF 130); GTW, Minute Book No. 10, 601.

20. *Wall Street Journal*, 17 May, 26 September 1990, and 2 March 1992; Peter Brimelow, "Agreeing to Disagree," *Forbes* 149 (2 March 1992): 62-63.

21. *Wall Street Journal*, 7 February, 20 June 1991, and 18 February 1992; Diane Francis, "Unions: The New Rich and Privileged," *Maclean's* 109 (4 November 1991): 13.

22. Cecil Foster, "Report from Canada," *Traffic World* 220 (October 1989), 47-48; CV, Directors Minutes, 26 June 1990.

23. Greg Gormick, "Canada's Troubled Railroads," *Railway Age* 192 (February 1991): 67-68; CN, Operating Statistics Year 1990, 1.

24. Cecil Foster, "Canadian Ports, Railroads Band Together to Battle Cheaper U.S. Competition," *Traffic World* 224 (22 October 1990): 26-29; *Toronto Globe and Mail*, 27 May 1991; Robert P. James, "Canada's Ports, Railroads at Risk Without Major Changes, Study says," *Traffic World* 228 (2 December 1991): 25-26; Ibid., 229 (17 February 1992): 39.

25. CN, Annual Report (1990): 4-7.

26. *CN Movin* 23 (March/April 1991): 18; Ibid., (September/October 1991): 14, 23; *Traffic World* 228 (21 October 1991): 21.

27. *GT Focus* (March/April 1992), 1; Ibid., (May/June 1991): 1; GTC, Minute Book No. 4, 320; Lorne C. Perry, interview, 9 August 1991; Yvon H. Masse, interview, 24 May 1989; Peter L. Schwartz, interview, 7 August 1989; Robert J. Bandeen, interview, 24 October 1991; Thomas J. Lamphier to the author, 24 March 1989.

28. J. H. D. Sturgess, interview, 7 August 1989; Yvon H. Masse to P. A. Clarke, 30 June 1989; Peter L. Clarke to Y. H. Masse, 5 July 1989, (PF 100); *CN, Canada-USA Transborder Traffic: CN Strategies for the Nineties* (Montreal: CN, 1989), vi, viii, 1, 21.

29. Walter Cramer to J. H. D. Sturgess, 13 June 1986; Kenneth W. Rooney to G. R. Gagnon, 8 February 1989, (PF 500); A. S. Eklove to John D. Guppy, 19 February 1991 (PF 105).

30. *GT Focus* (special ed. 1991): 1-3; Ibid., (November/December 1991), 8; GTW, Minute Book No. 10, 626.

31. GTW, Minute Book No. 10, 623, 637; CV, Directors Minutes, 8 October 1991; CV Ambassador (Summer 1991), 1; GTC, Minute Book No. 4, 318.

32. *CN Movin* 23 (July/August 1991): 17; *Keeping Track* 24 (July-August 1989): 2.

33. R. E. Lawless, Remarks for Grand Trunk Management Meeting, 18 December 1991; *Journal of Commerce*, 5 December 1991; *GT Reporter* 6 (November-December 1971): 1; *CN North America*, video tape (1992).

34. Ibid.

35. *Traffic World* 227 (9 September 1991): 42.

36. *Black Elk Speaks: Being the Life Story of a Holy Man of the Oglala Sioux, as Told Through John G. Neihardt* (Lincoln: University of Nebraska Press, 1972), 194.

EPILOGUE

Powerful forces at work in 1992 continued thereafter and, if anything, increased in intensity during the next three years. Fierce competition characterized the North American and even world markets. These realities coupled with deepening conservative sentiments on the political scene—in both Canada and the United States—as well as a growing devotion to marketplace solutions in these countries all had a predictable impact on the future course of Canadian National, its Grand Trunk Corporation, and the American properties held by CN through GTC.

The North American automotive industry, always cyclical in nature, rebounded and regained financial health during the years 1993-1995. Of particular and predictable importance to Grand Trunk Western were the fortunes of Ford and General Motors. GM remained the number one producer in the United States, but its recovery was slower than many analysts had hoped. And in 1993, GM's slice of the domestic market dropped to one-third; still impressive but clearly down from its earlier preeminence. Prognosticators vacillated over GM's ultimate place in the sun, but they were certain of one thing: the auto industry was in for even tougher competition. They pointed to the fact that by 1997 no fewer than twelve manufacturers would be producing vehicles in the United States—the

Big Three (GM, Ford, and Chrysler) plus seven Japanese and two German firms. As always, these manufacturers—each under severe competitive pressure—would demand constant and expensive attention from their transportation providers, including GTW.

Detroit-based GTW managers, however, no longer called the shots for this category of marketing or, for that matter, any other. CN's move to integrate management functions for the GTC roads within its own innards escalated when Ron Lawless was followed by Paul Tellier as head of CN. Successive early retirement plans reduced management personnel at Detroit's Brewery Park headquarters to a handful and collateral union agreements provided for similar reduction in hourly ranks; responsibilities were transferred to Montreal, Toronto, Edmonton, and elsewhere. At the same time, CN underwent its own downsizing and even contemplated marriage with arch rival Canadian Pacific. It was not to be. Canada's Parliament responded by authorizing privatization of CN which now incidentally, refers to itself officially as CN Rail, the ponderous CN North America moniker and muddy logo cast to the dust bin of history.

Plans by Canadian National to seek abandonment of certain light-density lines in Canada and to trim up to 11,000 jobs were mirrored at Central

Vermont when on-again-off-again plans to dispose of that historic property finally were resolved by sale to RailTex, a short line operator with several holdings around the U.S. and Canada. Operation by New England Central Railway, CV's successor, began on 4 February 1995.

Even as CN sought to reduce its bulk, managers looked to expanded opportunity for seamless and expedited service via the new Port Huron-Sarnia tunnel which entered service on 5 April 1995. This expansive investment to provide a nearly 28-foot interior diameter, underwater passage allowed easy handling of high-cube doublestack containers, multilevel auto racks, oversized loads, as well as the routine of traffic. Shippers applauded; and directors of the Port of Halifax, crestfallen earlier as steamship companies increasingly favored cities along the eastern seaboard of the United States, now took legitimate hope for their enterprise—especially in terms of the container business destined for Chicago and beyond. Major American railroads also took note of the tunnel's potential in making CN more competitive.

CN's marvelous new tunnel seemed an appropriate symbol for a revitalized railroad industry.

The laughing stock of Wall Street only a few years earlier, fortunes of the industry improved greatly during the 1980s and 1990s under the fresh breezes of deregulation and with aggressive and innovative management. The merger movement, well under way earlier, accelerated greatly in 1995 when Chicago & North Western merged into Union Pacific, when Atchison, Topeka & Santa Fe joined with Burlington Northern to forge Burlington Northern & Santa Fe, and when Union Pacific announced plans to acquire Southern Pacific. In the East, Conrail determined to sell or abandon about one-third of its already pared-down route structure, while CSXT and Norfolk Southern assiduously contemplated their respective strategic options. Many observers confidently predicted only two major railroads for the United States by the turn of the century.

What did that imply for Canadian National and its neighbor, Canadian Pacific? Where did they fit in or, indeed, did they have a place on the landscape of North American railroading in the twenty-first century? That question remains unanswered at the mid-passage of the 1990s. As radio announcers of yesteryear might have said: "Stay tuned for future developments."

APPENDIX A

GRAND TRUNK WESTERN RAILROAD

LOCOMOTIVE ROSTER

6-30-92

Unit	Model	Builder	Horsepower	Year Built	Assignment*
					* GTW unless otherwise noted
GTW 1000	CS9	GTW	900	1979	
GTW 1001	CS9	GTW	900	1980	
GTW 1002	CS9	GTW	900	1980	
GTW 1003	CS9	GTW	900	1980	
GTW 1502	SW1200	EMD	1200	1955	
GTW 1512	SW1200	EMD	1200	1960	
GTW 1513	SW1200	EMD	1200	1960	
GTW 1514	SW1200	EMD	1200	1960	
GTW 1515	SW1200	EMD	1200	1960	
GTW 1516	SW1200	EMD	1200	1960	
GTW 1517	SW1200	EMD	1200	1960	
GTW 1518	SW1200	EMD	1200	1960	
GTW 1519	SW1200	EMD	1200	1960	
CV 4134	GP9	EMD	1750	1958	
GTW 4135	GP9	EMD	1750	1958	
GTW 4136	GP9	EMD	1750	1958	
GTW 4137	GP9	EMD	1750	1958	

LOCOMOTIVE ROSTER (CONTINUED)

Unit	Model	Builder	Horsepower	Year Built	Assignment*
					* GTW unless otherwise noted
GTW 4138	GP9	EMD	1750	1958	
GTW 4139	GP9	EMD	1750	1957	
GTW 4427	GP9	EMD	1750	1954	
GTW 4428	GP9	EMD	1750	1954	
GTW 4432	GP9	EMD	1750	1954	
GTW 4433	GP9	EMD	1750	1954	
GTW 4434	GP9	EMD	1750	1954	
GTW 4438	GP9	EMD	1750	1954	
GTW 4439	GP9	EMD	1750	1954	
GTW 4444	GP9	EMD	1750	1956	
GTW 4446	GP9	EMD	1750	1956	
CV 4559	GP9	EMD	1750	1957	
GTW 4600	GPR9	EMD	1750	1956	
GTW 4601	GPR9	EMD	1750	1957	
GTW 4602	GPR9	EMD	1750	1957	
GTW 4603	GPR9	EMD	1750	1954	
GTW 4604	GPR9	EMD	1750	1956	
GTW 4605	GPR9	EMD	1750	1957	
GTW 4606	GPR9	EMD	1750	1957	
GTW 4607	GPR9	EMD	1750	1957	
GTW 4608	GPR9	EMD	1750	1957	
GTW 4609	GPR9	EMD	1750	1957	
GTW 4610	GPR9	EMD	1750	1956	
GTW 4611	GPR9	EMD	1750	1957	
GTW 4612	GPR9	EMD	1750	1957	
GTW 4613	GPR9	EMD	1750	1957	
GTW 4614	GPR9	EMD	1750	1957	
GTW 4615	GPR9	EMD	1750	1957	
GTW 4616	GPR9	EMD	1750	1956	
GTW 4617	GPR9	EMD	1750	1957	
GTW 4618	GPR9	EMD	1750	1957	
GTW 4619	GPR9	EMD	1750	1954	
GTW 4620	GPR9	EMD	1750	1957	
GTW 4621	GPR9	EMD	1750	1957	
GTW 4622	GPR9	EMD	1750	1957	
GTW 4623	GPR9	EMD	1750	1957	
GTW 4624	GPR9	EMD	1750	1957	
GTW 4625	GPR9	EMD	1750	1957	
GTW 4626	GPR9	EMD	1750	1954	
GTW 4627	GPR9	EMD	1750	1956	
GTW 4628	GPR9	EMD	1750	1957	
GTW 4629	GPR9	EMD	1750	1956	
GTW 4700	GP18	EMD	1800	1960	
GTW 4701	GP18	EMD	1800	1960	
GTW 4702	GP18	EMD	1800	1960	

LOCOMOTIVE ROSTER (CONTINUED)

Unit	Model	Builder	Horsepower	Year Built	Assignment*
					* GTW unless otherwise noted
GTW 4703	GP18	EMD	1800	1960	
GTW 4704	GP18	EMD	1800	1960	
GTW 4706	GP18	EMD	1800	1960	
GTW 4707	GP18	EMD	1800	1960	
GTW 4901	GP9	EMD	1750	1954	
GTW 4902	GP9	EMD	1750	1956	
GTW 4909	GP9	EMD	1750	1957	
GTW 4910	GP9	EMD	1750	1957	
GTW 4917	GP9	EMD	1750	1957	
GTW 4918	GP9	EMD	1750	1957	
GTW 4919	GP9	EMD	1750	1957	
GTW 4920	GP9	EMD	1750	1957	
CV 4926	GP9	EMD	1750	1957	
GTW 4930	GP9	EMD	1750	1957	
GTW 4931	GP9	EMD	1750	1957	
GTW 4932	GP9	EMD	1750	1957	
GTW 4933	GP9	EMD	1750	1957	
GTW 5700	GP38-2	EMD	2000	1972	
GTW 5701	GP38-2	EMD	2000	1972	
GTW 5702	GP38-2	EMD	2000	1972	
GTW 5703	GP38-2	EMD	2000	1972	
GTW 5704	GP38-2	EMD	2000	1972	
GTW 5705	GP38-2	EMD	2000	1972	
GTW 5706	GP38-2	EMD	2000	1972	
GTW 5707	GP38-2	EMD	2000	1972	
GTW 5708	GP38-2	EMD	2000	1972	
GTW 5819	GP38-2	EMD	2000	1978	
GTW 5820	GP38-2	EMD	2000	1978	
GTW 5821	GP38-2	EMD	2000	1978	
GTW 5822	GP38-2	EMD	2000	1978	
GTW 5823	GP38-2	EMD	2000	1978	
GTW 5824	GP38-2	EMD	2000	1978	
GTW 5825	GP38-2	EMD	2000	1978	
GTW 5826	GP38-2	EMD	2000	1978	
GTW 5827	GP38-2	EMD	2000	1978	
GTW 5828	GP38-2	EMD	2000	1978	
GTW 5829	GP38-2	EMD	2000	1978	
GTW 5830	GP38-2	EMD	2000	1978	
GTW 5831	GP38-2	EMD	2000	1978	
GTW 5832	GP38-2	EMD	2000	1979	
GTW 5833	GP38-2	EMD	2000	1979	
GTW 5834	GP38-2	EMD	2000	1979	
GTW 5835	GP38-2	EMD	2000	1979	
GTW 5836	GP38-2	EMD	2000	1979	
GTW 5844	GP38-2	EMD	2000	1977	

LOCOMOTIVE ROSTER (CONTINUED)

Unit	Model	Builder	Horsepower	Year Built	Assignment*
					* GTW unless otherwise noted
GTW 5845	GP38-2	EMD	2000	1977	
GTW 5846	GP38-2	EMD	2000	1977	
GTW 5847	GP38-2	EMD	2000	1977	
GTW 5848	GP38-2	EMD	2000	1977	
GTW 5849	GP38-2	EMD	2000	1977	
GTW 5850	GP38-2	EMD	2000	1978	
GTW 5851	GP38-2	EMD	2000	1978	
GTW 5852	GP38-2	EMD	2000	1978	
GTW 5853	GP38-2	EMD	2000	1978	
GTW 5854	GP38-2	EMD	2000	1978	
GTW 5855	GP38-2	EMD	2000	1978	
GTW 5856	GP38-2	EMD	2000	1978	
GTW 5857	GP38-2	EMD	2000	1978	
GTW 5858	GP38-2	EMD	2000	1978	
GTW 5859	GP38-2	EMD	2000	1978	
GTW 5860	GP38-2	EMD	2000	1978	
GTW 5861	GP38-2	EMD	2000	1978	
GTW 5900	SD40	EMD	3000	1969	
GTW 5901	SD40	EMD	3000	1969	
DWP 5902	SD40	EMD	3000	1969	DW&P
DWP 5903	SD40	EMD	3000	1969	DW&P
DWP 5904	SD40	EMD	3000	1969	DW&P
DWP 5905	SD40	EMD	3000	1969	DW&P
DWP 5906	SD40	EMD	3000	1969	DW&P
DWP 5907	SD40	EMD	3000	1969	DW&P
DWP 5908	SD40	EMD	3000	1969	DW&P
DWP 5909	SD40	EMD	3000	1969	DW&P
DWP 5910	SD40	EMD	3000	1969	DW&P
DWP 5911	SD40	EMD	3000	1969	DW&P
GTW 5912	SD40	EMD	3000	1970	
GTW 5913	SD40	EMD	3000	1970	
GTW 5914	SD40	EMD	3000	1970	
GTW 5915	SD40	EMD	3000	1970	
GTW 5916	SD40	EMD	3000	1970	
GTW 5917	SD40	EMD	3000	1970	
GTW 5918	SD40	EMD	3000	1970	
GTW 5919	SD40	EMD	3000	1970	
GTW 5920	SD40	EMD	3000	1970	
GTW 5921	SD40	EMD	3000	1970	
GTW 5922	SD40	EMD	3000	1970	
GTW 5923	SD40	EMD	3000	1970	
GTW 5924	SD40	EMD	3000	1970	
GTW 5925	SD40	EMD	3000	1970	
GTW 5926	SD40	EMD	3000	1970	
GTW 5927	SD40	EMD	3000	1970	

LOCOMOTIVE ROSTER (CONTINUED)

Unit	Model	Builder	Horsepower	Year Built	Assignment*
					* GTW unless otherwise noted
GTW 5928	SD40	EMD	3000	1970	
GTW 5929	SD40	EMD	3000	1970	
GTW 5930	SD40-2	EMD	3000	1975	
GTW 5931	SD40-2	EMD	3000	1975	
GTW 5932	SD40-2	EMD	3000	1975	
GTW 5933	SD40-2	EMD	3000	1975	
GTW 5934	SD40-2	EMD	3000	1975	
GTW 5935	SD40-2	EMD	3000	1975	
GTW 5936	SD40-2	EMD	3000	1975	
GTW 5937	SD40-2	EMD	3000	1975	
GTW 6200	GP38	EMD	2000	1966	
GTW 6201	GP38	EMD	2000	1966	
GTW 6202	GP38	EMD	2000	1966	
GTW 6203	GP38	EMD	2000	1966	
GTW 6204	GP38	EMD	2000	1966	
GTW 6250	GP38	EMD	2000	1969	
GTW 6251	GP38	EMD	2000	1969	
GTW 6207	GP38AC	EMD	2000	1970	
GTW 6208	GP38AC	EMD	2000	1970	
GTW 6209	GP38AC	EMD	2000	1970	
GTW 6210	GP38AC	EMD	2000	1970	
GTW 6211	GP38AC	EMD	2000	1970	
GTW 6212	GP38AC	EMD	2000	1970	
GTW 6213	GP38AC	EMD	2000	1970	
GTW 5709	GP38-2	EMD	2000	1972	
GTW 5710	GP38-2	EMD	2000	1972	
GTW 5711	GP38-2	EMD	2000	1972	
GTW 5712	GP38-2	EMD	2000	1972	
GTW 5713	GP38-2	EMD	2000	1972	
GTW 5714	GP38-2	EMD	2000	1972	
GTW 5715	GP38-2	EMD	2000	1972	
GTW 5716	GP38-2	EMD	2000	1972	
GTW 5717	GP38-2	EMD	2000	1972	
GTW 5718	GP38-2	EMD	2000	1972	
GTW 5719	GP38-2	EMD	2000	1972	
GTW 5720	GP38-2	EMD	2000	1972	
GTW 5721	GP38-2	EMD	2000	1972	
GTW 5722	GP38-2	EMD	2000	1972	
GTW 5723	GP38-2	EMD	2000	1972	
GTW 5724	GP38-2	EMD	2000	1972	
GTW 5725	GP38-2	EMD	2000	1972	
GTW 5726	GP38-2	EMD	2000	1972	DW&P
GTW 5727	GP38-2	EMD	2000	1972	DW&P
GTW 5728	GP38-2	EMD	2000	1972	
GTW 5729	GP38-2	EMD	2000	1972	

LOCOMOTIVE ROSTER (CONTINUED)

Unit	Model	Builder	Horsepower	Year Built	Assignment*
					* GTW unless otherwise noted
GTW 5730	GP38-2	EMD	2000	1972	
GTW 5731	GP38-2	EMD	2000	1972	
GTW 5732	GP38-2	EMD	2000	1972	
GTW 5733	GP38-2	EMD	2000	1972	
GTW 5734	GP38-2	EMD	2000	1972	
CV 5800	GP38AC	EMD	2000	1971	CV
CV 5801	GP38AC	EMD	2000	1971	CV
GTW 5802	GP38AC	EMD	2000	1971	CV
GTW 5804	GP38AC	EMD	2000	1971	
GTW 5805	GP38AC	EMD	2000	1971	
GTW 5806	GP38AC	EMD	2000	1971	CV
CV 5807	GP38AC	EMD	2000	1971	CV
CV 5808	GP38AC	EMD	2000	1971	CV
CV 5809	GP38AC	EMD	2000	1971	CV
CV 5810	GP38AC	EMD	2000	1971	CV
GTW 5811	GP38AC	EMD	2000	1971	
GTW 5812	GP38AC	EMD	2000	1978	
GTW 5813	GP38AC	EMD	2000	1978	
GTW 5814	GP38AC	EMD	2000	1978	
GTW 5815	GP38AC	EMD	2000	1978	
GTW 5816	GP38AC	EMD	2000	1978	
GTW 5817	GP38AC	EMD	2000	1978	
GTW 5818	GP38AC	EMD	2000	1978	
GTW 6214	GP38AC	EMD	2000	1970	
GTW 6215	GP38AC	EMD	2000	1971	
GTW 6216	GP38AC	EMD	2000	1971	
GTW 6217	GP38AC	EMD	2000	1971	
GTW 6218	GP38AC	EMD	2000	1971	
GTW 6219	GP38AC	EMD	2000	1971	
GTW 6220	GP38AC	EMD	2000	1971	
GTW 6221	GP38-2	EMD	2000	1975	
GTW 6222	GP38-2	EMD	2000	1975	
GTW 6223	GP38-2	EMD	2000	1975	
GTW 6224	GP38-2	EMD	2000	1975	
GTW 6225	GP38-2	EMD	2000	1975	
GTW 6226	GP38-2	EMD	2000	1975	
GTW 6227	GP38-2	EMD	2000	1975	
GTW 6228	GP38-2	EMD	2000	1975	
GTW 6250	SD38DC	EMD	2000	1969	
GTW 6251	SD38DC	EMD	2000	1969	
GTW 6252	SD38DC	EMD	2000	1969	
GTW 6253	SD38DC	EMD	2000	1971	
GTW 6254	SD38DC	EMD	2000	1971	
GTW 6400	GP40	EMD	3000	1968	
GTW 6401	GP40	EMD	3000	1968	

LOCOMOTIVE ROSTER (CONTINUED)

Unit	Model	Builder	Horsepower	Year Built	Assignment*
					* GTW unless otherwise noted
GTW 6402	GP40	EMD	3000	1968	
GTW 6403	GP40	EMD	3000	1968	
GTW 6404	GP40	EMD	3000	1968	
GTW 6405	GP40-2	EMD	3000	1968	
GTW 6406	GP40-2	EMD	3000	1972	
GTW 6407	GP40-2	EMD	3000	1972	
GTW 6408	GP40-2	EMD	3000	1972	
GTW 6409	GP40-2	EMD	3000	1972	
GTW 6410	GP40-2	EMD	3000	1972	
GTW 6411	GP40-2	EMD	3000	1972	
GTW 6412	GP40-2	EMD	3000	1972	
GTW 6413	GP40-2	EMD	3000	1972	
GTW 6414	GP40-2	EMD	3000	1973	
GTW 6415	GP40-2	EMD	3000	1973	
GTW 6416	GP40-2	EMD	3000	1973	
GTW 6417	GP40-2	EMD	3000	1973	
GTW 6418	GP40-2	EMD	3000	1973	
GTW 6419	GP40-2	EMD	3000	1973	
GTW 6420	GP40-2	EMD	3000	1973	
GTW 6421	GP40-2	EMD	3000	1973	
GTW 6422	GP40-2	EMD	3000	1979	
GTW 6423	GP40-2	EMD	3000	1979	
GTW 6424	GP40-2	EMD	3000	1979	
GTW 6425	GP40-2	EMD	3000	1979	
GTW 7010	SW9	EMD	1200	1956	
GTW 7012	SW9	EMD	1200	1952	
GTW 7017	SW1200	EMD	1200	1955	
GTW 7019	SW1200	EMD	1200	1955	
GTW 7262	SW900	EMD	900	1958	
GTW 7263	SW900	EMD	900	1958	
GTW 7264	SW900	EMD	900	1958	
GTW 7265	SW900	EMD	900	1958	
GTW 7266	SW900	EMD	900	1958	
GTW 7267	SW900	EMD	900	1958	
GTW 7268	SW900	EMD	900	1958	

* GTW unless otherwise noted

	UNITS		TOTAL UNITS 277 ASSIGNMENT		LEASED/OWNED	
	CS9	4	GTW	257	LEASED	189
	SW9	2	DW&P	12	OWNED	88
	SW900	7	CV	8		
	SW1200	11				

UNITS

GP7	29
GPR9	30
GP18	7
GP38	7
GP38AC	25
GP38-2	86
GP40	5
GP40-2	21
SD38DC	5
SD40	30
SD40-2	8

BIBLIOGRAPHY

Much of the essential material for this book derives from primary sources of the Grand Trunk Corporation and its subsidiary railroad companies. These are reposited, for the most part, in the general office building at Detroit with scattered holdings at Pokegama, Wisconsin (DW&P). President Files are identified as PF and Secretary Files as SF.

PUBLICATIONS AND ARCHIVAL MATERIALS OF THE GRAND TRUNK CORPORATION, SUBSIDIARIES, AND PARENT.

"Agreement Covering Joint Section—White River Junction-Brattleboro. Boston & Maine Railroad and Central Vermont Railway (January 1, 1930)." Dechief Research Library, CN, Montreal.

Apache Plastics. Minute Book No. 1

Canadian National. A Brief Resume as to the Central Vermont Railway, and Territory Served (1935). Dechief Research Library, CN, Montreal.

_____. Annual Reports, 1965-95.

_____. Overview—Grand Trunk Western,1969.

_____. *Movin'*, 1982-1992.

_____. Operating Statistics 1990.

Canadian National/DW&P. Time Table, 1 October 1923.

Central Vermont. *Ambassador,* 1990-92.

_____. Director Minutes, 1963-85

_____. Outline of the History of Receivership, Central Vermont Railway Company, 12 December 1927 to 31 January 1930. A report of E. Deschenes, comptroller, to George A. Gaston and J. W. Redmond, receivers, 1930. Deschief Research Library, CN, Montreal.

_____. Report Prepared for Hon. W. C. Kennedy, Minister of Railways and Canals, 1 March 1922. Deschief Research Library, CN, Montreal.

_____. Stockholder Minutes, 1975-92 Corporate Flight, Minute Book No. 1.

Corporate History of the Central Vermont Railway Company for Lines in the United States of America, 1 November 1916. General Manager office, CV, St. Albans.

Detroit & Toledo Shore Line. Minute Books Nos. 1-5.

Detroit, Grand Haven & Milwaukee Railway. Time Table, 20 April 1891.

Detroit, Toledo & Ironton, Corporate Records, vols. 16-31.

Domestic 2, Minute Book No. 1.

Domestic 3, Minute Book No. 1.

Domestic 4, Minute Book No. 1.

Duluth, Winnipeg & Pacific. Minute Books Nos. 4-7.

Grand Trunk Corporation. Annual Reports, 1971-91.

_____. Acquisition Evaluation, Chicago, Milwaukee, St. Paul & Pacific Railroad Company, 2 February 1982.

_____. GTC and Milwaukee II Objectives Can Be Achieved Through Cooperative Action, 2 February 1982.

_____. Headquarters Dedication, 16 October 1987.

_____. Minute Books Nos. 1-4.

_____. President Files.

_____. Press Releases, 1971-91.

_____. Public Relations and History files.

_____. Results of GTC/CN Study of Chicago, Milwaukee, St. Paul & Pacific Railroad Company, 15 February 1982.

_____. Secretary Files.

Grand Trunk Land Development Corporation. Minute Book No. 1.

Grand Trunk Milwaukee Car Ferry Company. Minute Book No. 1.

Grand Trunk Radio Communications Company. Minute Books Nos. 1-4.

Grand Trunk Technologies. Minute Book No. 1.

Grand Trunk Western. Agreement of Consolidation, 9 May 1928

_____. *GT Focus*, 1989-1994.

_____. Executive Minute Books.

_____. Federal Valuation Order No. 20— Narrative of Corporate History of the Affiliated and Controlled Lines of the Grand Trunk Railway Company of Canada in the United States. GTW Valuation Engineer, (n.d.).

Grand Trunk Western, Meetings of Stockholders and Board of Directors, Minute Books Nos. 1-10.

_____. *GT Reporter*, 1970-90.

_____. Vice President Files.

Hopper, A. B., and T. Kearney, comps. Canadian National Railways: Synoptical History of Organization, Capital Stock, Funded Debt and General Information as of December 31, 1960 (Montreal: Accounting Department, 20 October 1962).

Keeping Track. 1971-92. CN publication.

Meighan, Arthur. Grand Trunk Acquisition (1919). Dechief Research Library, CN, Montreal.

Railroad Ties. 1990-92. DW&P publication.

Relco Financial Corporation. Minute Book No. 1.

● ● ● ● ●

PUBLICATIONS AND REPORTS BY OTHER CORPORATIONS

Canadian Pacific. Annual Reports, 1960-91.

Chicago, Milwaukee, St. Paul & Pacific. Press Releases, 1979-85.

Conrail. Annual Reports, 1960-95.

First Monday / Third Monday (Internal communication from Chicago, Milwaukee, St. Paul & Pacific). 1980-85.

Soo Line. Annual Reports, 1961-88.

Soo Line. Quarterly Reports, 1981-85.

● ● ● ● ●

PERSONAL INTERVIEWS

Aldrich, James W. Director of Security, GTW, 24 October 1990.

Aydelott, G.B. Retired President and Chairman of the Board, Denver & Rio Grande Western Railroad, 22 September 1982, 9 February 1990.

Baisley, John J. Director of Materials Transportation, General Motors Corporation, 6 March 1990.

Bandeen, Robert A. President and Chairman, Cluny Corporation, 3 November 1989, 24 October 1991.

Brady, Thomas. General Manager—Customer Services, GTW, 8 March 1990.

Burdakin, John H. Retired President, GTC, 6 December 1988, 24 May 1989, 4 November 1989, 21 February 1991, 5 March 1991.

Casaroll, J.J. General Motors Corporation, 6 March 1990.

Cole, Basil. Counsel, Hopkins, Sutter, Hamel & Park, 21 March 1989.

Cramer, Walter H. Senior Vice President of Marketing, GTW, 11 August 1989, 6 March 1990.

Flanigan, J. W. Manager-Materials Transportation Economics, General Motors Corporation, 6 March 1990.

Haupt, Richard. Director-Transportation and Traffic, Ford Motor Company, 6 March 1990.

Lamphier, Thomas J. Retired President, Burlington Northern, 29 March 1989.

Lawless, Ron. President and Chairman, Canadian National, 7 August 1989.

Maas, Gerald L. Retired President, GTC, 23 January 1989, 9 February 1990, 6 March, 25 September 1991.

Masse, Yvon H. Senior Vice President and Chief Financial Officer, Canadian National, 24 May 1989.

McKnight, William J. Corporate Secretary, GTC, 15 March 1991.

Neumann, Richard L. General Manager, DW&P, 26 August 1991.

Opperthauser, Earl C. Retired Vice President-Law, GTW, 6 November 1989, 6 March 1990.

Perry, Lorne C. Assistant Vice President-Advertising, Canadian National, 23 May 1989, 9 August 1991.

Rixon, Robert L. Retired Director of Marketing, CV, 9 August 1989.

Rowe, William. Marketing Manager-Fuels and Materials, GTW, 30 August 1991.

Schwartz, Peter L. Assistant Vice President-Strategic Studies, Canadian National, 7 August 1989.

Sharp, Robert A. Retired President, Detroit, Toledo & Ironton, 3 May 1989.

Smith, William K. Former Director, GTW, 24 September 1989.

Sullivan, James R. Retired Vice President-Marketing, Conrail, 9 February 1990.

vom Eigen, Robert P. Attorney, Hopkins, Sutter, Hamel and Park, 21, 22 March 1989.

Walker, Robert A. Vice President-Corporate Planning, GTC, 7 March 1990.

Williams, John David. Vice President, Anthony M. Franco Inc., 6 March 1990.

Zaleta, Robert M. Director-Automotive Marketing, GTW, 31 May, 11 November 1991.

● ● ● ● ●

GOVERNMENT MATERIALS

Interstate Commerce Commission. Finance Docket 28640, decision, 7 September 1984.
_____. Official Transcript, Financial Docket 28640, 26 July 1984.

30 ICC 293 Valuation Docket 24C Central Vermont Railway

114 ICC 579-593 Valuation Docket 561 Central Vermont Transportation Co.

141 ICC 503-544 Valuation Docket 856 Duluth, Winnipeg & Pacific Railway.

143 ICC 1-123 Valuation Docket 478 Grand Trunk Western and Grand Trunk Western Milwaukee Car Ferry.

143 ICC 1-301 Valuation Docket 445 Grand Trunk Railway of Canada.

U.S. District Court for the Northern District of Illinois, Docket No. 77B8999, ICC Finance Docket No. 28640, "Report and Recommendation for the Future of the Milwaukee Road, 15 May 980"; "Trustees Revised Plan for Reorganization, September 15, 1981"; "Trustees's Amended Plan for Reorganization, 31 March 1983" with appendices 1, 2, 4.

U.S. Railroad Administration, *Final System Plan,* 2 vols. (Washington: Government Printing Office, 1975).

● ● ● ● ●

NEWSPAPERS

Burlington (Vermont) *Free Press*, 1981-92.
Chicago Tribune, 1979-85.
Des Moines Register, 1979-85.
Detroit Free Press, 1971-92.
Detroit News, 1971-92.
Financial Post, 1991.
Journal of Commerce, 1971-92.
Kansas City Business Journal, 1982-85.
Milwaukee Sentinel, 1981-85.
Minneapolis Star/Tribune, 1981-85.
New York Times, 1980-92.
Rail News Update, 1985-91.
St. Albans (Vermont) *Messenger*, 1929, 1971-92.
Globe and Mail, 1971-92.
Wall Street Journal, 1970-92
Washington Post, 1970-92.
Washington Post National Weekly Edition, 1985-89.

● ● ● ● ●

SECONDARY WORKS—BOOKS

Alder, Dorothy R. *British Investments in American Railways, 1834-1898.* Charlottesville, University Press of Virginia, 1970.

Baker, George Pierce. *The Formation of the England Railroad System: A Study of Railroad Combination in the Nineteenth*

Century. Cambridge: Harvard University Press, 1937.

Barriger, John W. *Super Railroads for a Dynamic Economy*. New York: Simmons-Boardmann, 1955.

Beaudette, Edward H. *Central Vermont Railway: Operation in the Mid-Twentieth Century* Newton, N.J.: Carstens, 1982.

Berton, Pierre, *The Impossible Railway: The Building of the Canadian Pacific—A Triumphant Saga of Exploration, Politics, High Finance and Adventure*. New York: Alfred A. Knopf, 1972.

_____. *The National Dream: The Great Railway, 1871-1881*. Toronto: McClelland & Stewart, 1970.

Bigger, E. B. *The Canadian Railway Problem*. Toronto: Macmillan, 1971.

The Biographical Directory of the Railway Officials of America, 1896-1985. Titles varies. Irregularly issued.

Black Elk Speaks: Being the Life Story of a Holy Man of the Oglala Sioux, as Told Through John C. Neihardt. Lincoln: University of Nebraska Press, 1972.

Chandler, Alfred D., Jr., Ed. and Comp. *Giant Enterprise: Ford, General Motors, and the Automobile Industry*. New York: Harcourt, Brace & World, 1964.

_____. *Henry Varnum Poor: Business Editor, Analyst, and Reformer*. Cambridge: Harvard University Press, 1956.

Creighton, Donald. *Dominion of the North: A History of Canada*. Toronto: Macmillan, 1957.

Currie, Archibald William. *The Grand Trunk Railroad of Canada*. Toronto: University of Toronto Press, 1957.

Derleth, August. *The Milwaukee Road: Its First Hundred Years*. New York: Creative Press, 1948.

Dorin, Patrick C. *The Canadian National Railways' Story*. Seattle: Superior Publishing, 1975.

_____. *The Grand Trunk Railroad: A Canadian National Railway*. Seattle: Superior Publishing, 1977.

Dubin, Arthur D. *Some Classic Trains*. Milwaukee: Kalmbach Publishing, 1964.

Dunbar, Willis. *All Aboard! A History of Railroads in Michigan*. Grand Rapids: Eerdman's, 1969.

Eagle, John A. *The Canadian Pacific Railway and the Development of Western Canada, 1896-1914*. Kingston: McGill-Queen's University Press, 1989.

Fleming, R. B. *The Railway King of Canada: Sir William Mackenzie, 1849-1923*. Vancouver: University of British Columbia Press, 1991.

Flink, James J. *The Automobile Age*. Cambridge: MIT Press, 1988.

Foss, Charles R. *Evening Before the Diesel: A Pictorial History of Steam and First Generation Diesel Motive Power on the Grand Trunk Western Railroad, 1938-1961*. Boulder: Pruett Publishing, 1980.

Fournier, Leslie Thomas. *Railway Nationalization in Canada: The Problem of the Canadian National Railway*. Toronto: Macmillan, 1935.

Fuller, Robert Paul. *New England Railroads, Past, Present and Future*. Portland: New England Transportation Research, 1977.

Harlow, Alvin Fay. *Steelways of New England*. New York: Creative Age Press, 1946.

Heaver, T. D., and James C. Nelson. *Railway Pricing Under Commercial Freedom: The Canadian Experience*. Vancouver: University of British Columbia Center for Transportation Studies, 1977.

Hewetson, Henry Eldon. *The Financial History of the Canadian National Railway*. Chicago: University of Chicago Press, 1946.

Hilton, George W. *The Great Lakes Car Ferries*. Berkeley: Howell-North, 1962.

Hofsommer, Don L. *The Southern Pacific, 1901-1985*. College Station: Texas A&M University Press, 1986.

_____. *The Quanah Route: A History of the Quanah, Acme & Pacific Railway*. College Station: Texas A&M University Press, 1991.

Holt, Jeff. *The Grand Trunk in New England*. West Hill, Ontario: Railfare Enterprises Limited, 1986.

Hughes, Jonathan. *American Economic History*, 3d ed. Glenview, Ill.: Scott Foresman/Little Brown Higher Education, 1990.

Hungerford, Edward, David W. Sargent, Jr., Lawrence Doherty, and Charles E. Fisher. *Vermont Central—Central Vermont: A Study in Human Effort*. Boston: Railway & Locomotive Historical Society, 1942.

Innis, Harold A. *A History of the Canadian Pacific Railway*. Toronto: University of Toronto Press, 1971.

Jackson, John N., and Jon Burtniak. *Railways in the Niagara Peninsula: Their Development, Progress and Community Significance.* Belleville, Ont.: Mika Publishing, 1978).

Johnson, Arthur M., and Barry E. Supple. *Boston Capitalists and Western Railroads.* Cambridge: Harvard University Press, 1967.

Jones, Robert C. *The Central Vermont Railway: A Yankee Tradition,* 6 vols. Silverton, Colo.: Sundance Publications, 1981-82.

King, Frank A. *Minnesota Logging Railroads.* San Marino: Golden West Books, 1981.

Kirkland, Edward C., *A History of American Economic Life,* 4th ed. New York: Appleton-Century-Crofts, 1969.

_____. *Men, Cities and Transportation: A Study in New England History, 1820-1900,* 2 vols. Cambridge: Harvard University Press, 1948.

Lamb, W. K. *History of the Canadian Pacific.* New York: Macmillan, 1976.

LaValle, Omer. *Van Horne's Road.* Montreal: Railfare, 1975.

Mackay, Donald. *The Asian Dream: The Pacific Rim and Canada's National Railway.* Vancouver: Douglas & McIntyre, 1986.

McDougall, John Lorne. *Canadian Pacific.* Montreal: McGill University Press, 1968.

Martin, Albro. *Enterprise Denied: Origins of the Decline of American Railroads, 1897-1917.* New York: Columbia University Press, 1971.

Ploss, Thomas H. *The Nation Pays Again.* Self published, 1983.

Prosser, Richard S. *Rails to the North Star.* Minneapolis: Dillon Press, 1966.

Rae, John B. *American Automobile Manufactures: The First Forty Years.* Philadelphia: Chilton Company, 1959.

_____. *The Automobile Industry.* Boston: Twayne Publishers, 1984.

Railroad Facts. Washington: Association of American Railroads, 1984.

Railroad Ten-Year Trends, 1980-1989. Washington: Association of American Railroads, 1991.

Regehr, T. D. *The Canadian Northern Railway: Pioneer Road of the Northern Prairies, 1895-1918.* Toronto: Macmillan Company of Canada, 1976.

Saunders, Richard. *The Railroad Mergers and the Coming of Conrail.* Westport, Ct.: Greenwood Press, 1978.

Schull, Joseph. *The Great Scot: A Biography of Donald Gordon.* Montreal: McGill-Queen's University Press, 1979.

Shaughnessy, Jim. *The Rutland Road.* Berkeley: Howell-North Books, 1964.

Stevens, G. R. *Canadian National Railways: Sixty Years of Trial and Error, 1836-1896* Toronto: Clarke, Irwin & Co., 1960.

_____. *Canadian National Railways: Towards the Inevitable, 1896-1922.* Toronto: Clarke, Irwin & Co., 1962.

_____. *History of the Canadian National Railways.* New York: The Macmillan Company, 1973.

Stover, John F. *American Railroads.* Chicago: University of Chicago Press, 1961.

Transportation in American: A Statistical Analysis of Transportation in the United States—Supplements, Updates and Corrections, 8th ed. Westport: Eno Foundation, 1990.

Trostel, Scott D. *The Detroit, Toledo & Ironton Railroad: Henry Ford's Railroad.* Fletcher, Ohio: Cam-Tech Publishing, 1988.

_____. *Henry Ford: When I Ran the Railroads: A Chronicle of Henry Ford's Operation of the Detroit, Toledo & Ironton, 1920-1929.* Fletcher, Ohio: Cam-Tech Publishing, 1989.

Turner, Gregg M., and Melancthon W. Jacabus. *Connecticut Railroads . . . an Illustrated History.* Hartford: Connecticut Historical Society, 1989.

Wilgus, William J. *The Railway Interrelations of the United States and Canada.* New Haven: Yale University Press, 1937.

Willis, James F., and Martin L. Primack. *An Economic History of the United States,* 2d. ed. Englewood Cliffs: Prentice-Hall, 1989.

Wilner, Frank N. *Railroads and Productivity: A Matter of Survival.* Washington: Association of American Railroads, 1985.

● ● ● ● ●

SECONDARY WORKS—CHAPTERS OR SELECTIONS IN BOOKS

Graffagnino, J. Kevin. "John Gregory Smith." In *Railroad in the Nineteenth Century,* edited by Robert L. Frey, 365-66. New York: Facts on File, 1988.

Kennedy, Charles J. "The Rutland Railroad." In *Railroads in the Nineteenth Century,* edited by

Robert L. Frey, 355-57. New York: Facts on File, 1988.

Redinger, Matthew A. "Henry Varnum Poor." In *Railroads in the Nineteenth Century*, edited by Robert L. Frey, 330-32. New York: Facts on File, 1988.

● ● ● ● ●

Secondary Works—Articles, Magazine, and Journals

Baskerville, Peter. "Americans in Britain's Backyard: The Railway Era in Upper Canada, 1850-1880." *Business History Review* 55 (Autumn 1981): 317-20.

Brimelow, Peter. "Agreeing to Disagree." *Forbes* 149 (2 March 1992): 62-63.

Brown, Robert R. "The Battle of the Gauges in Canada." *Bulletin No. 34*, Railway & Locomotive Historical Society (1934): 20-50.

Business Week. 1981-85.

Brumgard, James W. "The Recycled Geeps of Battle Creek." *Trains* 54 (September 1994): 58-64.

Calkins, Edmund A. "Railroads in Michigan Since 1850." *Michigan History* 13 (Winter 1929): 10.

Canadian Reports 2, no.3 (1990).

Chancellor, Andrea. "Doors to Canada Swing Wider." *Modern Railroads* 44 (May 1989): 34-35.

Conant, Michael. "Socialized Railroads in the U.S.A.: The Grand Trunk Western." *California Management Review* 19 (Summer 1977): 59-63.

Crain's Detroit Business. 1985-92.

Doherty, Lawrence. "General History of the Ogdensburg & Lake Champlain Railroad." *Bulletin*, Railway & Locomotive Historical Society (August 1942): 91-95.

Eagle, John. "Monopoly or Competition: The Nationalization of the Grand Trunk Railway." *Canadian Historical Review* 62, no. 1 (1981): 3-30.

Eltore, John. "Conrail Confronts New Uncertainties." *Modern Railroads* 49 (October 1989): 22-26.

Fairweather, S. W. "A New View of the C. N. R." *The Railroad Telegrapher* 56 (April 1939): 246-49.

Forbes. 1971-92.

Forbes, Charles S., and Jack B. Wood. "History of the Vermont Central—Central Vermont Railway System: 1843-1932." *The Vermonter* 37, nos. 11-2 (1932): 237-77.

Fortune. 1971-92.

Francis, Diane. "'Unions' The New Rich and Privileged." *Maclean's* 109 (November 1991): 13.

Gormick, Greg. "Canada's Troubled Railroads." *Railway Age* 192 (February 1991): 67-68.

Gorsky, John L. "Big Steam's Last Stand: Milwaukee Junction, 1960." *National Railway Bulletin* 56, no. 1 (1991): 4-11.

"GTW Consistently Wrings Profits from a 'Too Short' Corridor." *Railway Age* 181 (28 August 1980): 34-35.

Hartley, Scott. "Central Vermont . . . a Survivor." *Trains* 56 (February 1991): 30-42.

"Henry Ford's Railroad Experiment." *Railroad Magazine* 78 (July 1938): 9-28.

Hilton, George H. "Detroit River Car Ferries of the Canadian National Railways." *Journal of the Steamship Historical Society of America* 18 (1961): 99-102.

_____. "Great Lakes Ferries: An Endangered Species." *Trains* 35 (January 1975): 42-51.

Journal of Commerce. 1971-92.

Kuhn, Gordon H. "Conrail Strives to be 'Carrier of Choice.'" *Progressive Railroading* 34 (October 1991): 30-31.

Latimer, R. R. "The Challenge of Rate Freedom." *Railway Age* 180 (28 May 1979): 50-53.

MacKenzie, Kenneth S. "Term of Convenience to Legal Entity: The Canadian National Railways 1918 to 1923." *Canadian Rail* (May-June 1983): 76-87.

MacKenzie, Kenneth S., and J. Norman Lowe with Bill Palmer. "A Legacy Transformed." *CN Movin'* 21 (February 1989): 9-10.

Mailer, Stanley H. "In Minnesota CN is Spelled DW&P." *Trains*, 34 (March 1974): 20-28.

Malone, Frank. "Contract Rates are Catching On." *Railway Age* 183 (22 February 1982): 42-44.

_____. "Grand Trunk: Good Track is Good Business." *Railway Age* 183 (12 April 1982): 15-18.

_____. "GTW-DT&I: A Slow Transition to Avoid Merger Shock." *Railway Age* 181 (30 June 1981): 38-42.

_____. "Paducah & Louisville: The Making of a Winner." *Railway Age* 190 (November 1989): 40-42.

Miller, Luther S. "CN: Productivity is the Road to Profit, and CN Rail is Showing the Way." *Railway Age* 179 (25 December 1978): 22-30.

Mitchell, F. Stewart. "Loosening the Grip." *Modern Railroads* 36 (April 1981): 34-35.

_____. "Milwaukee II: A Transformation of Assets." *Modern Railroads* 36 (August 1981): 47-48.

Middleton, William D. "Henry Ford and his Electric Locomotives." *Trains* 26 (September 1976): 22-26.

Modern Railroads. 1971-91.

Navin, William E. "The Founding of the Rutland Railroad." *Vermont Quarterly* 14 (July 1946): 91-94.

North Western Lines. 1989-90.

Official Guide of the Railways. 1871-1971. Title varies.

Progressive Railroading. 1971-92.

Railway Age. 1928-92.

Richard Vance. "A Marriage of Equals." *CSX Quarterly* (Fall 1990): 9-25.

Roberts, Robert. "Deregulation: The Turning Point." *Modern Railroads* 35 (December 1980): 58-62.

Rohde, William L. "Border Line." *Railroad Magazine* 43 (August 1947): 8-33.

Scribbins, Jim. "Interview with John H. Burdakin." *The Milwaukee Railroader* 18 (September 1988): 4-7.

Shaffer, Frank E. "We Now Have the Tools." *Modern Railroads* 36 (April 1981): 36-39.

Shedd, Tom. ". . . Cigars are Out." *Modern Railroads* 33 (October 1978): 43-45.

_____. "Freedom Pays." *Modern Railroads* 31 (July 1976): 20-23.

_____. "Guilford Gets Rolling in Northeast." *Modern Railroads* 39 (March 1984): 30-34.

Smith, Douglas N. W. "The Best Route Through the Rockies." *Canadian Rail* (January-February 1981): 3-35.

Smith, Russell D. "The Early Years of the Great Western Railway." *Ontario History* 60 (December 1968): 207-14.

Talman, James J. "The Development of the Railroad Network of Southwestern Ontario to 1876." *Canadian Historical Association Annual Report-1953*, 53-56.

Thomas, David. "Tough Enough to Hurt." *Canadian Business* 55 (November 1982): 28-39.

Thoms, William E. "Dereg Comes to Canada." *Trains* 49 (December 1988): 26-27.

Traffic World. 1971-92.

Trains. 1971-92.

Trap, Paul. "Foreign Railroads in Michigan, 1857-1893. "*The Old Northwest: A Journal of Regional Life and Letters* 13 (Winter 1986): 371-97.

Uckley, John. "Hundred Years Tunnel." *Rail Classics* 19 (February-March 1990): 25-27, 56-65.

Welty, Gus. "Change!" *Railway Age* 185 (January 1984): 37-44.

_____. "Grand Trunk Western: Battling Toward Profitability." *Railway Age* 176 (8 September 1975): 30-32, 104.

_____. "Mandating AEI Tagging." *Railway Age* 192 (March 1991): 34-38.

_____. "The Meaning of Merger." *Railway Age* 185 (July 1984): 73-76.

_____. "Regional Railroad Planner's Guide." *Railway Age* 190 (May 1989): 81-84.

_____. "The Search for Productivity." *Railway Age* 185 (November 1984): 31-34.

Wylie, Cleland B. "Route of the Freight 400's." *Trains* 7 (January 1947): 14-25.

INDEX

Regional Transit Authority, 97
Reid, Gil (artist), 157, *158*
Relco Financial Corporation (Relco), 169, 170, 191
Renaissance Center (Detroit), 65
"Rent a Train," 157
Reyes, Bonnie, 169
Riegel, Donald W., Jr., 115, 116
Riley, John H., 115, 116
Rio Grande Industries, 179
Rixon, Robert L., 130-31, 133, 157
RoadRailer trailers (GM), 122, 124, 162
Rocket intermodal train, 69, 130, 131, *132*
Rogers Pass rail line tunnel, 182
rolling stock, paint and logos on, 41, *42*
Roscoe, Snyder & Pacific (railroad), 117
Rostenkowski, Dan, 102
Rouses Point (New York), 9, 26, 69, 129, 180
Royal Oak, Michigan train station, *62*
Rutland (Vermont), *15*
Rutland and Burlington Railroad, 8, 14
Rutland Railroad, 14, *15*, 80

S

Saginaw (Michigan), rail lines, 74, *75*, 81, *82*, 83, 125
Saint John, 8
Salomon Brothers and Pennco, 83, 85
Santa Fe. *See* Atchison, Topeka & Santa Fe Railway
Santa Train, *47, 157*
Sarnia, Ontario, Canada: rail lines, 10, 16, 20, 183; tunnel, 124, 184, 191
Sault Ste. Marie (Michigan), 19
"Savvy Single-Line Service" (CP), 190
SCAT. *See* Short Crew Automobile Train
Schmiege, Robert, 167
Seaboard Air Line, 80
Seaboard Coast Line (railroad), 80, 91, 114
Seaboard Coast Line Industries, 91, 14
Seaboard System, 179
"seamless transportation" (CN), 187, 189
SEMTA, *64*
Sharon (Vermont), 131, 188
Sharp, Robert A., 86, *86*, 90, 91
Shedd, Tom, 75, *124*
Sheldon Junction, 159
Shepherd, Gene, 160
Shore Line. *See* Detroit & Toledo Shore Line Railroad
Short Crew Automobile Train (SCAT), 145, 147
Silver Freight Car Award, 72
"single system" transportation (CN), 187, 189
Smith, John, 8, 14
Smith, William K., 137, 147
Smith, Worthington L., 97
Solandt, Omand, 34
Soo. *See* Soo Line Corporation; Soo Line Railroad

Soo Line Corporation, 182
Soo Line Railroad (Soo), 57, 80, 89, 99, 118, 135, 152; and CP, 181-82, 190; and DW&P, 162; and GTC, 167; and Spine Line, 102-4, 106-8
South Bend (Indiana), *48, 49, 170*
South Charlestown (New Hampshire), *159*
Southeastern Michigan Transportation Authority. *See* SEMTA
Southern Pacific (railroad), 67, 96, 97, 114, 173; mergers, 100, 179; TOPS computer, 67
Southern Railway, 85, 86, 87, 90, 114-15, 119, 167
South Lyon (Michigan), 125, 153
South Windham (Connecticut), 131
"Spine Line" (Rock Island), 101, 102, 103, 106, 108
Springfield (Ohio), 83, 122, 153
Staff Training College (CN), 34
Staggers Act, 113-14, 115, 117, 152, 153, 170, 179
St. Albans (Vermont), 68, 188; rail lines, 8, 14, *33*, 53, 131, 157, 159; enginehouse, 68
Stasio, Edward J., *149*, 173
stations. *See* individual depots
St. Clair Tunnel, 10, 20, *20*, 184-85, 189
steam locomotives. *See* locomotive types
Stempel, Robert G., 174
St. Lawrence and Atlantic Railroad, 8, 9, 10, 50, 188
St. Louis (Missouri), 16
St. Louis-San Francisco Railway, 40, 91
St. Paul (Minnesota), 97, 124, 182
Straight Talk (GTW newsletter), 172
Straight Talk About Grand Trunk Western and Proposed Labor Agreement, 145
Stroh Brewing Company, 124, 165
Sturgess, John H.D., 187, 188
Sullivan, James R., 71
Superior (Wisconsin), 135, 167, 182
Swanton (Vermont), 9
Syracuse (New York, 180

T

Tarr, Robert, 34
Taschereau, Pierre, 34
Tatro, Paul E., *168*; and GTC, 166, 168-69; GTW controller, 41, 98, 99, 106, 109, 129
Taylor (Michigan), 122
Taylor, Reese, 107
TCU. *See* Transportation Communications Union
Temperance Yard (Toledo), 153
Temple, Barker & Stone, 155, 156
Thornton, Sir Henry W., *21*, 22, 24, 30
3Rs Act, 80, 88
Thunder Bay, 52
Thunderbolt (train), 119, *120*
Tischler, Howard M., 41, 43, *44* , 63
Titanic (ship), 21

DATE DUE

AUG 09 1996		
JUN 22 REC'D		
DEC 17 1997		
DEC 17 REC'D		
MAY 07 1999		
APR 29 REC'D		
OCT 03 1999		
REC'D SEP 20 1999		
OCT 12 2000		
REC'D OCT 13 2000		
JUN 10 2010		
REC'D JUL 24 2004		

Demco, Inc. 38-293